NOT BY WAR ALONE

Published in cooperation with
The Center for International and Strategic Affairs
University of California, Los Angeles

NOT BY WAR ALONE

SECURITY AND ARMS CONTROL IN THE MIDDLE EAST

PAUL JABBER

UNIVERSITY OF

CALIFORNIA PRESS

Berkeley · Los Angeles · London

University of California Press
Berkeley and Los Angeles, California
University of California Press, Ltd.
London, England
© 1981 by
The Regents of the University of California

Printed in the United States of America

1 2 3 4 5 6 7 8 9

Library of Congress Cataloging in Publication Data
Jabber, Paul, 1943–
    Not by war alone.
    Bibliography: p.
    Includes index.
    1. Near East—Politics and government—1945–
2. Near East—Defenses. 3. Arms control.
I. Title.
DS63.J29   327.1′74′0956   80–11341
ISBN 0–520–04050–3

For EVA

CONTENTS

TABLES

PREFACE

Paradoxically, as this book goes to press, the United States is fast becoming Egypt's major supplier of arms, supplanting the Soviet Union as the power with preeminent influence on the banks of the Nile. This new relationship cements a process of rapprochement between Washington and Cairo that has over the past several years produced a gradual yet startling reversal of alliances between the single most important Arab state and the two major forces. In 1955, it was the American decision not to become Egypt's main weapons provider that was instrumental in opening the Middle Eastern heartland to Soviet influence and dealt a deathblow to Western efforts to restrain the Arab-Israeli arms race. A full generation later, this fateful decision has now been reversed, in international circumstances that, both in the Middle East and beyond, are in many ways reminiscent of the peak years of Cold War containment. Whether its emerging role as principal military benefactor both to Israel and to major Arab states will place the U.S. Government in a better position to moderate future military competition within the region remains to be seen. What is clear beyond doubt is the crucial role arms transfers continue to play in the making and breaking of inter-state relations.

This book evolved from a doctoral dissertation submitted to the Department of Political Science at the University of California, Los Angeles. Several present colleagues and former teachers read earlier drafts and provided helpful comments. I am particularly indebted to Malcolm H. Kerr, Bernard Brodie, and Robert Dallek.

My additional thanks to the Middle East Institute in Washington, D.C., for permission to reprint portions of Chapter 2, which originally appeared in an article published by the *Middle East Journal* in its Summer 1974 issue. Also, parts of Chapter 7 were first presented at a workshop on Middle East arms control sponsored jointly by the Institute and the U.S. Arms Control and Disarmament Agency.

Also, to the UCLA Academic Senate; to the Bureau of Educational and Cultural Affairs of the U.S. Department of State, through the American Research Center in Egypt (ARCE); to the staff of the ARCE in Cairo; to the Staff of the Adlai E. Stevenson Institute of International Affairs in Chicago, particularly its former President, William R. Polk; to the staffs of the Truman, Eisenhower, Kennedy, and Johnson presidential libraries; and to many individuals, some listed at the end of this work, in this country as well as in the United Kingdom, Egypt, and Lebanon, who were most generous with their time, my sincere gratitude for their various contributions to this study through travel grants, residence and research fellowships, interviews, and other forms of valuable assistance.

PART I

THE PROBLEM AND ITS
SETTING

CHAPTER 1   INTRODUCTION

> Arms sales are now regarded as the most significant diplomatic currency of all.
>
> John Stanley and Maurice Pearton
> *The International Trade in Arms*

The enormous sales of military equipment by the United States to foreign countries—particularly in the Middle East—during the decade of the seventies have naturally sparked considerable public debate over the wisdom of such policies and their potential consequences. With their country cast in the role of arsenal to the world (the United States contributed 42 percent of global military exports in the decade 1968–1977, with the Soviet Union in second place at 30.5 percent), Americans rightly question the morality of such sales and worry about hidden commitments to future interventions abroad, and possibly new Vietnams, they may entail.

In response to these legitimate fears, the United States Congress has attempted to exercise some control over arms exports. Under the International Security Assistance and Arms Control Act of 1976, the executive branch is now required to notify Congress formally of any projected sale of weapons in excess of $25 million, and the legislature has thirty days in which to veto such action. In 1975, ninety-eight congressmen and senators requested the administration to convene a suppliers' conference to cap the growing international arms trade, a call echoed by numerous private groups and associations. Partly in response to this public mood, and soon after taking office, President Carter announced in May 1977 a new set of restrictions on U.S. arms transfer policy, and stated that Washington "will henceforth view arms transfers as an exceptional foreign policy implement." The new controls included a commitment to reduce arms sales in subsequent years below the 1977 total, not to be the first supplier to introduce new and advanced weapons systems that would create significantly higher combat capabilities in a given region, not to produce new weapons systems exclusively for sale abroad, and

3

to tighten restrictions on practices that encourage weapons proliferation, such as co-production agreements, third-party transfers, and sales by private arms manufacturers.

In principle, opposition to active weapons salesmanship abroad can hardly be faulted, on either ethical or practical grounds. Arms kill and maim; wars often create more problems than they solve; arms races are basically unstable and lead to conflict; military acquisitions by Third World countries siphon off resources badly needed for economic development, social reform, food, and education; and stronger military establishments encourage soldiers to intervene in politics and may lead to military dictatorships. It is difficult to understand how the most cherished objectives of American foreign policy— peaceful settlement of disputes, democratic government, socioeconomic progress, in short, the makings of international stability—can be served by allowing $9.5 billion in foreign military sales during the 1977 fiscal year alone.

In practice, however, the issue is not so clear-cut. As is often the case, reality refuses to bend to the simple generalities of principle. In 1977, a typical year, the United States sold arms to no less than seventy-six countries, including some of America's closest NATO allies. Sales ranged from less than $500 worth of nonlethal supplies to Jamaica up to $5.803 billion worth of the most sophisticated heavy weapons to Iran. Unavoidably, the merits of these and other transactions cannot be intelligently debated in isolation from the particular circumstances that surround each of them, or by ignoring the complex multinational character of the world arms trade.

Two facts are central to this problem and must be recognized and given their full weight in any serious discussion of alternatives to current U.S. practices. First, arms sales are an explicit instrument of state policy, wielded directly by national governments as a legitimate means to the attainment of foreign policy objectives. Second, the United States is only one of several major powers with active military-export industries engaged in vigorous, sometimes bitter, competition for markets. Primarily these include the Soviet Union, France, and Great Britain. Sweden, Italy, Israel, and several other medium powers are also significant producers of some weapons, such as advanced combat aircraft, armor, naval units, and certain types of missiles.

These two elements, the political significance of arms deals and producer competition, have combined to yield a variety of incentives to sell arms that range over a broad spectrum and are a far cry from the simple profit motive of the private "merchant of death" of the past or the defense-related corporations of the present. These incentives include the desire to strengthen the military potential of allies and friendly regimes, to secure important quid pro quo's such as base rights, to preempt arms acquisitions by clients from rival suppliers, to extend the umbrella of symbolic deterrence over regions coveted by adversary blocs, to gain the allegiance of uncommitted governments, and to otherwise secure valuable ideological or political influence in the inner councils of foreign governments.

From the economic viewpoint, the incentives have been just as compelling. Included are the need to maintain a viable domestic arms industry with a minimum of subsidization by the taxpayer, to compensate partially for heavy defense expenditures, to develop and maintain national technological expertise in the production of advanced weapons, and to redress balance-of-payments problems.

In the Middle East, all these factors have been in evidence as stimulating the several arms races that region has witnessed over the past two decades, both in the Arab-Israeli conflict area and more recently in the Persian Gulf. In fact, beginning with the famous "Czech" arms deal between Egypt and the Soviet bloc in 1955, the supply of military equipment has provided the principal avenue of local competition between Russia and the West. The willingness to supply or accept arms became the measuring rod by which regional governments and external powers alike judged the staunchness of their friends and allies, the extent of their commitments, and even their ideological preferences.

However, neither these longstanding incentives nor the vast losses in equipment that resulted from the October 1973 war are sufficient to account for the tripling of arms sales to the Middle East in recent years. Two additional factors, of recent vintage and compelling power, must be added to this complex picture. Both relate to the area's major resource—petroleum—and the conditions created by the Organization of Petroleum Exporting Countries (OPEC) when it quadrupled oil prices by the 1973 Arab oil embargo.

One factor is the industrial countries' need to secure adequate and steady supplies of oil, which they have attempted to do in part by concluding with the producers very sizable agreements entailing directly or indirectly the exchange of oil for arms, as well as industrial goods and technology. The other is the desire to recover some of the vast capital flowing from the developed world into the coffers of the OPEC countries by selling them large quantities of the latest military equipment, often while sharply marking up the price tags on these weapons and ancillary services.

Against this background, sketched here in its barest outlines, what are the prospects for a significant stemming of the international arms trade? Given the nature of current international relationships, of which the continuing

Soviet-Western struggle in the less-developed world is only one important facet, as well as the range of domestic interests involved in most arms-producing countries, unilateral restraint is a most improbable solution. Nor, in some cases, is it advisable. Because of its strategic importance, its resources, and its impact on global stability, the Middle East conflict region presents the United States with some of the most agonizing choices.

Repeatedly in this decade, American diplomatic efforts, security commitments, and economic stakes have required aggressive arms supply practices, notwithstanding contrary official pronouncements. Orders by Jordan for Hawk air-defense missiles in 1975, by Saudi Arabia for the sophisticated F-15 Eagle air-superiority fighter in 1977, and by Iran for advanced airborne warning and control (AWACS) systems in 1977 are examples of arms deals that have provoked widespread congressional as well as public debate and opposition. Yet, as in the controversial—and ultimately futile and self-defeating—blocking by the U.S. Congress of arms to Turkey following the latter's invasion of Cyprus in 1974, the choice is often between the rock and the hard place.

Could Washington afford in 1975 to rebuff Jordan—a long-standing arms customer and friend of the U.S.—or to place a moratorium on sales to the Gulf area—as Senator Kennedy and other legislators were demanding at the time—while simultaneously pledging several billion dollars in military aid to Israel under the Sinai interim settlement package agreement then being negotiated by Secretary of State Kissinger, without jeopardizing the integrity of the delicate, evenhanded diplomatic role through which the United States has sought to promote a final peaceful settlement of the Arab-Israeli conflict?

Could Saudi Arabia, the largest petroleum exporting country and the key moderator of OPEC policies, be denied, without punitive repercussions, aircraft that were being supplied to Israel?

Can the Arab members of OPEC—and probably Iran as well—be expected not to stop the flow of oil again in some future regional crisis, if the West stops the supply of weapons viewed by these governments as essential to their security?

Can Israel be expected to make large-scale withdrawals from occupied Arab territories back into the narrow and highly vulnerable territorial confines of the pre-1967 borders without eliciting compensatory commitments of liberal future conventional weapons supplies?

In a region where nuclear military capabilities already exist and threaten to multiply, and where international mistrust, enmities, and irredenta abound, would a unilateral, imposed curtailment or outright denial of conventional military supplies contribute to regional and global security, or would it create greater jeopardy?

It is a fundamental assumption of this study that only multinational action by agreement among all the major arms exporters offers realistic chances for significant, lasting reductions in the international arms trade. The study's main purpose is to define critical requirements for the viability and effectiveness of such international accords by exploring some aspects of the relationship between the international transfer of conventional armaments, the general purposes of arms control, and the political objectives and security interests of arms suppliers and arms recipients. Specifically, the focus will be on a brief conceptualization of arms control for regions witnessing a high level of inter-state conflict, and a detailed examination of a relevant historical instance for insights into the workings of an actual arms control system, the performance of the participants in it, and its applicability as a prototype for future arms limitation arrangements.

The historical case to be examined is the system instituted by the United States, Great Britain, and France under the Tripartite Declaration of May 1950 to regulate the flow of arms to the Middle East. This system was aimed at preventing the outbreak of war in the region by maintaining a stable balance of military power through a rationing of the supply of armaments to the countries directly involved in the Arab-Israeli conflict. It effectively lasted until the Fall in 1955, when it was practically nullified by the announcement of a major arms transaction between Egypt and the Soviet bloc.

The specific choice of the tripartite case for study was dictated by a number of factors. The rationing system was a unique experiment in coordinated, long-term, multilateral arms control on a regional level. Similar supplier arrangements to curtail the flow of weaponry to the area were again proposed in the late sixties and in the seventies—principally by the United States. The instability of the Arab-Israeli strategic and political environment, the continuing arms buildup, and the almost total reliance of the local parties on external arms suppliers give the Middle Eastern arms race special significance, both as the most virulent example of a regional military contest and as a prime candidate for arms limitation. Last but not least, the period covered in this study, 1950–1955, was a seminal one in the contemporary political history of the Middle East, particularly from the standpoint of its foreign affairs. Insofar as Arab-Western relations were affected by the issue of arms supplies, the analysis herein will shed new light on the international politics of the region during these crucial years.

One of the more debated aspects of this stage in United States policy toward the Middle East is the failure of American diplomacy to prevent the consummation of the Soviet-Egyptian arms agreement, as well as Egyptian President Gamal Abdel Nasser's motivations in making such a sudden, daring, and far-reaching overture toward the Communist bloc. To the extent that they touch on it at all, most studies of the period analyze the arms deal exclusively in terms of the political circumstances in the spring and summer of 1955, such as the creation of the Baghdad Pact, the Israeli raid on Gaza in the previous February, the stirrings of nonalignment in the Third World, and the "Spirit of Bandung." The role played by these immediate political factors in Cairo's decision to turn to the East for arms was important and should not be minimized. These factors significantly affected Egypt's perception of its need for additional military strength, and they alerted its leadership to the viability of a policy of disengagement from an exclusively Western orientation for Egypt's external affairs. Since these events have been adequately covered in several published works, they will not be treated in much detail here, save to the extent that they directly affected the arms transfer process.

No full explanation of this turning point in the international relations of the Middle East can be reached, however, in isolation from its most relevant matrix: the arms supply policies of the major area suppliers during that period, regional arms control arrangements then in effect, and the impact of these policies and arrangements on the weapons-acquisition experiences and expectations of the governments at the receiving end—in this case, notably Egypt. It is this matrix that the present study seeks to describe and analyze. Furthermore, by placing the Egyptian decision within this expanded but directly pertinent context, the significance and implications of this episode for the general understanding of relations between arms exporters and Third World clients can be more accurately identified.

The structure of this work was largely dictated by three main interests: a *theoretical* concern for bringing to the fore the rather neglected area of regional arms control; an *historical* curiosity about the roots and course of determinant —but as yet not well studied—events in a crucial formative period of contemporary relations between the Middle East and the West; and a *policy-relevant* desire to "learn the lessons" of a concrete past experience in Middle East arms control and assess the future applicability of similar measures. Prescriptively, this study argues for increased attention to the regional approach to arms control, on grounds of greater feasibility and of more relevance to the problem of restraining armed conflicts than the global approaches of the past or those that can be realistically envisaged today.

Obviously, deriving definitive policy-relevant judgments about the advantages and drawbacks of supplier-imposed regional arms limitation systems for purposes of conflict management would require consideration of a multiplicity of empirical cases. What the present work attempts is essentially to survey and evaluate the available historical record in the single instance where this particular arms control device was implemented, and draw conclusions that— while hopefully apposite to the general problem of limiting arms transfers on a multinational basis—are of particular pertinence to the Arab-Israeli situation.

To argue for the validity of restrictions on arms transfers to conflict regions, both as a subject of inquiry and as a course of governmental action, does not imply a callous denial of legitimate grounds for waging conflict, or an unquestioning endorsement of the status quo. In fact, a principal underlying thesis of this work is that arms control can be easily misused by those who do the controlling to achieve ulterior political objectives or impede undesired change. This is particularly the case when such fundamentally asymmetric relationships are involved as those between rich, industrially advanced arms suppliers ("haves") and less-developed, technologically ill-equipped arms recipients ("have-nots"). A corollary of this thesis, developed particularly in the concluding chapters, is the need for control systems in the arms transfer field that are politically acceptable at both ends of the transfer process.

Moreover, conflicting goals can be pursued through nonviolent means. In the choice of instrumentalities to attain political ends, be they individual or national, armed conflict is only one option. In many cases it is the least effective option; in all cases it is the least desirable. In the difficult but imperative search for ways of managing and resolving international quarrels without resort to force or threats of force, primary attention should be paid to international efforts and instruments designed to control and limit the stockpiling and transfer of implements of war. This has become a widely accepted objective, yet most study and attention in the last few decades have concentrated on strategic nuclear arms control, and comparatively little work has been done on the requirements and dynamics of the control of conventional weapons.

Those few studies that have investigated problems related to the control of non-nuclear arms have laid their main emphasis on the practices and motivations of arms-exporting countries. They have paid inadequate attention to the perspectives of arms recipients—most of whom are developing countries, recently freed from colonial bondage or other forms of foreign influence, and with concerns and goals substantially different from those of the major powers. Furthermore, the bulk of the literature dealing with specific controls —often sponsored by agencies of government—as well as the pronouncements and initiatives by decision-makers of exporting countries often appear singularly insensitive or insufficiently attentive to the purely "political" components of any arms control proposal, i.e., those aspects that tie the proposal to the larger political context in which it will be implemented, and that will largely determine its ultimate success or failure. The analysis that follows will have served one of its principal purposes if it sheds some useful light on these neglected but critical issues.

CHAPTER 2 PROBLEMS AND PROSPECTS FOR ARMS CONTROL IN THE ARAB-ISRAELI CONFLICT

> We Arabs—we don't really expect to win our wars with Israel on the battlefield. But we have seen what effects these wars can have on Israel on the diplomatic front.
>
> Senior Egyptian diplomat, 1975
> Thomas Kiernan, *The Arabs*

> Israel and its neighbors are now entering a period of fierce nuclear competition.
>
> Shalhevet Freier
> Head, Israeli Atomic Energy Commission
> January 1976

For over thirty years, both sides in the Arab-Israeli conflict have relied on ever-increasing military power and its repeated use in all-out warfare in preference to negotiation as the best, if not the only, guarantee of security, the optimal instrument for reaching desired ends, and the most effective means for the eventual redress of grievances. Repeatedly reinforced by events often precipitated by its own logic, this doctrine of "military coercion" has been a primary conceptual obstacle to a peaceful settlement.[1] It has found past expression in four major wars and innumerable border clashes, raids, and other military skirmishes, with their grievous toll in blood and treasure. Continued reliance on this doctrine as the principal mode of interaction between the conflicting parties portends an even more baneful future, given the escalating cost, sophistication, and destructive power of the weapons acquired in recent years and those apt to be introduced over the coming decade.

1. For a relevant discussion of "coercive warfare" and "compellence," see Thomas C. Schelling, *Arms and Influence* (New Haven and London: Yale University Press, 1966), especially pp. 170–176.

ENDURING ELEMENTS OF MILITARY INSTABILITY

Though general agreement on a casual link between arms and war may be lacking, there is broad concurrence in the view that the large-scale buildup of armaments by the main parties to the Arab-Israeli dispute has been a highly destabilizing factor. The incidence of four wars between these countries within a span of two decades—not to mention the very substantial fighting during the 1969–1970 war of attrition in the Suez Canal area—fully attests to the volatility of the dispute and the active use made of existing arsenals in this most heavily armed part of the nonindustrialized world. Furthermore, the continually escalating Arab-Israeli arms race represents the most unstable type of weapons contests. As a study sponsored by the U.S. Arms Control Disarmament Agency concluded in 1970, it is an extremely competitive race, with adversary states as mutual pacesetters, procuring offsetting armaments in a continuous action-reaction process; new arms accretions have repeatedly involved generational jumps in the quality of armaments, at periodically faster rates, and with sharp increases in military expenditures; finally, each side aims, not at equilibrium, but at achieving a preponderance of power.[2]

Compounding the problem are geopolitical and demographic factors that have prompted both Israelis and Arabs to equip their military forces to fit symmetrical strategies built around the principle of surprise attack.[3] The emphasis laid on air power and sophisticated air defenses by Israel and Egypt is prompted by the need to assure the mastery of the skies required for successful ground action in the open terrains of Middle Eastern battlefields, or to deny mastery of the skies to others. Quick control of the air can be achieved only by knocking out the enemy's air force by surprise attack.[4] The consequent urge to embark on preventive wars or on preemptive strikes in

2. Amelia C. Leiss et al., *Arms Control and Local Conflict*, Vol. 3: *Arms Transfers to Less Developed Countries* (Cambridge, Mass.: Massachusetts Institute of Technology, February 1970), pp. 282–287, 311–315.

3. For a discussion of this, see Nadav Safran, *From War to War: The Arab-Israeli Confrontation, 1948–1967* (New York: Pegasus, 1969), pp. 249–252; Yair Evron, *The Role of Arms Control in the Middle East*, Adelphi Paper, No. 138 (London: International Institute for Strategic Studies, Autumn 1977), pp. 17–18; Steven J. Rosen and Martin Indyk, "The Temptation to Preempt in a Fifth Arab-Israeli War," *Orbis* 20 (Summer 1976), 265–286; and Robert J. Pranger and Dale R. Tahtinen, *Implications of the 1976 Arab-Israeli Military Status* (Washington, D.C.: American Enterprise Institute, 1976), pp. 1–12.

4. The Egyptian offensive across the Suez Canal in October 1973 did not require prior neutralization of the Israeli air force—in itself a very hazardous undertaking, given the advanced air defense system the Israelis also possess—because control of the skies over the envisaged area of operations along the eastern bank of the Canal was already achieved through the SAM defensive umbrella erected on the western bank.

crisis situations thus adds to the overall instability that has characterized inter-war periods. It also provides increased impetus to the arms race by putting enormous pressure on both sides to assure their capability for both offensive and defensive action through the constant qualitative and quantitative upgrading of stockpiles, as the region has witnessed since 1954–1955.

Another major factor contributing to the conflict potential of the arms race is its composite, or multitiered, character. The Syrian-Egyptian-Israeli competition—which accounts for by far the major input of weaponry into the immediate area of conflict (see Table 1)—forms only the core of a complex process in which Israel has been simultaneously reacting to arms acquisitions of other Arab opponents as well, most notably Jordan and Iraq, and, in more recent times, Libya and Saudi Arabia. In addition, some Arab states have been contributing to the race against Israel but have also been racing against one another and/or contiguous non-Arab states (such as Iran), often in quest of influence and bloc leadership as much as security.

A further significant booster to acceleration of the arms competition is what may be termed "anticipatory procurement" of major weaponry. Due to the complete dependence of the local parties on external sources of supply, they will tend to acquire more armaments than their immediate needs require whenever the opportunity arises, so as to build backup reserves against the day when political shifts, embargoes, rationing arrangements, or other restrictions might dry up these sources. Egypt's initial arms deals with the Soviet bloc in 1955 and early 1956, when weapons were purchased far in excess of the military's absorptive capacity, provide a clear example of this practice. Similarly indicative is the Israeli demand for U.S. arms, particularly combat aircraft and missilry, in the post-1967 period, which far exceeded American assessment of Israeli needs.[5]

Not less pernicious than the behavior of the regional recipients is the role

5. Beyond Tables 1, 2, and 3, the purpose of which is simply to illustrate long-range trends in the arms competition, no attempt is made here to detail the quantitative aspects of the competition in terms of both military equipment and expenditure. This would be superfluous, as such information has been compiled and amply examined on a country and regional basis by numerous sources. The most comprehensive are: Leiss et al., *Arms Control*; Stockholm International Peace Research Institute (SIPRI), *The Arms Trade with the Third World* (New York: Humanities Press, 1971), and the annual *Yearbooks*; International Institute for Strategic Studies (IISS), *The Military Balance* (London), also annual; Safran, *From War to War*; Evron, *Role of Arms Control*; Pranger and Tahtinen, *Implications*; and U.S. Arms Control and Disarmament Agency (ACDA), *World Military Expenditures and Arms Transfers 1967–1976* (Washington, D.C.: Government Printing Office, July 1978), and subsequent annual volumes.

Table 1. Military Expenditures of Selected Middle Eastern Countries, 1951–1976 (in current U.S. $ millions)

Annual Averages	1951–1955	1956–1960	1961–1965	1966–1970	1971–1973	1974–1976
Egypt	146.8	236.4	336.2	459.4	866.7	1,150.7
Israel	104.1	183.8	245.8	917.4	1,700.7	2,815.0
Iraq	53.5	92.9	193.4	555.0	970.7	1,670.7
Syria	25.8	65.2	107.2	274.2	421.7	804.3
Jordan	28.0	45.6	55.6	104.6	129.0	154.3

SOURCES: Yair Evron, "Arms Races in the Middle East and Some Arms Control Measures Related to Them," in *Dynamics of a Conflict*, ed. Gabriel Sheffer (New York: Humanities Press, 1975), Tables 2–6, for the years 1951–1960; and Arms Control and Disarmament Agency (ACDA), *World Military Expenditures, 1971*, and *World Military Expenditures and Arms Transfers, 1966–1975, and 1968–1977* (Washington, D.C.: Government Printing Office).

Table 2. Operational Inventories of Jet Combat Aircraft and Tanks on the Eve of War

	Jet Combat Aircraft			Tanks		
	1956	1967	1973	1956	1967	1973
Egypt	205	431	620	430	1,300	1,955
Israel	110	290	488	400	800	1,700
Syria	44	78	326	200	400	1,270
Iraq	34	150	224	135	395	945
Jordan	16	18	52	105	300	400

SOURCES: Amelia C. Leiss et al., *Arms Control and Local Conflict*, Vol. 3: *Arms Transfers to Less Developed Countries* (Cambridge, Mass.: M.I.T., February 1970); Nadav Safran, *From War to War: The Arab-Israeli Confrontation, 1948–1967* (New York: Pegasus, 1969); and International Institute for Strategic Studies, *The Military Balance, 1973–1974* (London).

of the primary arms suppliers. During the 1960s, the Soviet Union and the United States became so enmeshed in the political as well as the military dimensions of the local arms rivalry, and their intervention became so polarized once the U.S. became practically Israel's sole supplier in 1968, that this rivalry often took on the added character of a Soviet-American regional arms race by proxy.[6] Beginning with the War of Attrition in 1969, Middle Eastern battlefields became testing grounds for new weaponry, and the prestige of the suppliers from a military-technological standpoint became fully engaged; neither the Soviet Union nor the United States was willing to let its respective clients be defeated in a test that unambiguously pitted American technology against Russian technology on the battlefield. Moreover, because arms sales have been the venue for the Soviets' political entrance in the region,

6. On the multitiered character of the Middle East arms race, see J. C. Hurewitz, *Middle East Politics: The Military Dimension* (New York: Praeger, 1969), pp. 452–456; and Safran, *From War to War*, pp. 247–248.

and continued to be the mainstay of their Middle Eastern presence, a change of suppliers by a Middle Eastern government has come to be perceived by both the East and the West as tantamount to crossing the political threshold between one camp and the other. Furthermore, the tight arms-transfer relationship has gradually created for the *suppliers* a bigger stake in the outcome of the political disputes in the area; thus, throughout the sixties, both the Soviets and the Americans gradually slipped into a diplomatic stance of outright support for the side they were arming in the Arab-Israeli conflict. This polarization reached its apex following the Six-Day War of 1967, with the breach in relations between the United States and the major Arab countries on the one hand, and between Israel and the Soviet Union on the other, and was maintained and reinforced during the six years that preceded the October War. The vigorous American diplomatic sponsorship of a peaceful settlement in the wake of the 1973 encounter, and the concomitant rapprochement between Washington and Cairo have begun to reverse this trend, but any further outbreak of large-scale conflict between the Arabs and Israel is likely to reinforce it again.

Such heavy commitment of prestige and resources further magnifies the grim potential for superpower confrontation already inherent in a situation where interests are at stake that both nuclear giants regard as greatly important. To illustrate this danger, one need only compare the behavior of the superpowers in the latest Middle East war, when they started feverishly replenishing the dwindling arsenals of their respective clients within a few days of the outbreak of fighting, with the restraint and conflict-limiting collaboration they exhibited during the 1956 Suez War, the 1965 Indo-Pakistani War, and the Six-Day War of 1967.[7] In 1973, tensions between Moscow and Washington rose markedly as the fighting progressed. In a sense, the worldwide alert of U.S. military forces that climaxed the showdown on 25 October can be perceived, not as a radically new departure, but as one further long step toward globalization of a regional conflict that was already being fought almost exclusively with Soviet and American weaponry. Without a negotiated solution to the Arab-Israeli dispute, it is difficult to see how a disengagement of these two main suppliers from their interactive role in the regional arms race can be effected.

7. For an analysis of Soviet behavior, see Paul Jabber and Roman Kolkowicz, "The Arab-Israeli Wars of 1967 and 1973," in Stephen S. Kaplan et al., *Mailed Fist, Velvet Glove: Armed Forces as a Political Instrument* (Washington, D.C.: The Brookings Institution, September 1979). On U.S. actions, see William B. Quandt, *Decade of Decisions* (Berkeley and Los Angeles: University of California Press, 1978), chaps. 2 and 6.

STRATEGIC IMPACT OF THE 1973 WAR

The current halting movement toward peace should not be allowed to disguise the basic instability of the post-October War situation. Indeed, the latest war has brought about a potentially more volatile strategic environment than that which spawned it. Separation-of-forces agreements between the major combatants have helped prevent the day-to-day frictions likely to arise when hostile military forces face each other in close proximity. They may also provide an earnest of newly found goodwill on the part of the adversaries. Basically, however, the present situation lacks even those deceptively stabilizing elements that seemed to presage in 1970–1973 an indefinite "no war–no peace" stalemate, despite the 1979 Egypt-Israel treaty.

First, Israel's military superiority did not dissuade Egypt and Syria from seeking to alter the status quo by armed force. Greatly significant for the future strategic calculus is the fact that the challenge came at a time when the consensus of qualified opinion considered Israel's superiority so overwhelming as to rule out Arab attack. The misreading of intelligence information by both Israeli and U.S. services in the days that preceded the Arab offensive largely resulted from this mistaken assessment, on which Israel had based its security posture and its politico-diplomatic position since June 1967.[8] Not only did the Arabs seize the military initiative but they did so with relative success, achieving the limited objectives of gaining a foothold on the Sinai and inflicting severe losses on the Israelis in both manpower and equipment.[9]

Secondly, a psychological equilibrium has been reestablished within the Arab-Israeli military equation. While Israel obviously held the tactical advantage on both fronts at the end of the war, the 1973 hostilities ended on an ambiguous note. Despite heavy losses, neither the Egyptian nor the Syrian armies were defeated, and Egypt managed to regain control of a politically

8. For a good analysis of Egyptian prewar calculations and motives, see Donna Robinson Divine, "Why this War . . . ," *International Journal of Middle East Studies* 7 (October 1976), 523–543. A competent assessment of Israeli and American perceptions on the eve of war is in Avi Shlaim, "Failures in National Intelligence Estimates: The Case of the Yom Kippur War,' *World Politics* 28 (April 1976), 348–380. On Israel's strategic doctrines and the role of deterrence, see Dan Horowitz, "The Israeli Concept of National Security and the Prospects of Peace in the Middle East," in Gabriel Sheffer, ed., *Dynamics of a Conflict* (New York: Humanities Press, 1975), pp. 235–276.

9. These objectives and the larger aim of restoring a credible military option after the 1967 debacle had been spelled out by the Egyptians as early as 1969, and provided the rationale for the 1969–1970 war of attrition as well. For an analysis of the latter, see Ahmed S. Khalidi, "The War of Attrition," *Journal of Palestine Studies* 3 (Autumn 1973), 76–82.

and diplomatically very important foothold on the Sinai. Moreover, the Arabs were able to force Israel to fight on their terms for much of the war, and they succeeded in causing very heavy human casualties and material losses, relative to previous encounters. The Arab soldier proved his ability to fight well, plan and execute complex logistic and combined-arms operations with efficiency, and master modern arms technology.

Until the October War, Israel had found reassurance in the belief that such developments lay far in the future. One typical Israeli assessment held that "in contrast to the severe weaknesses of the Arab armies, the . . . IDF [Israel Defense Forces] has increasing technological superiority, a remarkable level of general training, and originality of the strategic and practical conceptions of the command. The army's fighting spirit is not less obvious. . . . As long as there is no radical change in the structure of Arab society, the qualitative difference between Israel and Arab military potential will persist and will perhaps increase to the detriment of the Arabs."[10] Many Arab observers came to share this evaluation after the 1967 defeat, and something akin to a martial inferiority-complex developed in the Arab psyche. In a widely read piece published soon after that debacle, Cecil Hourani dourly asserted: "The basic truth we must face is that the Arabs as a whole do not yet have the scientific and technological skills, nor the general level of education among the masses, which make possible the waging of large-scale modern warfare."[11] While it lasted, this perceptual element had a conflict-limiting effect in both camps. Its restraining hold has now been definitively broken.

Lastly, from an Arab vantage point, war worked where nothing else had. Starting with Nasser's acceptance of the American-engineered cease-fire that ended the War of Attrition in August 1970, and culminating in the United Nations Security Council debates of June–July 1973, the Egyptian leadership experienced enormous frustrations on the diplomatic front. A long campaign

10. Saul Friedlander, "Policy Choices before Israel," in Paul Y. Hammond and Sidney S. Alexander, eds., *Political Dynamics in the Middle East* (New York: American Elsevier, 1972), pp. 123–124. A similar assessment is made by Israeli General Y. Harkabi in "Basic Factors of the Arab Collapse during the Six-Day War," *Orbis* 11 (1967), pp. 677–691. General Dayan spoke in an identical vein to the graduating class of Israel's Army Command and Staff College only two months before the outbreak of the October War; see *Haaretz* (Tel Aviv), August 10, 1973.

11. Cecil Hourani, "The Moment of Truth," *Encounter* 29 (November 1967), 3–14. The article was first published in Arabic by the Beirut newspaper *An-Nahar* in a special supplement. A very dim view of present Arab capabilities was expressed in another influential book by the Syrian intellectual Sadiq Al-Azm, *Self-Criticism after the Defeat* [in Arabic] (Beirut: Dar Al-Tali'ah, 1968).

punctuated by repeated disappointments was unsuccessfully waged to induce active international—particularly American—participation in bringing about a settlement based on Israel's withdrawal from the occupied territories. In dramatic contrast, the October War swiftly sparked a worldwide sense of urgency that Sadat had vainly tried for three years to impart, catalyzed a measure of coordinated Arab action that soon threatened an energy crisis of global proportions, and brought the superpowers to the brink of confrontation. More importantly, the war forced the United States to engage in intensive diplomatic efforts that it had previously shunned, because of the strains on American-Israeli relations inherent in any vigorous attempt to achieve a settlement that would divest Israel of most of its 1967 territorial gains.[12]

From the perspective of Cairo, Damascus, Amman, Baghdad, and the Palestinians, the fundamental lesson of 1973 is clear. Should the current diplomatic momentum wane, and international—particularly American— interest in pressing for a political settlement slacken, or should the negotiating process fail to proceed beyond partial solutions that do not address fundamental Arab grievances, further recourse to arms—or the reactivation of a credible threat to do so—may be the optimal Arab choice.[13]

It is in this light that the widespread and punitively negative reaction within the Arab world to the March 1979 Israel-Egypt peace treaty must be assessed. This bilateral arrangement threatened to deprive the Arab bloc of any credible war option, by neutralizing its most potent military component, the Egyptian armed forces. Sadat's protestations notwithstanding, eastern-front Arabs feared that Cairo would prove less than zealous in its devotion to Palestinian rights and pan-Arab obligations once Israel evacuated Sinai.

12. Two excellent studies of U.S. post–October War diplomacy are: Edward R. F. Sheehan, *The Arabs, Israelis, and Kissinger* (New York: Reader's Digest Press, 1976); and Quandt, *Decade of Decisions*, chaps. 7–9. We now know (e.g., Quandt, p. 162) that, in the Fall of 1973, Washington was gearing up for another major Middle East diplomatic offensive in search of an acceptable compromise. This author, however, spent the summer of 1973 in Cairo, interviewing members of the Egyptian foreign-policy community, and the overriding impression he gathered was one of general Egyptian bafflement at the American position and almost total despair of any sincere U.S. effort at peacemaking.

13. For a typical optimistic Arab assessment of the "new balance of power," see Ghassan Tueni, "After October: Military Conflict and Political Change in the Middle East," *Journal of Palestine Studies* 3 (Summer 1974), 114–130. Mr. Tueni is a prominent Lebanese newspaper publisher, former cabinet minister, and ambassador to the United Nations as of this writing. An informed Israeli assessment of how the Arabs view the new relationship of forces is Moshe Shamir's "Arab Military Lessons from the October War," in Louis Williams, ed., *Military Aspects of the Israeli-Arab Conflict* (Tel Aviv: University Publishing Projects, 1975), pp. 172–178.

Most significantly, within Egypt itself, uncertainty among much of the politically relevant public over the real course the regime was charting for the
country has deprived Sadat of solid domestic support for his peace policies,
and casts serious doubts over their permanence.

Thus, paradoxically, the contemporary Arab-Israeli strategic balance
presents a Janusian double face. It offers better chances of a negotiated peace
than at any time since the emergence of Israel. However, if diplomacy proves
sterile, it presages an increase in both the scale and the costs of armed
violence.

How can Israel—the challenged party—prepare for this contingency within
the demographic and economic limitations particular to it ? Considering the
costs of the 1973 war, this may prove a task beyond its means unless it proves
willing to surrender basic social goals or to severely mortgage its freedom of
action in the foreign sphere.

Available statistics are not sufficient for an accurate estimate of the total
price the Israeli economy paid for the eighteen days of fighting in October
1973, but they are indicative of its magnitude. Israeli Finance Minister Pinhas
Sapir put the military bill at a staggering $7 billion, a figure larger than the
country's entire 1973 gross national product (GNP).[14] U.S. grant military aid
and the contributions of Jewish communities abroad helped defray these
costs, but only partially.[15] In addition to paying for direct war costs, lengthy
mobilization, and economic disruption, Israel has had to reequip its armed
forces with weaponry that is progressively more sophisticated and hence more
expensive. In the inter-war years, military outlays annually escalated from
$460 million in 1966 to $1.69 billion in 1972, making Israeli per capita defense
expenditures the highest in the world.[16] The burden of this massive effort on
the individual Israeli taxpayer, while grievous, was made tolerable by the
high rate of economic growth attained during this period, which allowed the
military portion of the GNP to remain fairly stable. Averaging about 18
percent over the period 1967–1973, however, this again was unmatched by

14. *Jerusalem Post*, March 15, 1974. According to Sapir, Israeli military equipment
losses in the first week of fighting alone had amounted to some $2 billion; *Guardian*
(London), October 20, 1973. See also Moshe Brilliant, "Israel's Economy Burdened
by War," *New York Times*, March 15, 1974.

15. Total U.S. government economic assistance to Israel in fiscal year (FY) 1974
was fixed at $2.65 billion, of which $2.5 billion was for military purposes; private
flows to Israel as a result of the war were estimated by the U.S. State Department at
$1.237 billion. See U.S. Congress, Senate, *Report No. 93-657*, 93rd Congress, 1st
Session.

16. ACDA, *World Military Expenditures and Arms Transfers, 1967–1976*.

any other country.[17] Such a rate of growth was achieved by allowing rampant inflation, accumulation of a giant foreign debt, and a steep increase in taxation. Following the 1973 war, these negative trends were intensified, while the economic growth rate, which was already expected in 1973 to level off, was substantially reduced by the effects of the latest war. Furthermore, a larger share of Israel's industrial output has been diverted to the defense sector, and no less than 25 percent of the total Israeli labor force has come to be employed either directly by the military establishment or indirectly in industry, construction, and other services for defense.[18] Average annual defense allocations in the 1974–1980 budgets (which reflect less than total ultimate expenditures) have amounted to some $3.775 billion.[19]

In short, Israel faces an augmented defense burden with increasingly limited indigenous resources. The policies of fiscal imbalance that permitted the maximal effort of the early- and mid-seventies cannot be continued indefinitely. By 1975, despite large-scale U.S. assistance amounting to 40 percent of the total Israeli defense budget in 1973–1975, the foreign exchange deficit was increasing at the ruinous rate of $4 billion per year, an amount that almost equalled the country's total annual exports.[20] Military purchases accounted for over one-third of this deficit.[21] Not surprisingly, in 1974–1976 the rate of growth in Israel's gross national product, which had been one of the highest in the world prior to the October War, fell to almost zero.[22]

In human terms, the cost of the latest round was equally onerous, and much more so than in the previous two encounters. Wounded and unaccounted-for personnel aside, the loss of some 2,838 dead out of a total Jewish population of some 2.8 million is equivalent to the loss of 220,000 soldiers for a population the size of the United States. This is equivalent to almost five times the number of combat deaths sustained by the United States in a decade of

17. This high percentage is *exclusive* of U.S. assistance and represents the true economic burden on the Israeli economy; David Kochav (Economic Advisor, Israeli Ministry of Defense), "The Economics of Defense—Israel," in Williams, *Military Aspects*, p. 180.

18. Ibid., p. 179.

19. See Table 1, above.

20. Williams, *Military Aspects*, p. 182. As Kochav points out, over the longer term this situation is further aggravated by the fact that about half of the U.S. aid consists of repayable loans.

21. Ibid., p. 182. For a discussion of the broader implications for the Israeli economy of stepped-up military imports after 1973, see Nadav Halevi, "The Economy of Israel: Goals and Limitations," *Jerusalem Quarterly*, No. 1 (Fall 1976), pp. 88–92; and Haim Darin-Drabkin, "The Economic Aspects of Defense," *New Outlook* 18 (March–April 1975), 51–54.

22. ACDA, *World Military Expenditures and Arms Transfers, 1967–1976*, p. 48.

conflict in Southeast Asia, and constitutes a very punishing blow for a community that, for obvious historical reasons, is very conscious of its demographic makeup and circumstances. In the Sinai campaign of 1956, by way of contrast, Israel sustained minimal casualties; and in the Six-Day War, she lost less than one thousand dead.[23]

In fact, the latest war and its inconclusive termination represents the type of conflict that Israel has by doctrine always tried to avoid and is organizationally and structurally least able to afford. It was initiated by the opponent, it came largely by surprise, and it was fought initially on Israel-held territory— all factors that worked to maximize Israeli material and human losses. It was of relatively long duration, Israel having failed to secure early mastery of the air over the battle areas. It ended indecisively, which, apart from important psychological implications, meant that for the first time the adversary had not been left with a shattered military machine to rebuild but, to the contrary, in an overall state comparable to that of the Israeli machine. It also meant that a higher level of mobilization of the reserves, who form the bulk of the armed forces, would have to be maintained at a heavy economic price, or the size of the standing army substantially increased. By 1977, the standing army had grown from 115,000 in 1973 to 164,000.[24]

But the most vexing aspect of this episode from an Israeli viewpoint must be that this enormous investment has been in vain. Despite its limited but tangible military victory on the battlefield, Israel emerged from the October War with a diminished feeling of security and in a politically weaker bargaining position. The new Egyptian willingness to negotiate without a preceding Israeli commitment to full withdrawal from the Arab territories, which President Sadat evinced in the immediate aftermath of the 1973 fighting and most forcefully expressed in his November 1977 visit to Israel, may be regarded as Israel's only war gain. But this was a bonus of the latest round in a limited sense only. Egypt became willing to sit at the bargaining table without preconditions because it now held several strong bargaining chips, whereas before October 1973 it had had none. The Cairo leadership no longer felt that a prior withdrawal pledge by Israel was absolutely necessary, because it believed that the withdrawal could now be secured through the application of regional and global economic and political pressures set in motion by the

23. For factual information on and a comparative military analysis of past encounters, see Trevor N. Dupuy, *Elusive Victory: The Arab-Israeli Wars, 1947–1974* (New York: Bobbs-Merrill, 1977); and J. Bowyer Bell, *The Long War: Israel and the Arabs Since 1946* (Englewood Cliffs, N.J.: Prentice-Hall, 1969).

24. IISS, *The Military Balance, 1977–1978*, p. 85.

latest war—pressures that simply would have been unavailable without that war. The soundness of this calculus was borne out in March 1979, with the signing of a peace agreement that indeed entailed total Israeli return of conquered Egyptian territory.

By any assessment, this costliest of wars resulted in a substantial deterioration of Israel's position. Herein lies the deep significance of the 1973 crisis, given Israel's peculiar philosophy of national security. In the words of General Y. Harkabi, one of the country's most influential strategic thinkers, "Israel's sensitivity to its security stems not only from the urge to ensure its existence but also to ensure the continuance of its 'success story.' Other states may exist if they are not successful. But Israel's success is imperative for its existence. This, at least, is the conviction of both its leaders and many of its people, who believe that otherwise it will not attract the necessary immigration and capital . . . [and] it is an operative factor of utmost importance." [25] This is why Israel must see to it that the October 1973 setback is not repeated.

One way of avoiding such repetition is through a comprehensive peaceful settlement. The outlook for successful negotiations have become brighter in the post-October War period than ever before because of a convergence of several factors that have created a new strategic balance between Arabs and Israelis. Applied in its most comprehensive sense, the term "strategic" embraces psychological, economic, and political as well as military components. Some psychological and military aspects have already been touched upon. The economic difficulties that the continuing conflict is imposing on Israel have also been outlined. On the Arab side, the material burdens of the confrontation have been markedly alleviated through the vast increase in oil revenues for the producing countries, and the willingness of these countries to share heavily in the financing of the Arab war effort.[26] Politically, the considerable growth of inter-Arab coordination and collaboration, and the intensified superpower involvement in the dynamics of the confrontation—both militarily and diplomatically—are also elements that help counterbalance

25. Yehoshafat Harkabi, "Obstacles in the Way of a Settlement," in Sheffer, ed., *Dynamics of a Conflict.*

26. For example, in the two years following the 1973 war, Egypt received $2.564 billion in Arab economic assistance; *Middle East Economic Digest*, January 16, 1976. Post-1973 Arab oil revenues invalidate the prognostications of some analysts that Israel was winning the arms race because her higher rate of GNP increase allowed her to progressively devote more money to the military sector than her major adversary (Egypt) without unduly straining her resources. For this argument, see Safran, *From War to War*, especially pp. 190–204; and John C. Lambelet, "A Dynamic Model of the Arms Race in the Middle East, 1953–1965," in *General Systems, Yearbook of the Society for General Systems Research* 16 (1971), 145–167.

the still clear Israeli superiority in the purely military arena. Furthermore, the oil factor has sharply reduced the American willingness to maintain previous levels of support for Israel, whether political or military, even in times of severe crisis. Thus, for Israel, the new situation is one that drastically limits the usefulness of "military coercion" as a strategy of action, and it has induced a stronger disposition to trade territorial conquests for less tangible Arab political concessions than was evident prior to October 1973.[27] For the front-line Arab states as well, particularly Egypt, the economic burden of arms competition, despite aid from oil-rich states, has reached a point where further increases have become well-nigh intolerable.[28] More importantly, the prospects for speedy Arab economic development in conditions of peace opened up by the enormous influx of oil money, and the widespread feeling that the Arab world can now deal with others—including the West and Israel itself—on a level of equality and with self-confidence, have created the right domestic political conditions for a moderate and conciliatory stance in Arab-Israeli diplomacy.

In case the diplomatic approach fails, however, a restitution of flexibility has been sought in further strengthening of military power. The results of the 1973 war were bound to speed up the momentum of the race even beyond its previous fast pace. On the Israeli side, the very substantial margin of military superiority universally perceived to have existed at the time was shown to be inadequate for deterrence. On the Arab side, despite the success of their initial offensive and their much improved battlefield performance, the Egyptian and Syrian forces could not register a military victory. A virtually irresistible incentive existed for all parties to seek a substantial increase in their military power.

This has been sought principally in further strengthening of the conventional forces. By 1976, the heavy October War losses in equipment had already been recouped, and the arms flow into the area continues apace (see Table 3).[29] Educated by experience, the adversaries will place even greater

27. An excellent analysis of the internal Israeli debate over the fate of occupied Arab territories is in Rael J. Isaac, *Israel Divided: Ideological Politics in the Jewish State* (Baltimore: Johns Hopkins University Press, 1976).

28. A well-rounded and sensitive discussion of Egypt's economic plight can be found in John Waterbury, *Egypt: Burdens of the Past, Options for the Future* (Hanover, N.H.: American Universities Field Staff, n.d.).

29. In addition to the standard sources listed above (see note 5, above), detailed data and analysis of the arms buildup can be found in Dale R. Tahtinen, *Arab-Israeli Military Status in 1976* (Washington, D.C.: American Enterprise Institute, 1976); and in Pranger and Tahtinen, *Implications*.

Table 3. Comparative Increments of Military Power In Israel and Selected Arab States, 1974–1980

	Combat Aircraft				Tanks				Active Military Personnel (thousands)			
	1974	1976	1978	1980*	1974	1976	1978	1980	1974	1976	1978	1980*
Egypt	672±	688	612	586	2,000	1,975	1,680	2,420	323.0	342.5	395.0	410.0
Syria	440	440	392	750	1,670	2,400	2,600	2,670	137.5	227.0	227.5	272.4
Jordan	50	66	76	76	490	490	500	540	74.9	67.9	67.9	75.0
Iraq	218±	299	339	379	1,390	1,390+	1,900+	2,000+	112.5	158.0	212.0	n.a.
Saudi Arabia	90	97	171	171	115	385	325	500	43.0	51.5	58.5	n.a.
Israel	466±	543	543	650	1,900+	2,765	3,065	3,240–5,040†	145.5	158.5	487.2‡	

SOURCES: International Institute for Strategic Studies, *The Military Balance* (London: IISS, n.d.); and Anthony Cordesman, "The Arab-Israeli Balance: How Much Is Too Much?" *Armed Forces Journal International* (October 1977).

* Estimate.
† Depending on the output of the domestic Israeli arms industry.
‡ Total mobilizable personnel within seventy-two hours.

emphasis than in the past on strategies of surprise attack for war initiation. The Arabs' ability to strike first in 1973 proved extremely successful, basically predetermining the entire course of the war. Enormous military incentives exist for Israel to restore a preventive or preemptive war posture. New military technologies have added another destabilizing ingredient. The advent of a new generation of conventional weapons—precision-guided munitions—which combine high accuracy with relatively low cost and afford considerable versatility in deployment has introduced novel elements of uncertainty that may be highly detrimental to stable deterrence.[30] If the Arab-Israeli conflict reenters a state of active confrontation, these factors will greatly increase military instability and raise the level of tension arising from inevitable frictions and incidents.

Future wars are not likely to be short and conclusive, however. They will not follow the blitzkrieg pattern of the 1956 and 1967 encounters, but the more protracted, costly, and indecisive 1973 model. Higher levels of military proficiency and of available armaments, as well as the recently battle-tested effectiveness of missile defense systems, militate against the type of lightning wars preferred—indeed, *required*—by the Israelis. This will give increased prominence to a heretofore relatively submerged but important element in the Middle Eastern military picture: Israel may opt for "going nuclear" to reestablish a credible deterrent.

ACROSS THE NUCLEAR THRESHOLD ?

The low visibility of the Israeli nuclear potential in the inter-war period of 1967–1973 was a direct consequence of the unchallenged military upper hand that Israel achieved in the aftermath of the Six-Day War and consolidated with the strengthening of the air force during and after the War of Attrition. Territorial depth and easily defensible borders complemented armed strength, creating a feeling of immediate security. This feeling was buttressed by optimistic prognostications regarding the future course of the military balance. The fast-growing Israeli GNP, the burgeoning local military industries, the still-widening technological advantage over the Arab world, and the increased level of American aid to and identification with Israel were all regarded as

30. On the technological breakthroughs in conventional weaponry represented by the new panoply of precision-guided munitions (PGMs), and the tactical and strategic implications thereof, see, among others, James Digby, *Precision-Guided Weapons*, Adelphi Paper, No. 118 (Summer 1975); and James L. Foster, "New Conventional Weapons Technologies: Implications for the Third World," in Uri Ra'anan et al., eds., *Arms Transfers to the Third World: The Military Buildup in Less Industrial Countries* (Boulder, Colo.: Westview Press, 1978).

pointers to continued Israeli supremacy.[31] Furthermore, the basic Israeli doctrine of deterrence through military superiority appeared to be working satisfactorily, particularly after the passing of President Nasser, as the Egyptians resorted to diplomacy and courted the United States. Under these conditions, a nuclear arsenal was superfluous, and a threshold capability held in reserve as a military option but nevertheless of interim usefulness as a bargaining lever and psychological weapon was much more advantageous.

Such calculations notwithstanding, there was rather general agreement on the notion that a nuclear deterrent might become essential: (1) if the Arab countries, particularly those surrounding Israel, achieved some degree of effective unity that radically enhanced their military capability; (2) if Egypt gained some form of access to nuclear weaponry; or (3) if the balance of conventional armaments shifted enough to encourage the Arab countries to seek a military confrontation.[32]

The events of October 1973 brought these preconditions very near to realization. Syro-Egyptian coordination forced Israel to fight simultaneously on two fronts for the first time since 1948, and there were other effective aspects of Arab solidarity. During the fighting, the Soviet Union supplied Egypt with a nuclear-capable short-range missile, the SCUD, and Soviet nuclear warheads for the missiles were reported aboard Soviet cargo ships in Egyptian harbors.[33] As for the general balance of power, Israeli superiority did not dissuade Egypt and Syria from war on October 6. Moreover, the qualitative changes in the strategic environment already discussed cast heavy

31. For arguments along these lines, see sources cited in note 26, above; also see J. C. Hurewitz, "Weapons Acquisition: Israel and Egypt," in Frank B. Horton III et al., eds., *Comparative Defense Policy* (Baltimore: Johns Hopkins University Press, 1974).

32. In a 1963 signed article appearing in the daily *Maariv*, General Moshe Dayan, who then held the Agriculture portfolio, stated that in anticipation of Egypt's development of atomic warheads for her locally produced surface-to-surface missiles, "we must diligently develop these weapons so that we don't lag" (*New York Times*, April 13, 1963). Outgoing Prime Minister Ben-Gurion made similar remarks later that year (ibid., November 16, 1963). Also see statements by the former chairman of the Israeli Atomic Energy Commission, Professor Ernst Bergman, in *Maariv*, May 13, 1966. For more on the internal governmental debate over nuclear policy in this period, see Shlomo Aronson, *Conflict and Bargaining in the Middle East* (Baltimore: Johns Hopkins University Press, 1978), pp. 45–54.

33. The SS-1c, or SCUD, is a 185-mile range ballistic missile capable of carrying kiloton-range nuclear warheads or conventional payloads. Besides the Soviet Union, it is operated by East Germany and Poland, with nuclear warheads under Soviet custody; IISS, *Military Balance, 1973–1974*, p. 72. For reports of missiles and warheads in Egypt, citing U.S. official sources, see *Washington Post*, November 21, 1973; and *Aviation Week and Space Technology*, November 5, 1973.

doubts on the future sufficiency of the Israeli Army as a deterrent, in addition to the economic burdens that the escalation of the conventional arms race has entailed. In fact, as a conflict-limiting device, the policy of regional military balance pursued by the United States over the last two decades has been a signal failure. While this may induce in the major suppliers a stronger interest in arms control as an alternative approach, it may also prompt Israel to seek in nuclear weapons a reinforcement of her weakened deterrent.[34]

The interplay between external arms supplies and the nuclear option has an additional facet. Israel's almost total reliance on the United States as its one source of conventional weapons was starkly emphasized during the October War. This inescapable reliance can only render Israel more vulnerable than ever to American pressures, which may be decisive in thwarting Israeli policies. The withdrawal from Sinai in 1957 and the acceptance of the second Rogers plan of June 1970 (which committed Israel to withdraw from most of the territories occupied in 1967) as a basis for negotiation are only two out-standing past examples of the effectiveness of determined American compulsion.[35] This state of affairs can generate a strong urge to ensure greater autonomy of decision-making in the future through self-reliance in the supply of strategic weaponry, on which ultimate security is dependent. This urge has found expression in the intensive effort to expand and diversify the local armaments industry in the wake of the 1967 French embargo—including the development of a supersonic fighter, the "Kfir," on the pattern of the Mirage V but with American jet engines, and a medium battle tank, the "Merkava."[36] The desire for greater autonomy may also impel the Israelis to opt for nuclear status if their only major ally and purveyor of arms insists on imposing conditions considered inimical to their vital interests.

The manufacture and deployment of nuclear weapons by one or more local

34. "Israeli military superiority in the Middle East is considered by Israeli planners to be an essential factor in deterring the Egyptians from a new 'round' of fighting. . . . The need to maintain this superiority has dictated Israeli behavior in the arms race" (Evron, *Role of Arms Control*, p. 14).

35. One author, citing Israeli Foreign Ministry sources, states that Prime Minister Eshkol contemplated with his advisors using the nuclear issue to persuade Washington to abandon the "imposed settlement" approach embodied in the first Rogers plan made public in late 1969; Aronson, *Conflict and Bargaining*, p. 98.

36. On Israel's efforts to develop the domestic military industries, see, among others, Hurewitz, "Weapons Acquisition"; Jac Weller, "Israeli Arms Production" *Ordnance* 55 (May–June 1971), 540–544; Dominique Verguèse, "Science and Technology: Israel's Key to Survival," *Le Monde Weekly*, July 29–August 4, 1971, p. 3; and Herbert J. Coleman, "Israel Aircraft Develops New Capabilities," *Aviation Week & Space Technology*, March 31, 1975, pp. 14–17.

parties to the Arab-Israeli dispute has long been a subject of grave international concern. While the Arab side has lagged behind in atomic research and plant construction, the development by Israel of a militarily significant nuclear option over the past two decades has been a continuing source of friction between Washington and Tel Aviv.[37] Besides a small reactor near Tel Aviv, which has a rating of 6 thermal megawatts and is of negligible military value except as a training ground for scientists and technicians, Israel has a large research reactor at Dimona, in the northern Negev, which has an output of 26 thermal megawatts and thus can produce sufficient plutonium per year for at least one bomb of a yield similar to that used on Nagasaki. The Dimona reactor was constructed in cooperation with France, and Israel has complete control over it. Thus, if Israel can obtain natural uranium on the world market without safeguards—which is entirely possible, since supply has overtaken demand and there is no tight overall international control—or increase home production of uranium from phosphates, Dimona can be entirely self-sufficient.[38]

Once the required plutonium has been fabricated in the reactor core, the next step toward nuclear weapons would be the construction of the chemical plant needed to separate out the plutonium. The available evidence does not indicate that a separation facility has been set up. It is considered feasible to build such a plant in secrecy, however, and the necessary equipment can be easily acquired from private parties, as the Indian experience in building the Trombay chemical separation plant has shown. Moreover, a small facility can be built in a relatively short time if a crash program requires it, and Israel has already moved in that direction with her "hot laboratories" (facilities equipped for remote-control processing of irradiated materials). Indeed, several years ago it was suggested that enough plutonium for at least one bomb may have

37. A detailed description of the Israeli nuclear effort and possible strategic roles is in the author's *Israel and Nuclear Weapons* (London: Chatto & Windus, 1971). On U.S.-Israeli frictions, see, inter alia, Aronson, *Conflict and Bargaining*, pp. 41–42, 51.

38. On Israel's local uranium production potential, see "'Go Nuclear,' Expert Urges," *Jerusalem Post*, December 14, 1973, in which a leading Israeli nuclear scientist, Dr. Shimon Yiftah, advocates the building of nuclear stations for power production. In 1975, Yiftah stated that Israel possessed up to 60,000 tons of uranium and could extract 60 tons annually at the Arad Chemical works for use in nuclear reactors; *Los Angeles Times*, October 9, 1975. It is reported that, in 1968, Israel's intelligence services engineered the illicit diversion to Haifa of 200 tons of uranium oxide fuel being transported by sea from Holland to Italy under loose EURATOM safeguards, Elaine Davenport et al., *The Plumbat Affair* (Philadelphia: J. B. Lippincott, 1978). This amount of natural uranium would have provided Dimona with sufficient fuel for some ten years of operation.

already been separated in the laboratory.[39] It should be noted in this context that the construction of a chemical separation plant, in view of the extensive investment involved, would not be warranted by the minimal needs of the existing Israeli nuclear program, and could be explained only in terms of acquiring an independent military option.[40]

The delivery of nuclear warheads in the Middle East is not a formidable problem. The distances to be covered are not great, populations and industry are concentrated in small areas—in Egypt as well as in Israel—and only a small number of bombs would be needed, whether for actual warfare or for blackmail and/or deterrence purposes. Regional air defenses—though increasingly formidable—are inferior to adversary penetration capabilities; the improvements in Egypt's air defenses do not detract significantly from the credibility of the Israeli air force's potential to deliver one or two nuclear payloads over Egyptian area targets. Israel has gone a long way toward acquiring an effective nuclear delivery system in the process of developing a strong air force for conventional warfare purposes, and even unorthodox means such as commercial airliners or helicopters should not be discounted.

Nor has the missile alternative been overlooked. Local tests with home-manufactured solid-fuel rockets were carried out as early as 1961 in Israel as part of a program given high priority because of "grave defense problems," in the words of the then-Deputy Defense Minister Shimon Peres.[41] In 1963, the French arms manufacturer, Dassault, was commissioned to develop a surface-to-surface mobile missile system at an expense of reportedly over $100 million. The product, code-named "MD-660," is an SRBM (short-range ballistic missile) with a range of about 300 miles, and is capable of carrying a 1200-pound warhead. Though delivery of this sytem was apparently delayed somewhat by the French arms embargo imposed in 1967, it was later reported to be in production in Israel itself under the name "Jericho," though not yet operationally deployed.[42]

39. Leonard Beaton, "Why Israel Does Not Need the Bomb," *New Middle East* (London), No. 7 (April 1969), pp. 7–11.

40. A decade ago, the cost of a small chemical separation plant was put at $40 million; C. F. Barnaby, ed., *Preventing the Spread of Nuclear Weapons* (London: Souvenir Press, 1969), p. 21. India's first separation plant was said to have cost only $7.5 million; William Van Cleave, "Nuclear Technology and Weapons," in Robert M. Lawrence and Joel Larus, eds., *Nuclear Proliferation: Phase II* (Lawrence, Kansas: University Press of Kansas, 1974), p. 47.

41. As quoted in the *New Scientist* (London), March 28, 1963.

42. IISS, *Military Balance, 1973–1974*, p. 32; and Aronson, *Conflict and Bargaining*, p. 51.

It is not easy to assess with any degree of exactitude Israel's aims in developing a missile system at such expense. In terms of cost-effectiveness, a relationship that Israelis have had constantly in mind when allocating their limited resources, it is hard to justify this project except in the context of a possible nuclear weapons program. No explanations of the rule envisaged for the missile have been given, and, at first glance, it appears that a sophisticated and, regionally, very significant means of delivery has been developed together with a nuclear weapons option that can be converted into a capability at short notice. Although this force would be very limited at first, in view of the small number of warheads that can be assembled with present plutonium-producing facilities, it would be sufficient to radically affect the military balance in the area.

Repeated U.S. efforts first launched under the Kennedy Administration to bring the Israeli atomic program under effective external supervision have failed,[43] and the Israelis have pointedly refrained from excluding the possibility of developing nuclear weapons as a future military policy if circumstances warrant it. Israel has remained adamant in its refusal to subscribe to the nuclear Non-Proliferation Treaty. The implied threat by Israel's leaders in their arms negotiations with the United States of going nuclear if their conventional weapons needs are not satisfied has been a complicating factor for U.S. Middle East policy, and is a major incentive for a continued American commitment to maintaining Israel's regional military superiority.[44]

The nuclear-weapons option presents Israel's decision-makers with a definite policy alternative in their selection of means to attain their security objectives. Israel does at present have the technological capacity to exercise this option; whether she will seriously contemplate doing so will of course depend almost exclusively on the impact such a step will be expected to have

43. See Michael Bar-Zohar, *The Armed Prophet: A Biography of Ben-Gurion* (London: Arthur Barker, 1966), p. 283; Aronson, *Conflict and Bargaining*, pp. 42, 51; and U.S. Congress, Senate, *Senate Delegation Report on American Foreign Policy and Nonproliferation Interests in the Middle East* (June 1977), p. 2.

44. On American-Israeli quid pro quo's, see Aubrey Hodes, "Implications of Israel's Nuclear Capability," *Wiener Library Bulletin* (London) 22 (Autumn 1968), 2–8; Geoffrey Kemp, "U.S. Military Policy: Dilemmas of the Arms Traffic," *Foreign Affairs* 48 (January 1970), 278–279; and S. Flapan, "Israel's Attitudes to NPT," a paper presented at the SIPRI Symposium: "Review of Nuclear Proliferation Problems," (Tallberg, Sweden, 15–18 June 1973), p. 23. The problems raised by the trade-off of nuclear abstention for conventional weaponry acquisition are discussed in Richard Burt, *Nuclear Proliferation and Conventional Arms Transfers: The Missing Link* (Santa Monica, Calif.: California Seminar on Arms Control and Foreign Policy, December 1977).

on her ongoing confrontation with the Arab countries. Would acquisition of nuclear weapons make Israeli-Arab relations more stable or less so? Is it likely to aid in the achievement of Israel's political objectives, or will it defeat such purposes? This will in turn be largely determined by the reactions of the Soviet Union and the United States to the Israeli move.

The deterrent effect and political benefits derivable from a nuclear posture naturally require for their full realization that the acquisition of nuclear weapons be revealed. For the new factor to have the desired impact on the situation, the opponent must be made aware of it and cognizant of the new relation of forces. The current Israeli posture has three components: a public avowal at the highest political levels of an advanced capability to build nuclear devices;[45] an ambiguous pledge not to be the first to "introduce" nuclear weapons into the region, coupled with a proviso that the first such introduction by others will be immediately matched by Israel; and a nuclear establishment with sufficient plant, scientific manpower, and technological skills to endow both the avowal and the proviso with high credibility. The ambiguity has been defended by Israelis on grounds that it maximizes freedom of action, provides bargaining leverage with the United States for conventional arms and political support, does least damage to Israel's international image, and is sufficient to deter the Arabs from undertaking extreme hostile acts such as attacks on population centers in wartime. Furthermore, it is expected to discourage the Arab governments from actively seeking a nuclear capability of their own, presumably by fostering hopes that the initiative is theirs and nuclearization can be avoided so long as they themselves refrain from taking the nuclear path.[46]

The policy of "keeping the Arabs guessing" that Israel has followed for a decade would be too risky if the credibility of a nuclear deterrent were to become the mainstay of Israeli security. Assuming that the capacity for weapons development at short notice exists, the basic choice for Israeli decision-makers is no longer whether to assemble the weapons but whether to openly assume a nuclear posture. Barring some fortuitous security breach, it would be extremely chancy to speculate whether actual warheads are in hand at any particular point in time. Not only does the secrecy surrounding Israeli nuclear activities present obvious obstacles, but also the difficulty of

45. The most explicit and authoritative avowal was made by Israel's President Ephraim Katzir in December 1974; *Maariv*, December 2, 1974.

46. For further description, see Yair Evron, "Israel and the Atom: the Uses and Misuses of Ambiguity, 1957–1967," *Orbis* 17 (Winter 1974), 1326–1343; and Alan Dowty, "Israel and Nuclear Weapons," *Midstream* 22 (November 1976), 7–22.

meaningfully determining when an advanced option becomes an actual weapons stockpile allows little scope for certainty. Arguably, from the standpoint of deterrence and psychological impact on the adversary, Israel has already introduced nuclear weapons into the conflict, since its principal opponents credit the Jewish state with a nuclear capability.[47] But only the willful disclosure of a military capability, which may assume any of several more or less direct forms—credibility being the essential requirement—will signal, to friends and enemies alike, a declared commitment to a nuclear security posture, with all the implications thereof.[48]

If the economic burdens of the military confrontation are to be assuaged by exercise of the nuclear option, a very major change in the structure of the country's military defense system would be necessary. A substantial diminution of the conventional component in the Israeli forces and a military doctrine calling for earlier wartime use of nuclear weapons than as a last-gasp measure to head off total military collapse would be required. Domestic opponents of a nuclear military capacity have often voiced the concern that reliance on a nuclear deterrent would leave Israel defenseless against low-scale conventional military threats, such as border clashes, limited enemy probes or incursions, and guerrilla warfare, to which the country has been continuously exposed, and which are hardly deterrable with threats of nuclear retribution. It is not likely, however, that the sacrifice in the conventional forces would have to be of such magnitude as to cripple the Israeli Army's ability to respond to these limited threats. The small nuclear-weapon stockpile of probably not more than ten 20-kiloton warheads that Israel can produce at the present time from her indigenous program should not cost more than $200–$300 million over and above the substantial investments already incurred in building plutonium-producing facilities and acquiring a missile delivery system.[49]

47. Both Egypt's President Sadat and Palestine Liberation Organization Chairman Yasser Arafat, for example, have stated their belief that Israeli nuclear arms have been produced. See, inter alia, *New York Times*, December 17, 1974, and April 4, 1975.

48. For a discussion of advantages and disadvantages of a nuclear posture, including reactions by extraregional nuclear powers, see the author's "Israel's Nuclear Options," *Journal of Palestine Studies* 1 (Autumn 1971), 21–38.

49. For estimates of nuclear weapons production costs, see the "Report of Secretary-General U Thant on the Effects of the Possible Use of Nuclear Weapons and on the Security and Economic Implications for States of the Acquisition and Further Development of These Weapons," 10 October 1967, text in ACDA, *Documents on Disarmament, 1967*; see also Barnaby, *Preventing the Spread*, pp. 27–29. For an analysis of the Israeli case at 1970 prices, see Jabber, *Israel and Nuclear Weapons*, pp. 82–85.

Naturally, this relatively minor outlay would be only a first step that would have to be followed by further, and progressively costlier, research and development. Once a country puts together a rudimentary nuclear force, it will soon feel compelled to develop less vulnerable and more accurate delivery systems and more sophisticated and versatile atomic warheads. It is questionable, for instance, whether the first generation of Israel's nuclear warheads will be compact and light enough to fit within the payload limits of the Jericho (MD-660) missile. Given the high level of military expenditure that Israel has attained, however, it will not have to place all its security eggs in the nuclear basket, as it will be able to maintain, in addition, conventional means adequate to meet a large spectrum of military contingencies. The deterrent effect of adding the nuclear component, on the other hand, could be very substantial.

The strong possibility of a regional nuclear arms race getting under way as Egypt and other Arab countries pool their resources to acquire or develop a nuclear deterrent of their own began to materialize in the second half of the seventies with the purchase of nuclear reactors by several Arab states and the activation of atomic research, planning, and training bodies, both within individual countries and on an inter-Arab level.[50] While only two small research reactors exist in the Arab world at the present time—one in Baghdad and the second in the outskirts of Cairo, both producing negligible fissionable material—Iraq, Libya, and Egypt have placed orders for large research and power reactors with France, the Soviet Union, and the United States, respectively.[51] By the late 1980s, the Arab bloc may have an installed nuclear capacity of over 2,300 megawatts electrical, which, while formally dedicated to peaceful purposes, will offer opportunities for national stockpiling of plutonium-rich nuclear wastes and surreptitious diversion to military uses. Although the production of electric power through nuclear energy in an area rich in fossil fuels offers scant economic attraction for the present, the desire to acquire technological know-how and the possible bonus of military spin-offs has already spurred joint Arab activities in the nuclear field. In November 1970,

50. Prominent members of Israel's defense community have declared the Arab-Israeli nuclear race as already under way. "Israel and its neighbors are now entering a period of fierce nuclear competition," stated Shalheveth Freier, the head of Israel's Atomic Energy Commission, in early 1976; *Nuclear Engineering International*, January 1976, p. 9.

51. For details of nuclear-related activities in the Arab states, see the author's "A Nuclear Middle East: Infrastructure, Likely Military Postures, and Prospects for Strategic Stability," in Milton Leitenberg and Gabriel Sheffer, eds., *Great Power Intervention in the Middle East* (Elmsford, N.Y.: Pergamon, 1979).

an Arab Cooperation Agreement for the Use of Nuclear Energy for Peaceful Purposes became effective, and since then a Joint Arab Scientific Board for the use of nuclear energy has been formed.[52]

In November 1973, the influential editor of the Cairo daily *Al-Ahram*, Mohamed H. Heikal, devoted his weekly article to the issue of an Israeli nuclear threat, a threat that he considered to have become much more proximate in the wake of the October War. He stressed the need for a comparable Arab atomic capability, since "deterrence is the only effective strategy for this age, in the sense that the possession of this type of weapons by both sides in a conflict is the only guarantee against their use." Heikal urged the summit conference of Arab leaders that was to convene in Algiers later that month to consider this question, asserting that it would require the pooling of resources of several Arab countries. He listed the requirements for building an Arab bomb as: a single Arab Board under high-level supervision, one hundred scientists, not more than $500–$750 million, access to existing facilities throughout the Arab world, and an adequate period of time.[53] A few weeks later, he again took up the theme of a need for an independent Arab nuclear force:

I earnestly hope that this subject be taken seriously, and that we prepare for it, with the foreknowledge that the use of nuclear weapons is fraught with enormous dangers, but also aware that our struggle with Israel—despite all that may be said about the coming peace conference—is a long, long, long struggle, and that this struggle may witness moments of madness that should not catch us by surprise. Moreover, if the Arab Nation truly aspires to an influential world role, this it cannot attain without an independent nuclear umbrella. This has been well understood by both China and France—and I daresay India and Japan as well, given their preparedness to build the bomb within months once a political decision has been taken.[54]

The start of nuclear competition would greatly escalate for all parties both the financial cost of maintaining an adequate nuclear force and the risks inherent in any further outbreak of conflict. On the other hand, once a balance is achieved, it would tend to decrease the likelihood of such outbreaks occurring.[55]

52. The text of the Agreement appears in *Economic Review of the Arab World* (Beirut) 6 (September 1972), 51–64.

53. *Al-Ahram*, November 23, 1973. Heikal was removed from his position by President Sadat in early 1974.

54. Ibid., December 14, 1973.

55. The chances for stability of a Middle Eastern nuclear balance are discussed in Jabber, *Israel and Nuclear Weapons*, pp. 141–144; and Jabber, "A Nuclear Middle East."

Table 4. Projections of Nuclear Reactor Capacity and Stockpiles of Separable
Plutonium 239 in the Middle East

Country	Current Capacity MWt	Estimated Capacity MWe		International Atomic Energy Agency (IAEA) Forecast MWe		Kilogram Accumulations of Separable Plutonium	
		1985	1990	1990	2000	1985	1990*
Israel	32	960	1,910	3,900†	15,300†	385	2,450
Egypt	2	600	4,200	5,000	12,600	142	2,985
Libya	—	1,040	1,040	—	—	350	1,580
Iraq	2	623	623	1,100	2,600	142	859
Kuwait	—	50	1,250	1,300	3,200	36	1,090
Syria	—	—	600	500	1,900	—	472
Saudi Arabia	—	—	600	200	1,400	—	188
Morocco	—	—	600	400	1,600	—	280
Tunisia	—	—	200	200	1,600	—	94
Lebanon	—	—	—	—	1,000	—	—
Sudan	—	—	—	—	800	—	—

* The lower estimate for reactor capacity was used in each case.
† These estimates for Israel are from Atomic Industrial Forum, *INFO News Release*, May 19, 1975.

THE OUTLOOK FOR ARMS CONTROL

Left uncontrolled, present trends in the armaments field—both conventional and nuclear—presage at least a continuation and more likely an
intensification of military instability in the Middle East area. In determining
what arms control measures fall within the realm of practical applicability to
the Arab-Israeli situation, a perhaps platitudinous but analytically important
assumption must be postulated, viz., that the nature of control options will be
governed by the political state-of-relations between the contending parties.
Within the context of a comprehensive Arab-Israeli political solution, a
plethora of arms control measures can be envisaged, given the improved
atmosphere and expected normalization of Israeli-Arab relations, the for-
saking of military pressure that agreement to a political settlement of standing issues implies, and the presumed desire of each party to ensure that the
other side keeps its share of the bargain by instituting supervisory and other
limitations on its ability to mount a significant military threat. As demonstrated by the Israeli-Egyptian 1979 treaty, easiest to negotiate will be tension-
limiting measures such as demilitarization of border regions, international
policing or inspection of sensitive points, and communications links (hot lines)
between the parties as part of any political settlement package. Also, arrangements probably would be made to regulate the qualitative and quantitative

inflow of new weaponry into the area, both to discourage the buildup of what may be perceived by either side as an imbalancing superiority, and to increase military stability by injecting only arms that enhance the defensive capabilities of the recipients and their ability to deter surprise attacks. Furthermore, partial disarmament steps such as reductions in stockpiles of costly weapons and dismantling or civilianization of military industries could become feasible in time, and regionally self-imposed curbs on arms production and acquisition and on military budgets under some form of mutual inspection might be negotiated.[56]

In the event that such a truly dramatic turnabout in the course of the Arab-Israeli dispute fails to materialize, or if only a partial settlement is negotiated that does not resolve all the major issues at stake but leads the region into a stage of uneasy "cold war" in which the possibility of future military confrontations is muted but not abated, arms control options will become severely restricted. In such circumstances, only two processes directly related to the arms race would appear open to some form of control: (1) local acquisition of nuclear weapons, and (2) the influx of conventional armaments from outside the region.

In the nuclear field, as no Arab country has developed a nuclear program capable of producing bombs, it is Israel, with a time-lead of eight to ten years in this regard, that poses the immediate problem. Were Israel to accede to the Nuclear Non-Proliferation Treaty (NPT), a measure of control over the small Israeli capability could be afforded by international supervision, provided adequate account is given of the weapons-grade plutonium already stockpiled.[57] In exchange, those Arab countries that have not already ratified or acceded to the treaty may be expected to agree to do so upon Israeli accession. Barring enormous pressures by the United States, however, sweetened by very substantial compensations in other areas, perhaps including large supplies (or commitments) of conventional weaponry, such Israeli surrender of the advantages of the nuclear option is not to be expected. The psycho-

56. A more detailed description of arms control measures supportive of strategic stability in peacetime appears in Chapter 8, below.

57. Such accounting may be a source of difficult problems. For instance, in 1970, in a story widely assumed to have been based on authoritative U.S. information, it was reported that in 1968 "some fissionable material from the Dimona reactor was diverted from normal peaceful uses and disappeared. It is not known whether this was diverted to weapons use, but that is the strong presumption here" (Hedrick Smith, "The U.S. Assumes the Israelis Have A-Bomb or Its Parts," *New York Times*, July 18, 1970). It is worth noting that in 1967, while the NPT was still in the negotiating stage, Egypt stressed that any acceptable safeguards system "must be extended to . . . all nuclear activities, past and present" (ACDA, *Documents on Disarmament, 1967*, p. 156).

logical-deterrence value of the potential nuclear capacity would be undercut, its usefulness as a bargaining counter in conventional-arms procurement efforts would be greatly diminished, and a future decision to "go nuclear" if circumstances warrant it would become much more difficult to implement. Furthermore, Israelis have argued that the guarantees against nuclear blackmail or attack provided by the superpowers through the Security Council to treaty members are not adequate.[58]

The Israeli government attitude toward any proposals that might restrict the nuclear option has been consistently negative. It is common practice to severely limit any debates of the issue in the Knesset, and public discussion of Israeli nuclear activities has been actively discouraged. Requests for parliamentary discussion have been customarily warded off by having a cabinet member move to transfer the subject to the Foreign Affairs and Security Committee. The meetings of this committee are always held *in camera*, and membership in it is in practice barred to Knesset members belonging to political groupings considered "unreliable" by the security community.

On the other hand, the Arab position has been constantly favorable to the NPT and to other measures likely to inhibit the introduction of such weapons into the Middle East conflict. Awareness of the advanced Israeli capability and of their own inadequacy in the nuclear field have mainly dictated the Arabs' attitude.

On the declaratory level, Arab leaders have alternated between threats of preventive war if Israel developed the atom bomb[59]—this was before the 1967 debacle drained such threats of their credibility—and belittlement of the Israeli capacity to mount an effective nuclear military strategy.[60] In the

58. See the statement of May 29, 1968, by Ambassador Tekoah at the U.N. (ACDA, *Documents on Disarmament, 1968*, p. 403); the intervention by Israeli representative Mordechai Kidron at the U.N. Conference of Non-Nuclear-Weapon States (Geneva, 29 August–28 September, 1968), A/CONF. 35/SR.1–20, 1 November 1968; and also the article by Bar-Ilan University Professor David Vital, "Double-Talk or Double-Think? A Comment on the Draft Non-Proliferation Treaty," *International Affairs* (London) 44 (July 1968), 419–433. For a more detailed analysis of the Israeli reluctance to join the NPT, see Jabber, *Israel and Nuclear Weapons*, pp. 126–128; and Yoram Nimrod, "Non-Nuclear Deterrence," *New Outlook* 19 (April–May 1976), 34–42.

59. Examples are the speeches by Nasser in Port Said on December 23, 1960, and in Cairo on February 22, 1966; also, *Al-Ahram*, September 25, 1964, and October 15, 1965.

60. In the early 1960s, an Israeli nuclear option was seen in the Arab press as either mere propaganda, aimed at discouraging the Arabs and inducing them to make peace on their enemy's terms, or as being beyond Israel's technological ability. Later on, Israel's capacity to produce nuclear weapons began to be acknowledged, but the

sixties, some attempts were made under Nasser to upgrade the Egyptian atomic program, albeit unsuccessfully,[61] and the possibility of obtaining nuclear warheads from external producers was explored, also without positive results.[62]

In the wake of the October 1973 war, several Arab states have launched civil nuclear expansion programs, with Iraq taking an active lead.[63] No installations of potential military significance are likely to become operational before 1983, however. At the same time, Arab officials and military commentators have begun to openly recognize the existence of an Israeli nuclear option and its strategic regional impact. Illustrative of this trend is the recommendation adopted by the Security Committee of the Egyptian Parliament on July 12, 1977 that an Arab institute for nuclear energy be established "in order to create an Arab nuclear capacity capable of facing up to Israel's increasing nuclear activity."[64]

The arms control approach to neutralization of the perceived Israeli danger has been actively pursued, particularly by Egypt, which, as a leading member of the nonaligned bloc at the Geneva disarmament forum (the ENDC, later CCD), has played a prominent role in disarmament efforts. A good summary statement of the predominant Arab position as regards the Non-

---

usefulness of a nuclear arsenal as a viable instrument of war or pressure in a Middle Eastern context was dismissed. See *Al-Ahram* and *Al-Gumhuriyya* (Cairo), July 19, 1970; also see statements by Mohamed Heikal—who at the time was Minister of National Guidance—on Egyptian television (*Al-Ahram*, July 22, 1970).

61. According to Heikal, the failure to mount a larger program was primarily due to lack of adequate financial resources and to deficiencies in management; *Al-Ahram*, November 23, 1973.

62. In 1966, Cairo reportedly approached the Soviet Union with a request for purchase of A-bombs in case of Israeli acquisition of these weapons. Moscow refused but was said to have offered Nasser a guarantee of nuclear protection, which the latter reportedly turned down as inadequate; *Al-Gumhuriyya*, February 6, 1966; and *New York Times*, February 4 and 21, 1966. After the Six-Day War, a similar request was relayed to Peking. The Chinese advice was to seek "self-reliance"; *Al-Ahram*, November 23, 1973. In 1970, Libya's new ruler, Colonel Al-Qaddhafi, reportedly sought to purchase a nuclear bomb that would be held at the disposal of the Arab states as a deterrent against Israel's nuclear capability, but he found no sellers; Mohamed Heikal, *The Road to Ramadan* (London: Collins, 1975), pp. 76–77.

63. For details of announced Arab nuclear projects and their military potential, see Jabber, "A Nuclear Middle East," pp. 77–86.

64. *Al-Ahram*, July 13, 1977. See statements by Sadat and Egyptian Foreign Minister Fahmi, in *Al-Ahram*, June 23, 1974; *Al-Anwar* (Beirut), January 1, 1975; *Arab Report and Record*, April 16–30, 1976; and *Der Spiegel* (Hamburg), March 28, 1976. Also see PLO Chairman Arafat on the CBS television program "Sixty Minutes," March 27, 1977; and Hassan Agha, "Egypt, Israel and the Atom Bomb," *Al-Tali'ah* 11 (September 1975), 19–29.

Proliferation Treaty can be found in the speech that Egyptian Ambassador M. Awad Al-Quni delivered to the First Committee of the U.N. General Assembly in May 1968, while the proposed treaty was under consideration. Al-Quni made the following major points: (1) his country considered the proposed treaty as adequate to the task of halting the horizontal spread of nuclear weapons, and it should therefore be adopted; (2) the security guarantees envisaged by the three nuclear sponsors should be further strengthened by an undertaking to "provide or support immediate assistance" to non-nuclear parties that are victims of nuclear attack or threat of attack; and (3) it was "of utmost importance that the treaty include the potential nuclear states—states which are on the threshold of becoming nuclear—in order to be meaningful."[65]

The security guarantees offered by the United States, the Soviet Union, and Great Britain eventually remained unchanged, i.e., the nuclear guarantors would only act through the U.N. Security Council in case of nuclear aggression or threat of aggression against a signatory to the NPT. This exposed any envisaged action to the possibility of a veto, thereby greatly undermining the value of the guarantee in the eyes of the potential victims.[66] This, and Israel's failure to subscribe to the treaty, resulted in the Egyptian decision to sign the NPT while withholding ratification, presumably pending Israeli accession. As of February 1978, twelve Arab countries had signed the treaty and eight of these had also ratified it.[67] Iraq, one of the two Arab states possessing nuclear reactors, had in February 1972 completed negotiations with the International Atomic Energy Agency (IAEA) on a safeguards agreement and placed its facilities under international supervision.

It can be safely predicted that further progress toward nuclear arms control in the Middle East will depend almost exclusively on Israeli policy. Heretofore, Israel's lukewarm attitude has been largely related to the absence of any proximate Arab nuclear menace. This situation is likely to

65. The full text of the Egyptian statement is in ACDA, *Documents on Disarmament, 1968*, pp. 397–402.

66. It is worthy of note that the Arab bloc representative on the Security Council at the time, Algeria, abstained in the vote on the resolution on "Security Assurances to Non-Nuclear Nations." For the full text, see ibid., p. 444.

67. The breakdown is as follows: signature only, Egypt, Kuwait, Yemen Arab Republic, and the People's Democratic Republic of Yemen; ratification, Iraq, Jordan, Lebanon, Libya, Morocco, Sudan, Syria, and Tunisia. It may be significant that, among the holdouts, two—Saudi Arabia and Algeria—have the best geographic conditions in the Arab world for nuclear weapons testing and dispersion. Neither country adheres to the 1963 Partial Test Ban Treaty.

change in the medium-term future, however, as huge financial resources become available to the Arab world from oil and the overall process of industrialization is accelerated. Indeed, it is likely that Arab states will seek a military nuclear capability as a shortcut or precondition to a larger "influential world role," or as a deterrent against infringement of vital interests by extraregional powers, as well as for counterbalancing the Israeli capability.

On the other hand, the hazards of a nuclear arms race notwithstanding, an Israel fearful of eventual Arab superiority in conventional military power may prefer creating an Arab-Israeli "balance of terror" rather than surrendering a potential weapon that may provide a credible final line of defense against the opponent's advantage in population and resources. Ultimate deterrence is the one strategic role that most Israeli observers are willing to conceive for their nuclear capability. Hence, the prospects for nuclear arms limitation will be inextricably linked to progress in the area of conventional-arms control.

Here, as already indicated, only those processes open to substantial influence by external suppliers are likely to be susceptible to restraints so long as the main protagonists in the conflict have not reached a final accommodation. It is not by accident that past efforts, initiatives, and proposals have pointed in this direction. The practically total reliance of the regional parties on weapons suppliers in the Soviet bloc, Western Europe, and North America has been a basic feature of the Middle Eastern military situation—as well as of all others in the nonindustrial world—and has enabled the major suppliers to impose restrictions on the arms flow.

In 1949, Great Britain, France, and the United States announced at the United Nations their opposition to the heavy influx of armaments into the area; and one year later, they instituted the rationing system under the Tripartite Declaration to impede "the development of an arms race between the Arab States and Israel." Since the breakdown of this arrangement in 1955, Western governments have regularly reiterated the view that measures for curtailing the warring capabilities of Israelis and Arabs are necessary to reduce regional instability. As local manufacturing potential is very limited, this curtailment could be achieved through agreed-upon limitations on the shipment of weapons by suppliers. In recent years, specifically since the war of June 1967, the United States government has expressed particular interest in joining with the Soviet Union to impose restrictions on the supply of arms to their respective clients as a means of enhancing prospects for political settlement of the dispute. The Nixon Administration repeatedly stated its willingness to discuss with the Soviets practical arrangements to this end.[68] Shortly after the October 1973 war, Secretary of State Kissinger restated this position, adding that any limitation measures "must include all those countries which might transfer their arms to one or more of the combatants and not just the parties in the last war."[69] The Carter Administration has made the curbing of both nuclear and conventional arms spread a priority item in its foreign policy, and high-level talks have been conducted with West European and Middle Eastern governments to elicit restraint.[70]

The Soviets have occasionally voiced similar concerns. In 1956 and 1957, both prior to and following the Suez crisis, they demanded a total cutoff in arms supplies. In February 1957, Moscow sent similarly worded notes to Washington, London, and Paris, that spelled out a comprehensive proposal on noninterference in the internal affairs of the Middle East. The fifth of six principles that would rule future Great Power policy was "reciprocal refusal to deliver arms to Middle Eastern counties."[71] The U.S. dismissed the proposal as a move clearly intended to dismantle the Baghdad Pact for regional defense and neutralize Western predominance in the area. The Soviet position on the more recent U.S. control suggestions has emphasized the priority of securing Israeli withdrawal from the territories occupied in 1967 before any arms limitations can be negotiated. However, Moscow has not expressly rejected Washington's overtures. In 1968, it put on the record its willingness to consider arms control measures for the area,[72] and the joint communique issued after the May 1972 summit meetings in Moscow between Nixon and Brezhnev contained a declaration by both superpowers of their willingness to work for a negotiated settlement of Arab-Israeli conflict that "would permit, in particular, consideration of further steps to bring about a military relaxation

68. President Nixon said that the U.S. was ready to discuss practical steps with the Soviets in his 1970 foreign policy report to Congress; text in ACDA, *Documents on Disarmament, 1970*, p. 32; similar sentiments were expressed in subsequent reports. See also the statements by former Secretary of State William Rogers made shortly before the 1972 Moscow summit meetings; *New York Times*, March 8, 1972. Congress urged the President to pursue these efforts in an amendment to the Military Sales Act of 1971, Public Law 91–672, January 12, 1971.

69. *New York Times*, November 13, 1973.

70. U.S., Congress, House of Representatives, Committee on International Relations, *Conventional Arms Transfer Policy: Background Information* (Committee Print, February 1, 1978).

71. Text in ACDA, *Documents on Disarmament, 1945–1959*, Vol. 2, pp. 742–746.

72. This was done in a Memorandum to the Eighteen-Nation Disarmament Committee entitled "Memorandum of the Soviet Government Concerning Urgent Measures to Stop the Arms Race and Achieve Disarmament," July 1, 1968; text in ACDA, *Documents on Disarmament, 1968*, pp. 466–470.

in the area." [73] In February 1975, for the first time on record since the Six-Day War, the Soviet Union reportedly took the initiative in raising the possibility of a superpower agreement to limit the arms flow to the Middle East following Israeli withdrawal from occupied territories. [74]

The only serious effort up to the present time to reach a Soviet-American understanding is the series of bilateral talks begun in 1978 following the establishment of a working group on conventional arms transfers. Aimed at developing a set of mutually agreed-upon criteria for arms supply policies, the heretofore secret negotiations are known to include discussion of regional mechanisms for implementation of supply restraints.

Since the beginning of the Arab-Israeli dispute, major arms suppliers have been aware of the benefits derivable from coordination of their arms-transfer policies. They have applied restrictions on the arms flow that were either explicit and formal, as in the rationing of the early fifties, or tacitly agreed upon, as in the case of some advanced weapons systems, notably after the 1967 war. [75] In following this course, they have not been motivated by an altruistic desire to spare the people of the region from the ravages of war or to enable them to devote more of their resources to developmental tasks. Too many domestic economic, political, and strategic interests are well served by vigorous arms-exporting programs. In the particular case of the Soviet Union, its entire presence in the Arab Middle East is almost exclusively predicated on its role as a generous and dependable purveyor of military equipment. Rather, the interest of the suppliers in arms control stems primarily from their desire to minimize the risks of undesired entanglement in regional conflicts that their otherwise profitable arms exports are likely to fuel, and in some instances even provoke. For both Washington and Moscow, the desirability of joint controls was further underscored by the severe jolt to Soviet-American relations occasioned by the October 1973 war.

Restraints imposed by major suppliers on weapons transfers to the Arab-Israeli area are a distinct future probability; hence the importance of investi-

73. Text in *New Times* (Moscow), No. 23 (1972), pp. 36–38.

74. *New York Times*, February 18, 1975.

75. Egyptian anger at the Soviet reluctance to provide some advanced offensive weaponry in the 1970–1972 period (including jet fighter-bombers of a quality similar to the Israeli F-4 Phantoms, and surface-to-surface missiles) was the principal of several factors that led to the ejection of the Soviet presence from Egypt in July 1972. The Egyptian leadership strongly suspected that the U.S. and the Soviets had reached some sort of understanding on limiting arms supplies to the area. Later, President Sadat would say, "It was clear that the stalemate—no peace, no war—suited the superpowers. There was some agreement between them about the level of arms supplies" (quoted in the *Sunday Times* [London], December 9, 1973).

gating the broadly similar arms rationing system that was operative in the region in 1950–1955, to develop insights into the workings of the system and the conditions attendant on its early success and eventual demise. An assessment of the control regime established under the 1950 Tripartite Declaration may provide useful guidelines for any prospective Middle East arms limitation. It should also have a more general prognostic value, since any future curtailment of the international arms traffic through international agreements will, in all probability, feature as a major component the same operational method that lay at the core of the tripartite system: the coordination among producers of limitations on their arms exports within norms that will be conducive to military stability and power balance among recipients.

CHAPTER 3   MULTILATERAL APPROACHES TO ARMS-TRANSFER LIMITATION

> The essential feature of arms control is the recognition of the common interest, of the possibility of reciprocation and cooperation even between potential enemies with respect to their military establishments.
>
> Thomas C. Schelling and Morton H. Halperin
> *Strategy and Arms Control*

The causal link between arms and conflict has long been a subject of contention among students of international affairs. Does the presence of arms lead to war? Or are arms buildups only a symptom of conflicts essentially rooted in political disputes born of territorial, ideological, racial, or economic grievances, and consequently have a marginal effect on the incidence of war?

Intuitive thinking, deductive reasoning, statistical tools, and the records of history have been marshalled by analysts on both sides of the issue with contradictory results.[1] The controversy is likely to be long-lasting, and its subject matter may not prove ultimately amenable to generalization, given the crucial role of human perceptions in the inter-state conflict process, perceptions that are largely shaped by the unique circumstances of each particular case. In all probability, both views described above are partially true, and the actual mechanisms of conflict include both processes. In quarrels marked by the presence of inflated military establishments, war may be the end result of a

---

1. For the view that "great armaments lead inevitably to war," see Emmanuel Kant's classic essay on "Eternal Peace"; Philip Noel-Baker, *The Arms Race* (London: Atlantic, 1958), chaps. 6 and 7; and Lewis F. Richardson, *Arms and Insecurity* (Chicago: Quadrangle, 1960). An opposing judgment is found in Samuel P. Huntington, "Arms Races: Prerequisites and Results," *Public Policy, 1958* (Cambridge, Mass.: Harvard University, Graduate School of Administration, 1958).

vicious process whereby an arms race is sparked by mutual suspicions arising from an initial dispute and is thereafter fuelled by its own action-reaction dynamics to a point of oversaturation in both arms and tension where any incident is apt to trigger the hostilities.[2]

In judging whether the control of arms levels is a potentially effective tool for conflict limitation, however, the basic issue is shortchanged when posed in these terms. The more significant and apposite question is not whether countries go to war primarily because they have the wherewithal to wage it. Rather, granting that almost all disputes have some foundation in political issues (ideology, territory, etc.), what effect do variable levels of armament exert on the choice of means to pursue political ends ? Arms may not *create* conflicts, but to what extent do they *exacerbate* existing disputes and *open up* military options ?

THE RELEVANCE OF ARMS CONTROL

In order to justify the usefulness of arms restraints, not as the be-all and end-all of peaceful conflict-resolution techniques but as a major component of any such approach, it is sufficient to assume that the mere availability of implements of war in most cases will increase the chances of resorting to violence for the settlement of outstanding disputes. While this assumption is easily suggested by common sense and reasonable expectation, it also stands on the strength of its widespread acceptance as valid by national leaders.[3] Furthermore, it is supported by a number of empirical investigations.[4]

2. As suggested by Hanna Newcombe, "The Case for an Arms Embargo," *War/ Peace Report* 11 (March 1971), 17–19. This thesis is different from the not uncommon "circularity" argument, which in fact evades the issue. Inis Claude, for instance considers that "this is a circular problem, in which causes and effects, policies and the instruments of policy, revolve in a cycle of interaction and are blurred into indistinguishability" (*Swords into Plowshares* [New York: Random House, 1956], p. 298). Only slightly less ambivalent is J. David Singer's position as stated in "Threat-Perception and the Armament-Tension Dilemma," *Journal of Conflict Resolution* 2 (March 1958), 90–105. Huntington, on the other hand, proposes in "Arms Races" (p. 63) that a sustained arms race is less likely to end in war and that "the danger of war is highest in the opening phases of an arms race, at which time the greatest elements of instability and uncertainty are present." The Arab-Israeli conflict provides examples supportive of both theories. The Sinai War closely fits Huntington's model, while the Six-Day War illustrates Newcombe's.

3. In Singer's economical formulation, for most decision-makers:

Threat Perception = Estimated Capability × Estimated Intent

The opponent's capability is universally measured in terms of military potential first and foremost.

4. See, among others, Richardson, *Arms and Insecurity*; Alan G. Newcombe,

The philosophy of arms control is intrinsically bound up with the premise that significant accretions to a nation's armed strength will, at a minimum, cause among its potential or actual opponents anxieties as to its intentions, heighten existing tensions, generate or reinforce hostile attitudes, elicit similar remedial counteraction, and encourage decision-makers to think in terms of military solutions to their problems. Arms limitation measures and agreements can critically affect these diverse facets of adversary relationships. Hence, their introduction need not wait on prior resolution of underlying political differences. Arms control can be both inherently valuable and a useful if not necessary prelude to settlement of the underlying dispute, for each and all of the following reasons: (1) increasing armaments in and of themselves may precipitate military action; (2) a concomitant of foreclosing or diminishing violent alternatives is an increase in the possibility of resort to diplomatic and other peaceful means; and (3) shared restraints help to generate mutual confidence in hostile camps and a reevaluation of enemy intentions, thereby weakening perceptions of threat basic to all conflicts and often chiefly responsible for their prolongation.

Arms control does not always spell arms *reduction*, however; hence the need for a concept broader than "disarmament". In some instances, a legitimate arms control measure may entail an increase in the possession of some weapons. This follows from the basic assumption that arms limitation is a means, not an end, and that the primary desideratum in any conflict situation is not simply a reduction in the absolute numbers of available weaponry but the establishment of conditions favoring pursuit of nonviolent avenues to conflict resolution. In situations where the neutralization of the politics of force requires the creation of a military balance of mutual deterrence or the offsetting of unilateral offensive superiority, it may be necessary to augment the net level of armaments on hand or effect increases in some weapon types and reductions in others.

Advocates of unqualified disarmament have long been uncomfortable with the arms control approach, and in some instances have been actively opposed to it. Many of their objections are valid and stand as a warning against the easy misuse of arms control. In their view, any steps that do not expressly aim

"Toward the Development of an Inter-Nation Tensionmeter," Peace Research Society (International), *Papers* 13 (1970), 11–27; Norman S. Alcock, "An Empirical Measure of International Threat: Some Preliminary Implications for the Middle East Conflict," Peace Research Society (International), *Papers* 15 (1970), 65–66; Michael D. Wallace, "Status, Formal Organization, and Arms Levels as Factors Leading to the Onset of War, 1820–1964," in Bruce M. Russett, ed., *Peace, War, and Numbers* (Beverly Hills, Calif.: Sage Publications, 1972), pp. 49–69.

at discarding or reducing existing weapons—with general and complete disarmament as the ultimate goal—represent further instances of power manipulation for unilateral advantage, precisely that misguided mode of international
conduct that disarmament is designed to exorcize. Such steps are also counter-
productive in that, by creating a false feeling of increased security, they often
may lull decision-makers into relaxing their arms limitation efforts short of
any substantial shedding of the instruments of violence, wherein lies long-
term security in any meaningful sense. A slightly less critical but still important drawback of "non-disarming" control measures is that they leave the
economic strains inherent in high military outlays untouched if not actually
augmented. The economic dimension is particularly relevant in conflicts involving less-developed countries. It is certainly pertinent in the Middle East,
where average defense expenditures in the countries directly involved in the
Arab-Israeli confrontation (Israel, Egypt, Syria, and Jordan) amounted in
1970–1976 to 28 percent of the gross national product for Israel and 13 percent
for the Arab states.[5]

To delineate plainly that particular portion of the arms limitation spectrum
with which this study is primarily concerned—the control of arms transfers to
regional crisis areas—it is important to draw the following broad distinctions
between arms control options:

1. A basic distinction must be made between control measures that are
global in character and in potential participation on the one hand, and measures that have a regional scope on the other. The problem of restraining the
international trade in arms has been approached mainly on a global level. This
is true of diplomatic negotiations, as discussed more amply below. It is also
applicable to the growing but still limited literature in the field. The salient
characteristic of contemporary treatments of this subject is the macroscopic
level of analysis common to most such studies. There is an evident urge to deal
with the arms traffic phenomenon on a macroanalytic level in order to obtain
general, universally valid conclusions about arms-transfer magnitudes and
trends, supplier incentives and risks, recipient motives and needs, the prospects for control, the impact of the traffic on stability, the traffic's relationship to arms races, and its effects on the incidence of wars.[6] This urge is

---

5. ACDA, *World Military Expenditures and Arms Transfers, 1967–1976*. See Table 1
for figures on military expenditures in 1951-1976.

6. Among the more useful works are: John L. Sutton and Geoffrey Kemp, *Arms to
Developing Countries 1945–1965*, Adelphi Paper, No. 28 (London: Institute for
Strategic Studies, 1966); Lewis A. Frank, *The Arms Trade in International Relations*
(New York: Praeger, 1969); George Thayer, *The War Business: The International*

understandable, both because the problem is indeed universal in its scope and because of the gaps in existing knowledge about the arms trade, deriving from the official secrecy that cloaks many of its facets. The prevailing consensus that emerges from these studies is, in the words of one assiduous observer of the arms traffic, that "realistic prospects for greater multilateral regulations of arms transfers between the industrial and less industrial states remain slim. So long as the demand for arms remains high and the rewards for supply seem to outweigh the dangers, it is difficult to see what set of circumstances will bring about a major change in the current behavior of the nations engaged in the process."[7]

One unfortunate upshot of this macroscopic approach, however, has been the insufficient consideration and study given to specific regional conditions—political, economic, and social, as well as strategic—which may critically affect conclusions reached on the strength of an analysis of gross worldwide indicators. Thus, the tendency has been to downgrade prospects for achieving arms trade limitations on a regional basis, mainly because analysis-in-the-large suggests that this is "a world from which the traffic in armaments is ineradicable."[8] Yet the problems of limiting the arms trade on a world scale—cer-

---

Trade in Armaments (New York: Simon and Schuster, 1969); Stockholm International Peace Research Institute (SIPRI), *The Arms Trade with the Third World* (New York: Humanities Press, 1971); Amelia C. Leiss et al., *Arms Control and Local Conflict*, Vol. 3: *Arms Transfers to Less Developed Countries* (Cambridge, Mass.: Massachusetts Institute of Technology, February 1970); John Stanley and Maurice Pearton, *The International Trade in Arms* (London: Chatto & Windus, 1972); ACDA, *The International Transfer of Conventional Arms*, A Report to the Congress Pursuant to Section 302 of the Foreign Relations Authorization Act of 1972; Robert E. Harkavy, *The Arms Trade and International Systems* (Cambridge, Mass.: Ballinger, 1975); Philip J. Farley et al., *Arms Across the Sea* (Washington, D.C.: The Brookings Institution, 1978); Uri Ra'anan et al., eds., *Arms Transfers to the Third World: The Military Buildup in Less Industrial Countries* (Boulder, Colo.: Westview Press, 1978); and Andrew Pierre, ed., *Arms Transfers and American Foreign Policy* (New York: New York University Press, 1979). Studies that focus on the region as a possible unit for arms control measures are: M.I.T., Center for International Studies, *Regional Arms Control Arrangements for Developing Areas: Arms and Arms Control in Latin America, the Middle East, and Africa*, prepared under contract to ACDA (September 1964); and Jacques Huntzinger, "Regional Recipient Restraints," in Anne H. Cahn et al., *Controlling Future Arms Trade* (New York: McGraw-Hill, 1977) pp. 163–197. A much earlier but equally influential work on the arms trade is H. C. Engelbrecht and F. C. Hanighen, *Merchants of Death: A Study of the international Armament Industry* (New York: Dodd, Mead, 1934).

7. Geoffrey Kemp, "The International Arms Trade: Supplier, Recipient and Arms Control Perspectives," *Political Quarterly* (London) 42 (October–December 1971), 389.

8. Colin S. Gray, "Traffic Control for the Arms Trade?" *Foreign Policy*, No. 6 (Spring 1972), p. 169.

tainly a tall order—are different from those problems that arise in using arms control locally for purposes of conflict resolution or regulation. These differences are not only of scale, purpose, and technique; they are also normative. The issue of unfair discrimination, for instance, a major sticking point raised by nonproducers whenever arms transfer regulation is discussed, loses much of its justification in the latter case; and if the arms control measures are agreed to by the recipients, it becomes totally groundless. To the extent that this distinction applies, it is less relevant to speak of the obstacles to arms limitation posed by general stimuli to supply and procurement—as most of the literature does—than of (a) incentives and disincentives for suppliers and recipients within the particular context of the conflict situation in which the actors find themselves, and (b) the problems of devising an adequate arms control system and means for its implementation.

2. At the regional level, a further differentiation is necessary between measures applicable in times of normal inter-state relations and those that are especially relevant in a crisis-control situation, for purposes of limiting an ongoing conflict or as confidence-building components of negotiated settlements. Agreements of the first type, feasible in periods of regional stability and normalcy, such as the different proposals discussed at meetings of the Organization of American States for limits on military expenditures by member countries,[9] are most unlikely among parties to an active conflict. Conversely, measures such as the British-American embargo on arms supplies to the South Asian subcontinent at the time of the 1965 India-Pakistan War, or the demilitarization of border areas in the context of a settlement to an existing conflict, are arms control steps that would not be resorted to in regions enjoying a state of peaceful, cooperative relations. The distinction is also valid in terms of such elements of the control system as the machinery required for implementation, adherence of affected parties (control measures for crisis situations may be imposed by extraregional powers or the United Nations without the acquiescence of target countries), and the operational guidelines, as well as the time frame designed for the system.

3. There are several other dimensions along which distinctions can be drawn

9. In March 1971, for example, Colombia proposed the formation of a special commission that would, among other things, consider "the adoption of a criterion of proportionality between the arms, territorial area, population, and economic potential on the one hand, and the basic requirements of national security on the other hand" of the twenty-three OAS member States (ACDA, *International Transfer of Conventional Arms*, p. C-51). In December 1974, eight Latin American states signed the Declaration of Ayacucho, which committed them to work toward ending the acquisition of arms "for offensive military purposes" (*New York Times*, December 13, 1974, p. 1).

between different arms control options. The main ones are: (a) nuclear/conventional/chemical/bacteriological; (b) bilateral/multilateral; (c) supplier/recipient; (d) use/possession; and (e) tacit/formal. These dimensions are crosscutting, and any number of combinations can be made to typologize and classify possible arms control arrangements, only a few of which have been attempted or internationally considered to date with serious intent.

These distinctions are not of formalistic value only. In addition to their taxonomic function, they provide general guidelines for policy determination and for ex post facto analysis that seeks to evaluate the scant experience yet garnered in the field of arms limitation. While in many instances the appropriateness of specific control measures for particular situations is clear and needs no belaboring, failure to take due account of this factor in borderline cases may doom arms control devices to ineffectiveness and ultimate frustration. As the case under study in Part II of this book will show, the British-French-American arms rationing scheme instituted in 1950 for the Arab-Israeli area is an example of a measure that may have been adequate for a crisis situation but was implemented in a manner that did not take account of the dynamic nature of the conflict and was more appropriate to a stable politico-military context, with results that not only defeated the original purpose of the tripartite arrangement but also gave added impetus to the burgeoning arms race in the region.

PAST MULTINATIONAL EFFORTS TO CONTROL THE TRANSFER OF ARMS

As we look over the record of arms control initiatives, negotiations, and agreements since World War II, it is clear that international efforts have been concentrated on strategic nuclear weapons. Politicians, decision-makers, diplomatic agents, journalists, academics, and other students of international security affairs have treated the issues of disarmament and arms limitation in a context almost exclusively dominated by the presence of nuclear weapons. Such is the magnitude of the destructive potential which a continuously improving military technology has created that the threat of nuclear war and the need to develop ways and means of averting it have overshadowed concern for the role that conventional armaments continue to play in international affairs. Though the nuclear equation has come to determine the relationship between the major powers, this is not the case in relations among non-nuclear countries. This emphasis on the nuclear aspects of international conflict management has tended to divert attention away from the abiding impact of conventional-weapons buildups on international politics in many parts of the world, and also away from more intensive study of the advisability and availability of control measures to curb the negative aspects of such impact.

Before the onset of the atomic age, the effect that the movement of arms from producing states—which have consistently been a small group of industrialized countries—to clients abroad had on the stability of the international system, on the balance of power between two or more possible opponents, and on the security and integrity of individual states or political regimes had been an object of major concern. This concern was heightened in the latter part of the nineteenth century, mainly by the feared effects of arms trafficking on the colonial hold of the European great powers in Africa and Western Asia. This resulted in the Brussels Act of 1890, which is the only international agreement ever to have been implemented that regulated the arms trade to a particular region on a global basis. Signed by seventeen states, including the European colonial powers and the United States, it decreed the exclusion of all firearms save flintlock guns and gunpowder from the African continent between the latitudes of 20 degrees North and 22 degrees South—roughly the area between South Africa and the Sahara—except under guarantees. It also restricted possession of firearms to license-holders only, so that it was more than just a trade-restricting measure. The Algeciras Act of 1906, to which the United States and thirteen other countries subscribed, sought to supplement the 1890 Act by banishing gunrunning from North Africa.[10]

Interest in controlling the arms trade reached its apex in the third and fourth decades of this century, when public opinion and many policymakers came to perceive a close relationship between the increased production and transfer of arms on the one hand and the fueling of arms races and outbreak of wars on the other. There was a widespread tendency to blame the large private arms manufacturers of the day, such as Krupps, Skoda, Vickers, and others for the calamity of the First World War, as well as for a host of lesser international evils. Against this background, fitful and largely unsuccessful attempts were made, particularly under the aegis of the League of Nations, to establish some degree of supervision over the arms traffic.

Two aborted efforts stand out: the Convention of St. Germain-en-Laye of 1919, and the 1925 Geneva Convention for the Supervision of the Arms Trade. The St. Germain Convention was worked out as part of the postwar diplomatic settlement at Versailles. It was meant to implement the undertaking in Article 23 of the League of Nations Covenant by the member states "to

10. Jeanne Kuebler, "Traffic in Arms," *Editorial Research Reports* (Washington, D.C.: Congressional Quarterly Service, April 28, 1965), p. 308; Stanley and Pearton, *Trade in Arms*, p. 18.

entrust the League with the general supervision of the trade in arms and ammunition with the countries in which the control of this traffic is necessary in the common interest." The Convention prohibited all arms trade between nations, with exceptions—which under the wording of the Convention could be extremely liberal—subject to government licensing; provided for full publicity for arms deals; and sought to complement previous agreements by banning all arms sales to the Near East area. Its failure was principally due to American refusal to ratify it.

The 1925 Geneva Convention was the product of a full-dress conference, attended by not less than forty-four states and lasting over a month (May 4 to June 17), that was wholly devoted to the search for controls over the arms trade. Yet, its provisions were less far-reaching than those of the St. Germain pact. Its main thrust was away from comprehensive controls, thus acknowledging the strong reluctance of both supplying and purchasing governments to impair their freedom of action in this sensitive field. In the words of the President of the Conference in his opening speech, the "Conference recognizes that there is a legitimate trade in arms. . . . The aim is not to throw any obstacles in the way of this legitimate trade, but to obviate the possible threat of illicit and dangerous traffic to compromise the good name of such legitimate trade."[11] Full governmental control over arms sales and publication of arms transactions were the document's principal features. It also failed to become operative because of insufficient ratification.

Thus, the major control measures envisaged in these early agreements emphasized giving publicity to arms deals through registration, the establishment of "prohibited zones" into which no armaments would be introduced without strict safeguards, and the cessation of arms exportation without licensing.[12]

Insofar as the arms trade was carried on by private manufacturers and dealers, the problem posited by weapons transfers during this period differed in its nature from the contemporary situation. Financial profit was the major incentive and determinant; to arms traders the larger political or security interests of governments were of marginal concern. Often, their activities were officially tolerated, if not actively encouraged, because of their contribution to foreign trade balances. In 1925, while the trade-control conference was meeting in the Palais des Nations, arms manufacturers were holding their own privately sponsored International Conference of Gunmakers to urge abandon-

11. Quoted in SIPRI, *Arms Trade with the Third World*, p. 95.

12. More detailed exposition here of these multinational efforts is redundant, as the record has been amply examined in multiple published works. See, among others, SIPRI, *Arms Trade with the Third World*, pp. 86–100.

ment of projects for international supervision in favor of existing agreements.[13] But if efforts to impose international controls were frustrated, during the nineteen-thirties the objective of curbing the private arms traffic was substantially fulfilled, as most arms-producing states began gradually adopting legislation that required licensing of arms exports. During the Second World War, this regulatory system was tightened and improved, and the overall governmental hold over domestic armament industries was greatly amplified.[14]

But the postwar world did not see a decrease in the magnitude of the arms traffic. It witnessed instead a crucial change in the nature of arms transfers: they became an explicit instrument of state policy, wielded directly by national governments as a legitimate means to the attainment of foreign-policy objectives.[15]

By the same token, the task of imposing a measure of control over the arms transfer process has also become proportionately more difficult and its requirements more complex. The total volume of arms supplies increased spectacularly in the postwar era in the wake of the decolonization process, with the emergence of a large number of new states and the complete emancipation of others, all eager to acquire the military accoutrements of sovereignty. At the same time, the configuration of international relations was radically altered. It was no longer unicentral, with Europe at its heart. It was now fractionated, with several regional subsystems gradually making their appearance. These, though often influenced by the overarching East-West superpower confrontation which came to dominate the period for a time, developed their own regional dynamics, patterns of power relations, conflicts, military conditions, and weapons requirements. Of course, the willingness of the industrialized countries to provide arms to customers abroad met a corresponding eagerness

13. John E. Wiltz, *In Search of Peace* (Baton Rouge, La.: Louisiana State University Press, 1963), p. 77.

14. The licensing system and its loopholes are examined in detail by Stanley and Pearton, *Trade in Arms*, chap. 3.

15. Many works describe and analyze incentives that prompt arms producers to favor continued supply to foreign clients. Particularly helpful are: Stanley and Pearton, *Trade in Arms*, chap. 4 and passim; SIPRI, *Arms Trade with the Third World*, pp. 17–41; Kemp, "International Arms Trade," pp. 377–382; Kemp, "U.S. Military Policy: Dilemmas of the Arms Traffic," *Foreign Affairs* 48 (January 1970), pp. 274–284; Farley et al., *Arms Across the Sea*, chaps. 2–4; Lawrence G. Franko, "Restraining Arms Exports to the Third World: Will Europe Agree?" *Survival* 21 (January–February 1979), 14–25. ACDA, *International Transfer of Conventional Arms*, chap. 2, which lists some of the criteria guiding U.S. policy; and Amos A. Jordan, *Foreign Aid and the Defense of Southeast Asia* (New York: Praeger, 1962), chap. 2, which outlines the purposes of U.S. military assistance as perceived in the confident period of the early 1960s.

on the part of the newly emergent states to absorb practically all that suppliers cared to make available, and more. In addition, the pressures behind this insatiable demand, caused largely by the insecurity of weak states in a world where armed might remains the final arbiter of all disputes, have been further strengthened in many less-developed countries by the accession to power of soldier-politicians, for whom military aggrandizement is a preferential priority when not a requirement of sheer political survival.[16]

These novel, variegated conditions make the easy panaceas for worldwide control of arms diffusion that formed the substance of international debate in previous decades no longer relevant. Yet, such anachronistic approaches continue to be propounded. This partially accounts for the total lack of progress in coming to grips with the arms transfer problem through consideration of realistic measures that tackle its more detrimental manifestations with some promise of success. A serious gap exists between the evolving reality and the conceptually static formulas periodically dragged out to cope with it. One example will suffice to illustrate this.

The main control feature of the proposed 1925 Geneva Convention, capping efforts to control the arms trade in the inter-war years, was the call for a recording system that would give publicity to all arms transfers. This was to be achieved by universal licensing of arms exports and public release of export licenses through the League of Nations.[17] The expectation was that this would do away with the destabilizing effects of secrecy on arms races and on the evaluation by adversaries of mutual intentions, and that it would substantially discourage the equally destabilizing traffic conducted by private arms makers independently of any governmental supervision. Furthermore, by submitting export practices to the full glare of public exposure, advocates hoped to mobilize the restrictive influence of peace-minded public opinion. The Convention never came into force, partly because of the American refusal to ratify it,[18]

16. Recipient incentives also have been examined in most of the works cited in the previous footnote. Worthy of note as well are: General J. N. Chaudhuri, "The International Arms Trade: The Recipient's Problems," *Political Quarterly* 43 (July–September 1972); and Ali A. Mazrui, "African Radicalism and Arms Policy," *African Scholar* 1 (1970), 3–4.

17. Text in the *Acts of the Conference on the Supervision of the International Trade in Arms and Ammunition and Implements of War*, Geneva, 4 May–17 June, 1925, League of Nations publication A.13.1925.IX.

18. Washington refused to participate officially in the Conference, sending only an observer, because of its sponsorship by the League of Nations. The Senate had not ratified the St. Germain Convention on the same grounds. Moreover, most weapons production in the United States was by private manufacturers, against whose interests these conventions were largely aimed, and whose financial well-being was considered

but also because many nonproducers of arms considered the exclusion of provisions for the control of arms manufacturing as well as trade highly discriminatory and detrimental to their security.[19]

Four decades and dozens of armed conflicts later, the only specific measures
suggested in a general negotiating forum in the nuclear age for dealing with
this problem echoed precisely the same approach proposed and rejected in the
1920s under much more favorable world conditions. Malta in 1965, and Den-
mark (with Iceland, Malta, and Norway as co-sponsors) in 1968 proposed in
the United Nations the consideration of publicity as a means of curbing the
international arms trade. The Maltese proposal even included an experimental
revival of the League of Nations' "Yearbook on the Trade in Arms, Ammunition and Implements of War," published from 1924 to 1938.

Not surprisingly, these motions met stiff opposition, with counterarguments
reminiscent of those heard at Geneva in 1925, now further strengthened both
by the number of the objectors—which included many of the principal developing countries—and by the vastly changed international context in which the
motions were made. The exorbitant costs of the strategic nuclear arms race
and the risks it embodies for world security, these opponents could claim, now
laid the onus of creating a more stable environment through arms control
squarely on the shoulders of the larger industrial and military powers, who
are also the main producers and suppliers of convential weaponry. Furthermore, there were now small but growing *regional* weapons production capabilities, which accentuated the asymmetry of controls on transfers only. Also,
the manifest inability of the United Nations to impose effective sanctions or
systems of supervision on sovereign states in an era of heightened sensitivity
to external intervention in the affairs of smaller nations has served to underline
the very touchy problems that noncompliance with an essentially voluntary
reporting arrangement would raise. Finally, the substantial legitimacy that has
accrued to movements of national liberation and other armed rebel groups in
the Third World struggling against the remnants of colonialism or subservient
domestic regimes has inspired some governments and sectors of public opinion

---

vital to the U.S. national interest. See Denna F. Fleming, *The United States and World
Organization, 1920–1933* (New York: Columbia University Press, 1938), pp. 67–70,
221; Acts of the 1925 Conference, p. 251; and Engelbrecht and Hanighen, *Merchants
of Death*, pp. 268–270. Ratification finally came in 1935, signalling a considerable shift
in the American position on arms-transfer control at the time; but by then the political
climate in Europe and the Far East had turned this into a dead issue.

19. A brief review of the positions and statements of these governments can be
found in SIPRI, *Arms Trade with the Third World*, pp. 95–98.

to ponder whether a trade registration system that would dry up sources of arms to these movements without placing similar restrictions on government-to-government transactions would amount to active support of an undesirable status quo.

It came as no surprise that the Maltese proposal was soundly defeated when put to a vote in the First Committee of the General Assembly, receiving only nineteen favorable ballots out of the total membership of the U.N. Perhaps more significant was the fate of the Danish proposal. Very limited—almost innocuous—in scope, it simply envisaged requesting the Secretary General to investigate the views of member states regarding arms trade registration. In the end, however, it was not even put to a vote by its major sponsor, in view of the generally hostile reception the idea had generated.

The rehashing of outmoded formulas for global restraints represented by the Maltese and Danish proposals is only partly to blame for the lack of progress in conventional arms control. The fact that only these measures were the subject of formal international debate is a reflection of the deep suspicion harbored by nonproducers of arms toward any measures that would limit their ability to acquire the instruments of self-defense. The statement of the Nigerian representative during the 1968 debate on the Danish registration proposal is typical: "It is one thing to limit the production of arms in the world as a whole but another to impose a limit on trade in conventional arms alone. . . . It would be tantamount to a discriminatory measure against a vast number of states which do not produce arms but yet need them at least for internal security purposes, while the few which can produce arms would still be free to produce and stockpile them in unlimited quantities." [20] In fact, arms suppliers have not betrayed any sense of urgency in curtailing a very lucrative business. This general evasiveness has been symbolized by the conspicuous and consistent absence of conventional arms control as a separate item on the agenda of the Conference of the Committee on Disarmament (CCD) in Geneva, the world's major disarmament forum, or on the agenda of the Political and Security Committee of the General Assembly.[21]

Only very recently has the international climate at governmental levels begun to change, prompted by the massive growth in the arms trade during the

---

20. Quoted in SIPRI, *Arms Trade with the Third World*, p. 108.

21. The efficacy of registration in curbing arms transfers is in any case disputable. It has been argued with plausibility that disclosure of weapons acquisitions may in some cases feed rather than dampen suspicions, tensions, and arms races, particularly in situations where existing arms balances may be upset by relatively minor transfers. See, for instance, Frank, *Arms Trade in International Relations*, pp. 224–251; and Gray, *Traffic Control*, p. 156.

seventies, including transfer commitments of some $140 billion from pro-
ducers to developing countries alone since the turn of the decade. In June
1978, the 149 United Nations members participating in the U.N. Special
Session on Disarmament called in their Final Document for consultations
"among major supplier and recipient countries on the limitation of all types
of international transfers of conventional weapons."

REGIONAL ARMS CONTROL

The regional approach clearly is a more practicable alternative at the present
time, and is likely to remain so for the foreseeable future. Moreover, it should
deserve priority, for the threats that conventional arms races pose are not
uniformly spread but peak at a few discrete locales under conditions of intra-
regional confrontation. Even a global measure such as registration of all arms
transfers *and* production would not bring more general security or lower the
level of international tensions better than the defusing and stabilization
through arms restraints of the military confrontations in, for instance, the
Middle East and central Europe.[22] It is these flashpoints that both contain the
greatest risk of adversely affecting worldwide security by precipitating external
intervention in crisis situations, and also account for the bulk of armament
transfers. The talks on multiple force reductions in Europe that began in
October 1973 are a substantial step in the right direction.

In general, the chances for success in negotiating arms control arrangements
for regions in crisis should be maximized by the fact that incentives for
restraint on the part of both suppliers and recipients of arms are also maximized there. For the suppliers, this is a function of their recognition that the
potential advantages and profits they may derive as sources of arms are out-
weighed by the risks of involuntary entanglement or overcommitment and
the economic penalties that may be incurred if their clients' resources are
unduly strained by the vicissitudes of the conflict. In the Middle East, for
instance, the former risks were underlined in October 1973 by the Soviet-
American confrontation that threatened to develop in the final hours of the
fourth Arab-Israeli war, and which brought American forces throughout the
world to the state of general alert. The latter penalties were exemplified
when the U.S.S.R. had to write off a large portion of the weapons that Egypt
imported for re-equipping her forces after the 1967 war, and when the United

22. In 1976, these two regions spent the following sums on arms imports: Europe
(NATO plus Warsaw Pact countries), $3.757 billion, or 28 percent of the world total;
Middle East, $4.414 billion, or 33 percent of the world total. See ACDA, *World
Military Expenditures and Arms Transfers, 1967–1976.*

States began to grant combat material to Israel free of payment to make up for the heavy Israeli losses in the October 1973 encounter.

For arms recipients involved in regional conflicts, the prospect of partial relief from the economic burdens of the arms race should provide enough incentives to interest them in control measures. More importantly, arms control may afford them a level of security higher than that achievable by active military competition. For this to be true, however, control arrangements will have to be negotiated with the participation or approval of these local recipients, in order to ensure that when these controls are enforced they are not perceived by any one of the parties as a threat to its relative power position. In other words, successful regional arms control must be consensual arms control, difficult as that may be to achieve. Unilateral imposition by arms suppliers will not do. As the case study of the Middle East tripartite system in Part II of this book will show, the resulting arrangements lend themselves all too easily to manipulation by the suppliers for the furtherance of ulterior political objectives. In the best of cases, an imposed system will be *perceived* as such a means of political pressure by the recipients, who will try their utmost to undermine it by withholding their essential cooperation, as well as by outright evasion.

Officially, the United States has been an active proponent of the regional approach to arms limitation.[23] In August 1970, the American representative submitted a working paper to the CCD that delineated some guidelines for regional arms control. The guidelines included undertakings by local parties not to produce or acquire the armaments they had agreed to regulate, and undertakings by potential suppliers not to supply such armaments. The controls would extend to "all States in the region whose participation is deemed important by other participants"; the objective of the control system would be the maintenance of a stable military balance; and there would be safeguards or supervisory arrangements to ensure compliance with the agreement.[24]

---

23. Among major suppliers, the United States was joined in this by Sweden, a significant arms producer and one of the more energetic members of the CCD, in 1971; ACDA, *Documents on Disarmament*, 1971 (Washington, D.C.: Government Printing Office, 1972), p. 82. Great Britain has also indicated her willingness to back such schemes, and the Soviet Union has engaged in U.S.-U.S.S.R. talks begun in 1977 on conventional arms restraints in preliminary consideration of regional limitations; *New York Times*, May 12, 1978.

24. In July 1976, the director of ACDA suggested to the CCD further specific examples of regional constraints: numerical ceilings on particular types of advanced weapons already present in a region, and agreements to forego acquisition of destabilizing systems, such as surface-to-surface missiles and long-range strike aircraft.

One other principle, perhaps the most important, stipulated that the initiative for the arms control arrangements should come from within the region concerned. It would be up to one or more of the local recipients of arms to call for or negotiate restraints that the external suppliers would be asked to respect. In other words, the onus of limiting regional arms races is placed exclusively on the self-denying abstinence of the participants. A similar reliance on voluntary limitations is evident in the supplementary suggestions offered in the same working paper for situations where the institution of a full-fledged multilateral arms control system is particularly difficult. These suggestions included unilateral undertakings by regional governments to refrain from acquiring certain types of advanced weaponry that would upset the military balance, and to disclose information regarding national production and procurement of armaments, in order to mitigate tensions generated by suspicion. Precisely what sort of regional conditions would preclude formal arms control agreements was not made clear, either in the working paper or in the statement by the American delegate on presenting the document to the CCD.[25] It stands to reason that negotiated arrangements would be most difficult to obtain in regions characterized by a high level of inter-state conflict.

In general, it is hard to quarrel with these principles. Any control system will be likely to incorporate most if not all of them. Only the notion of voluntarism is open to serious question. Given the sensitivity of nonproducing countries to any limitation proposals, the need to stress regional initiative so as to render the idea of international controls acceptable to them is understandable. Reliance on spontaneous restraint in the accumulation of military force may even be realistic for areas enjoying a low level of inter-state animosity—such as Latin America, where regional arrangements for both conventional and nuclear arms control have been indigenously proposed and, in the nuclear case, implemented. It is not realistic, however, to expect countries engaged in active conflict to initiate such moves without strong prodding if not outright pressure by the major external suppliers. Even if a party to conflict favors arms restraint on economic or long-term security grounds, it will be extremely reluctant to take the initiative, because of the fear that the adversary may interpret that as a sign of military weakness or loss of nerve, or because it may be a very unpopular and politically hazardous posture to adopt at home.

The arms-supplying countries cannot persuasively take the comfortable position that they should continue to make arms available to their clients for as long as these clients wish to purchase them, while piously proclaiming

25. ACDA, *Documents on Disarmament, 1970*, pp. 420–426.

a lively interest in arms control. A primary role certainly exists for them in generating regional arms control schemes, particularly for crisis areas. To exercise such a role should not mean coercing the regional recipients into unwilling participation in a control regime that they perceive to be detrimental to their interests. How to steer the middle course by establishing a mutually acceptable arms control system is, in many ways, the central question of this study.

The dialectical tension between the arms control requirements of international stability and the arms-acquisition—or sales—imperatives of national security is the critical relationship upon whose satisfactory resolution depends the viability of any arms-transfer control project. The Middle Eastern tripartite attempt—a unique experiment in this field—fell short of this goal and collapsed in failure. The key questions now are: how and why?

PART II

LESSONS OF THE PAST:
THE 1950–1955 ARMS RATIONING
REGIME

CHAPTER 4　SUPPLY AND CONTROL: ARMS AND THE TRIPARTITE DECLARATION OF MAY 1950

> Rarely has so large an undertaking been so unlucky in its timing or had so short-lived an effect.
>
> Dean Acheson
> *Present at the Creation*

On September 27, 1955, Egypt's Premier, Gamal Abdel Nasser, announced the conclusion of an arms purchase agreement with the Soviet bloc that, by the fall of 1956, had resulted in the accession of some $250 million worth of modern weapons to the Egyptian armed forces. Though first announced as a Czech-Egyptian deal, it soon became apparent that the agreement had been concluded with the U.S.S.R. The transaction thus marked the sudden spillover of Soviet power and influence into the Middle-East—precisely the breakthrough that Western diplomacy had assiduously attempted to forestall for almost a decade. Ironically, the breakthrough came a few months after the birth of the Baghdad Pact. Later known as CENTO, this regional defense organization had been created after years of repeated efforts by Britain and the United States to close the Middle East gap in the defensive chain of containment erected around the Soviet bloc in the opening years of the Cold War.

The arms deal not only leapfrogged the Baghdad Pact; it was partly precipitated by the Pact, and stands in this respect as a symbol of the cross-purposes that have plagued Western policies and intentions toward the Arab world for several decades. Moreover, it was not just a major arms transaction. Its effects on the balance of Great Power influence in the Middle East, on Arab-Western relations, and on the Arab-Israeli conflict were truly momentous. These effects have been amply reviewed in numerous published works and will be touched on only indirectly in this study. It is sufficient to note that

63

by opening the way to successive stages of Soviet penetration into the area, with a concomitant contraction of Western influence and with jeopardy to Western interests there, and by greatly increasing the virulence of the Arab-Israeli confrontation, the arms deal and the events that prompted it became a major turning point in the modern political history of the Middle East and a milestone in East-West relations.

These events also offer a prime example of the decisive impact that the politics of arms transfer may have on world affairs. The arms deal delivered a mortal blow to the policy of weapons transfer and regional arms control that the major Western powers had pursued in the Middle East since the Palestine War of 1947–1949, and that became institutionalized with the issuance of the Tripartite Declaration on "Security in the Middle East" by the United States, Great Britain, and France on May 25, 1950. To understand the reasons behind the failure of this tripartite policy, we shall analyze its origins, the instruments and manner of its implementation, and the web of events that led to its demise in September 1955. In the course of the analysis, the primary focus will necessarily be on the relations between Egypt, Great Britain, and the United States, although due emphasis will be given to the crucial roles played by both France and Israel. This is dictated by the purposes of our inquiry and by the nature of the events under review, as will soon become apparent.

The Tripartite Declaration was issued following a series of meetings in London by the Foreign Ministers of France, Great Britain, and the United States in May 1950. It announced a coordinated policy in the sphere of arms supply to the Arabs and Israel: arms would be given, but only moderately, and for defensive needs; supplies would be regulated so as not to fuel an arms competition. Also included was a strongly worded guarantee of the territorial status quo, which applied not only to internationally recognized state boundaries but also to the armistice arrangements that in 1949 had concluded the first Arab-Israeli war, and which would be maintained by direct Great Power intervention if necessary.

Because the Palestine conflict has so thoroughly dominated the international politics of the region, and because the territorial issues have long outlived the Western arms policy announced in 1950, subsequent historiography has put the accent on the "guarantees" clause while altogether neglecting the weapons regulation aspects of the tripartite undertaking. The nature of the Declaration as basically an arms control instrument was thereby totally obscured, although its preamble unambiguously emphasized the issue of "the supply of arms and war material" as its main concern. A closer look—cast here for the first time—at its origins and the purposes of its major sponsor, the United States, will show that the armaments problem did provide the primary incentive and was the issue on which the Declaration made its most significant impact during its short operative existence.

THE BACKGROUND OF POLICY

As the Arab Middle East emerged from the convulsions of World War II and was plunged barely two years later into the even more traumatic conflict over the future of Palestine, the circumstances of the region spelled a sure recipe for political turbulence and violent change. By and large, the newly independent states were economically poor, technically and industrially undeveloped, administratively inept, and militarily weak. Politically, the local regimes were mainly representative of oligarchic interests, and were both unequipped and unwilling to respond to the diverse challenges of their various societies. These challenges were sharpened by the transition to nominally full independence with its concomitant obligations and responsibilities, which were further compounded by the rise in overall popular expectations following the hard wartime years. Several of these regimes were further handicapped by the fact that they served largely at the pleasure of the dominant foreign power. This was particularly the case in Egypt, Jordan, and Iraq, where treaty arrangements gave Great Britain an overwhelming military presence and other special privileges.

In Syria and Lebanon, France, the former mandatory power, retained economic interests and some residual influence, but her political position had been practically destroyed when she had to grant the two countries full independence—and in 1946 finally withdraw her military forces—only under direct and explicit British pressure.[1] Of the two remaining sovereign Arab states, Yemen lived in self-imposed medieval isolation in the southwest corner of the Arabian peninsula, oblivious to the external world and possessing nothing that would lure covetous outsiders. Oil-producing Saudi Arabia, where the Arab-American Oil Company [ARAMCO] had been formed in 1936, allowed the United States a privileged position and a small military contingent at the Dhahran air base.

Nonetheless, Britain was the paramount regional power, and she would remain so for the rest of the forties and into the fifties. Even after India left

---

1. A brief account of the 1945–1946 Franco-British tussle over their respective positions in the two Levant states appears in George Kirk, *The Middle East 1945–1950* (London: Oxford University Press, 1954), pp. 106–113.

the Empire in 1947, London continued to regard the Middle East as vitally important, both for its oil wealth and as the hub of communications to the far-flung areas still under British control in East Africa, West Asia, and the Far East. Britain had military forces stationed in most countries of the area, and its diplomatic influence was felt in every Middle Eastern capital. Its real grip on events was not nearly as firm as appearances suggested, however. Two forces were relentlessly conspiring to pull the rug from under the imperious but aging British lion.

One of these forces was the rising tide of Arab nationalist sentiment, which British and American support for the Jewish cause in Palestine had turned militantly anti-Western. After Britain dumped the festering Palestine problem on the United Nations in February 1947, she would proceed on the basis that her military presence in Egypt and Iraq, as well as the future of the Anglo-Egyptian condominium over the Sudan, were the only issues of contention in British-Arab relations. Once these were resolved, Britain believed, an amicable modus vivendi under her continuing aegis could be reestablished. The malaise was deeper and more widespread, however, and its symptoms would affect the politics of the area right down to the present time. Palestine in particular had so envenomed these relations, and created such vast reservoirs of anger and mistrust, that no such compromise would prove feasible. Henceforth in the Arab world, any and all opposition to the West would become a virtue, regardless of its merits or consequences, while cooperation with the West or even the semblance of it would be treasonous and often tantamount to political suicide for those who risked it. By sponsoring a Jewish "national home" in Arab lands, Britain had forfeited any claim to Arab goodwill, and a belated and all too hesitant attempt to reverse course in the forties could not redeem it. She had also caused nationalist pressures on her remaining strongpoints in the area to increase severalfold.[2]

The second undermining force was domestic: the war had so exhausted Britain economically that she could maintain her extensive military commitments abroad only with extreme difficulty and provided that circumstances did not require substantial increases in expenditure. The precarious situation came to a head in the winter of 1946–1947, when the harsh weather and a rise in world commodity prices forced the Cabinet to adjust foreign policy to economic realities. February 1947 witnessed the decision to leave India and

2. An excellent analysis of this period is in Elizabeth Monroe, "Mr. Bevin's 'Arab Policy,'" St. Anthony's Papers, No. 11, *Middle Eastern Affairs: Number Two* (London: Chatto & Windus, 1961), pp. 9–48.

to turn the Palestine situation over to the United Nations.[3] The problem in the Middle East was compounded by increasing Soviet pressure on Turkey and Greece, in the opening rounds of the Cold War. Moscow's attempt to reestablish its historical sphere of influence in northern Iran the year before had failed, but not without alerting the West to its active interest in promoting traditional Russian claims in the soft underbelly area later to be known as the Northern Tier. Stalin now turned to political pressure—backed by military threats—on Ankara for concessions in the Dardanelles, and to strong support of the Communist-led guerrilla war in Greece. The British had primary responsibility for financial and military support of both countries, and in early 1947 they could no longer fulfill this. On February 21, in a message to the U.S. State Department, London requested Washington to take over.

This was a step of far-reaching consequences. In Secretary of State George Marshall's opinion, "it was tantamount to British abdication from the Middle East with obvious implications as to their successors."[4] Indeed, for a time it did look much like an abdication. Britain seemed intent not only on curtailing her financial aid to Greece and Turkey but also on disengaging militarily from her positions in southern Europe. Later in the year, the State Department was hard put to convince London not to withdraw its military forces from Greece (and Italy) forthwith, as the British had served notice they would do. In August, Prime Minister Attlee found it necessary to give assurances to Parliament that "despite this acceleration in the rate of withdrawal from overseas stations, and although certain calculated risks are being taken, there is no change in our foreign policy or in the defense policy which underlies our foreign policy."[5]

At any rate, Washington had decided to step into the breach. On March 12, the Truman Doctrine was enunciated by the President before a joint session of Congress. Calling the Doctrine a "serious course upon which we embark," he said that "it must be the policy of the United States to support free peoples who are resisting attempted subjugation by armed minorities or by outside pressures," and he went on to request authorization for $400 million in aid to Greece and Turkey, and for sending military and civilian personnel in an advisory capacity.[6] The policy of global containment of Communism

---

3. In the years 1946–1947, Palestine cost the British Exchequer £100 million. Ibid., p. 35n.

4. Walter Millis, ed., *The Forrestal Diaries* (New York: Viking, 1951), p. 245.

5. Great Britain, Parliament, *Parliamentary Debates* (House of Commons), August 6, 1947, col. 1503.

6. Text in U.S., Department of State, *Bulletin*, March 23, 1947.

was on. Moreover, the United States had made her entrance as a Middle Eastern power. Within the span of a decade—which would close with the Suez misadventure—Britain's presence in the entire Arab area (outside of South Arabia and the Gulf) would become a mere shadow of its former self.

At the time, however, the British did not see themselves as abdicators but rather as gentry in financial distress looking for a wealthy relative to bail them out. Below the Northern Tier, they fully intended to remain in control; and if Palestine had become too costly and too chaotic to hold, Egyptian and Iraqi nationalist demands could and would be renegotiated in such a way as to placate the nationalists by rendering the British military presence less visible (and its costs more bearable), while Britain's real influence would remain undiminished.[7] Furthermore, Middle Eastern oil was vital to Britain's economic prosperity; and with the breakdown of the wartime alliance with the Soviets, it was once more strategically imperative to keep the region under Western control. It was obvious, though, that Britain would not be able to continue her traditional guardianship unless the United States agreed to share in the financial burden, stopped making things difficult for her in places such as Palestine, Iran, and Egypt, and lent the necessary political backing and moral support.[8]

In short, London's immediate aim was to hitch the fresh and robust American horse to the stalled British wagon. In Washington, things were seen from a rather different angle. While there was a concordance of views in many aspects touching on regional security, there was no desire for an Anglo-American condominium. Briefly, the American attitude toward the Middle East was dictated by three basic factors. The most important was a policy

7. Renegotiation of the 1936 Treaty with Egypt resulted in the Sidqi-Bevin agreement of October 1946, and renegotiation of the 1930 Treaty with Iraq resulted in the Portsmouth Treaty of February 1948. In both cases, however, violent nationalistic opposition resulted in the scrapping of the new agreements.

8. In 1946–1948, Anglo-American relations were considerably strained by differences over Palestine, stemming from President Truman's strong support for the Zionist position. In Iran, the British had been in favor of granting the Soviets an oil concession in the north, for fear that otherwise their own oil interests would be jeopardized by Soviet agitation. As for Egypt, London expected greater U.S. support for its policy of maintaining troops in the Canal area. For a brief discussion of these and other differences, see Kirk, *Middle East 1945–1950*, pp. 5–17. Also see the memorandum of a conversation between Foreign Secretary Bevin and the Director of the Office of Near Eastern and African Affairs at the State Department, Loy Henderson, on September 9, 1947; in U.S., Department of State, *Foreign Relations of the United States, 1947*, Vol. V: *The Near East and Africa* (Washington, D.C.: Government Printing Office, 1971), pp. 496–502.

determination, first reached in 1946 at the time of the Iranian crisis,[9] that "[t]he security of the Eastern Mediterranean and of the Middle East is vital to the security of the United States"[10] and must be protected against Soviet encroachment. All else would be subordinated to this overriding objective. Second, there was a definite desire to see the British continue to have primary responsibility for Middle Eastern defense. The rapid dismantling of the American military machine after the close of World War II had been in response to a strong public expectation of a "return to normalcy"; replacing the British would be extremely unpopular and, in the short term, impractical as well.[11] Moreover, Washington had no particular wish to be saddled with the multiple problems of the area. America had primary responsibility for European reconstruction, it was felt, and the Marshall Plan was enough of a burden. Finally, the internal State Department documents revealed a rather ill-defined but clear sentiment that the political stability of the Arab area and the future cooperation of the local regimes could only be secured by establishing Arab-Western relations on a new basis that would be relatively free from traditional British imperialistic practices and would accommodate a modicum of nationalist aspirations.[12] There was a resolve not to participate in British regional economic initiatives[13] and to steer clear of policies that would associate the United States too closely with British interests. Irritation at the constraints imposed on the expansion of American economic activities by entrenched British influence played no small part in fueling this sentiment.

THE "PENTAGON TALKS" OF 1947

Defense of the Middle East against Communism, continued reliance on the British in the military sphere, and dissociation from British imperialism were

9. In September 1946, it was announced that American naval units would henceforth be permanently present in the Mediterranean; Millis, ed., *Forrestal Diaries*, pp. 210–211.

10. State Department memorandum, *Foreign Relations 1947*, p. 575.

11. "We are playing with fire while we have nothing with which to put it out," Secretary Marshall would tell a National Security Council meeting that discussed the Middle East in February 1948; Millis, ed., *Forrestal Diaries*, p. 373.

12. See particularly the extensive memoranda on "The British and American Positions," and on "Specific current Questions," *Foreign Relations 1947*, pp. 511–521 and 521–560.

13. For example, the British Middle East Office, set up in Cairo in 1945 as a successor to the wartime Middle East Supply Center. The Office was to provide agricultural, labor, health, and statistical advice to interested governments, foreshadowing U.S. foreign aid programs. Its services were only rarely sought on local initiative, however, and it was boycotted by the host country, Egypt, because of its imperialistic stigma.

the tenets of American policy. Whitehall was greatly disturbed at the future implications of the U.S. position, a feeling that the flow of American arms, men, and money into the area, which began after the announcement of the Truman Doctrine, did nothing to assuage. While the situation in Palestine was coming to a head as the United Nations debated the partition of the mandated territory in the fall of 1947, Foreign Secretary Bevin decided the time had come for both Western powers to coordinate their Middle East policies and reach an understanding on the nature of their complementary relationship there.

At Bevin's initiative, a series of meetings were held in Washington from October 16 to November 7, during which high military and diplomatic officials from both countries undertook a comprehensive review of the situation and reached a loose agreement on several aspects of their respective future roles in the area. The talks were conducted under a heavy veil of secrecy, and by mutual consent Palestine was left off the agenda. On this matter, the lines were clearly drawn and no possibility of a joint approach appeared in sight, particularly as U.S. policy on this one subject emanated directly from the Oval Office. Among the American participants were Robert Lovett, Loy Henderson, and George Kennan from the State Department, and Lt. General Lauris Norstad and Vice Admiral Forrest Sherman from the Pentagon. The British delegation was led by the Ambassador in Washington, Lord Inverchapel, and included among others the Assistant Under-Secretary of State at the Foreign Office, Michael Wright, and the Chief of Staff to the Minister of Defense, Lt. General Sir Leslie Hollis. The understandings that resulted from the policy review were expressed in twenty-five joint statements that were later concurred in and endorsed at the highest political levels, by the British Cabinet on the one hand, and the National Security Council (NSC) and President Truman on the other, thereby becoming established policy.[14]

In perspective, the importance of these conversations lies mainly in the attempt to "codify" the general guidelines of Anglo-American policy toward the Middle East. True, both governments decided not to formalize the results of the talks into an Agreement, but to consider them officially as merely an exchange of "recommendations that substantially coincided."[15] Also, several of the understandings reached were later unravelled by changing conditions and the gradual shifting balance of regional power and influence

14. Documentation on these talks was published in *Foreign Relations 1947*, pp. 485–626.

15. Memorandum by the Private Secretary to Bevin, December 4, 1947, ibid., p. 625.

from British to American hands. Nonetheless, on regional defense, arms supplies, and the question of the British base at the Suez Canal, there would be a remarkable continuity and consistency in Anglo-American policy for several years. The 1950 Tripartite Declaration and the abortive 1951–1952 proposals for a Middle East Defense Organization (MEDO), for instance, would be formal and open expressions of this coordinated approach.

In the sphere of regional defense, the two governments agreed that the area was "vital" to their security and its protection required that "the British maintain their strong strategic, political, and economic position in the Eastern Mediterranean and the Middle East, including the sea approaches to the area through the Straits of Gibraltar and the Red Sea," and that both countries "pursue parallel policies in that area."[16] Washington thereby secured a commitment by the British to continue their military role—which they in fact were not about to surrender—while Britain obtained an American endorsement of her policy of keeping troops in Egyptian, Iraqi, and other bases.

This linkage was made clear in the understanding on the "Retention of British Military Rights in Egypt,"[17] which affirmed the British right to keep the Suez Canal base during peacetime " in such a condition that [it] could be effectively and speedily used " in case of war or threat of war. The statement further specified that, in view of Egyptian resistance, this objective might best be achieved by the conclusion of regional defense pacts between Britain and the Arab states. The United States offered "to exert all its influence with the Egyptian Government in supporting the British during the negotiations." It also offered, as an inducement, to "consider favorably certain Egyptian requests for military advisers, various military supplies, other kinds of technical and financial assistance, etc.," subject to British approval.

As for arms supplies to the area in general, a separate statement declared that United States policy was "to confine arms sales to countries of the Middle East to reasonable quantities required for the maintenance of internal security," Greece and Turkey excepted.[18] In the future, however, it might be desirable to step up supplies to enable these countries to assume responsibility for their own defense. In the meantime, both powers agreed to maintain full exchange of information on the subject.

16. From "General Statement by the American Group" at the conclusion of the talks, ibid., p. 583. The British group submitted an identical statement.

17. Ibid., pp. 584–586.

18. Ibid., p. 613.

TERRITORIAL GUARANTEES AND REGIONAL SECURITY

If at the end of 1947 the feeling was that the line had been held against Moscow's pressures in the Middle East by the resolve shown in Iran, Turkey, and Greece, and that the seemingly intractable problem of Palestine might at last prove soluble by the Solomonic expedient of partition,[19] by 1950 the outlook from the standpoint of Western chanceries was again one that called for gloomy concern.

In Palestine, partition had not worked. Upon expiration of Britain's mandate on May 14, 1948, the Jews had announced the creation of their state, and the Arabs had fulfilled their pledge of resorting to war to impede it. Military ineptitude, unpreparedness, and lack of coordination had then combined with petty intrigues and dynastic ambitions among the political leadership to produce a disastrous Arab defeat. In the end, Israel had come into control of almost four-fifths of Palestine, and some 800,000 Arab Palestinians had been displaced to the neighboring countries or to parts of Palestine, such as the Gaza Strip and the West Bank, that ultimately came under Arab jurisdiction. Armistice arrangements had been worked out between the belligerents (except Iraq), but the peace remained tenuous, as border clashes and raids recurred and the Arab states continued to consider themselves in a state of war. The work of the U.N. Conciliation Commission was fruitless. While the Arabs now were generally willing to accept the terms of the 1947 partition proposal, the Israelis saw no reason to undo a fait accompli accepted by the Great Powers and highly beneficial to themselves. In April 1950, a meeting of the Council of the Arab League initialled a Joint Defense Alliance, and League members undertook not to sign separate peace treaties with Israel.

Equally disastrous was the political effect of the unexpected debacle on the Arab regimes. Mutual recriminations over the defeat, and the subsequent struggle in the Arab League over Jordanian King Abdullah's annexation of the West Bank, had fuelled and further embittered the complex of interlaced suspicions that—quite apart from the Israeli problem—Arab governments had of one another's annexationist designs.[20] Moreover, popular unrest was

19. The U.N. General Assembly voted on November 29 to divide the country into an Arab and a Jewish state, while Jerusalem and its environs would be internationalized.

20. For years, schemes of unification of Greater Syria (Syria, Lebanon, Palestine, and Jordan) and/or Iraq under the Hashemites in Baghdad or Amman, and Saudi fears of Hashemite ambitions in the Arabian Peninsula (from which Abdul-'Aziz Ibn Sa'ud had evicted them in the 1920s), on top of the traditional rivalry between Egypt and Iraq for Arab leadership, and the concerns of Christian Lebanon over Syria's unitarian designs, had created great instability in inter-Arab relations, which re-emerged after the temporary, and never more than paper-thin, show of unity in the first

widespread, and resentment among the below-the-top ranks in the military was rampant. The successive coups d'etat of March, August, and December 1949 in Syria were only the beginning of a series of convulsions that would rock the structure of Arab politics to its foundation and bring to grief the entire bankrupt "leadership of '48."

The political fluidity and fragmentation of the region, the animosity toward the West that nationalists increasingly sensitive to its encroachments and its paternalism were breeding, and the weakness of local military establishments gave cause for heightened anxiety, particularly in Washington, from a wider perspective as well. The Cold War had received new impetus in the late forties, with the Berlin blockade and the "loss" of mainland China to Communism. A crisis was brewing in Korea. The East-West confrontation was shaping up as a struggle of global proportions. On February 16, 1950, at the White House, Secretary of State Dean Acheson had made a celebrated speech, in which he had asserted that "the only way to deal with the Soviet Union, we have found from experience, is to create situations of strength." [21] If so, it was later pointed out, then the Middle East was "a region that seemed to call preeminently for creating a 'situation of strength' . . . , [for it] seemed almost to invite a Soviet push that would split the free world along its North-South axis, deny it the abundant oil resources of Iran, Iraq, and the Arabian peninsula, and open a path for the extension of Soviet influence westward across Africa and eastward into Pakistan and India." [22]

For such a "situation of strength" to emerge, a large-scale infusion of military and financial aid was obviously required. But strengthening individual local regimes was not sufficient, nor even salutary, by Western reckoning, without some arrangement that would ensure that the aid would be used exclusively for regional defense against Soviet aggression, rather than to further intraregional quarrels and ambitions or to launch a second round against Israel. Reliance on the crumbling network of British bilateral military alliances was probably no longer feasible, to judge from the troubles in Egypt over the Suez base. Might not a collective security system, somewhat along the lines of the just-concluded NATO pact, provide the necessary underpinning

Arab-Israeli war. For a good discussion of these conflicts, see Majid Khadduri, "The Scheme of Fertile Crescent Unity: A Study in Inter-Arab Relations," in Richard N. Frye, ed., *The Near East and the Great Powers* (Cambridge, Mass.: Harvard University Press, 1951), pp. 137–177; and Patrick Seale, *The Struggle for Syria* (London: Oxford University Press, 1965), chaps. 2, 4, and 6.

21. Text in U.S. Department of State, *Bulletin*, March 20, 1950.

22. Richard P. Stebbins et al., *The United States in World Affairs, 1950* (New York: Harper, 1951), p. 307.

for a joint defense effort, allow for a continued British military presence on a basis other than unilateral occupation, and prove a stabilizing factor in regional politics as well?[23]

These issues were reviewed at two regional conferences of U.S. diplomatic envoys in the Middle East, held in Istanbul in November 1949 and in Cairo in March 1950. They were also studied within the State Department, the Pentagon, and the NSC in April–May 1950, in preparation for a meeting of the American, British, and French foreign ministers scheduled for mid-May in London to precede a gathering of the North Atlantic Council. It was expected that Secretary Bevin would raise several aspects of British and American policy in the Middle East at the meeting, as Whitehall had for months pressed the need for better coordination by the Allies of their respective positions.[24]

The United States had agreed in the 1947 talks that Britain should seek to replace her treaties by a regional defense structure if no bilateral arrangements with Middle Eastern governments proved feasible. Frozen for the duration of the Palestine war, this idea had been the object of informal diplomatic soundings and had been discussed in the Arab press throughout 1949. The Foreign Office now seized upon the looming Soviet "world threat" and the example of NATO to try to convince the Egyptians that British troops should remain at the Suez base, and that the renegotiation of the 1936 Treaty should be conducted on the basis of a coordinated regional defense under British command.[25] Egyptian sponsorship of an exclusively Arab collective security pact had been partly a response to this increasing pressure for a regional defense partnership that, in the estimation of Egyptian and other Arab nationalists, served no other purpose than perpetuation of Britain's military presence.[26]

At this point, however, Washington was unwilling to support a regional pact that would be primarily reliant on American aid, as any British-sponsored arrangement would have to be. There was thus an American shift on this

23. On U.S. thinking along these lines, see J. C. Hurewitz, *Middle East Dilemmas* (New York: Harper, 1953), especially pp. 92–93; and John C. Campbell, *Defense of the Middle East* (New York: Harper, 1958), especially pp. 204–206.

24. M. A. Fitzsimons, *Empire by Treaty* (Notre Dame, Ind.: University of Notre Dame Press, 1964), p. 98.

25. Minutes of the talks between British and Egyptian officials starting in June 1950 were published by the Egyptian government in *Records of Conversations, Notes and Papers exchanged between the Royal Egyptian Government and the United Kingdom Government, March 1950–November 1951* (Cairo: Ministry of Foreign Affairs, 1951).

26. See statements by Egyptian Premier An-Nahas to Britain's Chief of the Imperial General Staff, Field Marshal Sir William Slim, in ibid., pp. 12–13.

matter since the 1947 talks. The reasons can be gleaned from a Department of State memorandum prepared for Secretary Acheson's guidance in the ministerial meetings.[27] Committed to the security of Israel, the Truman Administration now had to balance considerations of Arab strength to counter Soviet aggression against the likelihood that Western aid would be used in a revanchist war against the new state. Israeli officials had warned against this eventuality, and indicated they might resort to preventive war.[28] Moreover, the Arab states had stolen a march, having come forward with their own pact, which would stiffen their resistance to any Western proposals. Not that this new creation of the Arab League was of much use to the West. Not only was there much discord among its members; there was also "a fundamental difficulty[:] the area lacks a power center on the basis of which a pact could be built."[29] Finally, the critical situation in Europe and the Far East had so engaged available U.S. resources, both military and financial, that the alternative option of a Near East pact with Western participation could not be broached at this time.[30] The Joint Chiefs of Staff in particular were adamantly opposed to any further extension of American commitments abroad.

This attitude soon changed again. The outbreak of the Korean war in June caused both a reassessment of the seriousness of the strategic threat to the areas on the periphery of the Soviet bloc and a rapid increase in American military power. Consequently, in 1951, the United States joined Britain in co-sponsoring the Middle East Command proposals. As of May 1950, however, it is worth noting that the recommended policy was that

We are not in a position to consider any security pacts with Greece, Turkey, Iran or other Near Eastern countries at the present time because we cannot tell whether our capabilities at this time are adequate to defend our vital interests in Europe. Only an increase in Europe's own defensive strength, resulting from the North Atlantic Treaty and the Military Aid Program, would permit us to consider further security arrangements.[31]

27. U.S. Department of State Archives, "Regional Security Arrangements in the Eastern Mediterranean and Near Eastern Areas," Top Secret, May 11, 1950; also published in *Foreign Relations 1950*, Vol. V, pp. 152–158.
28. See, for example, the remarks of the Chief of Staff of the Israeli Army to the American Ambassador, in James G. Mcdonald, *My Mission in Israel, 1948–1951* (New York: Simon and Schuster, 1951), pp. 195–196.
29. U.S. Department of State Archives, "Regional Security," p. 4.
30. According to McDonald, this was explicitly conveyed to the U.S. ambassadors assembled at Istanbul by the Assistant Secretary of State for the Near East, George McGhee, who chaired the conference; McDonald, *My Mission in Israel*, p. 200.
31. U.S. Department of State Archives, "Regional Security," p. 6.

For Britain, once the Arab-Israeli war was over, the first objective became salvaging the scattered remains still afloat from the sinking wreckage of her Middle East policy. Her position was very anomalous. The war had confirmed her as Foreign Enemy Number One in Arab lands, for Arabs everywhere blamed her above all others for the loss of Palestine. At the same time, she had treaty obligations with several major Arab states that rendered her partially responsible for their defense, committed her to their assistance in case of war, and required her to supply them with military equipment and training.[32] This situation had been tenable in the past, despite the resentment of the local populations at the continued presence of British troops and bases. With the Arabs now ranged against a strong and aggressive Israel, however, this was no longer the case, for any substantial hostilities would almost inevitably lead to British involvement.[33] Such involvement would in all cases redound to British disadvantage, for, on the one hand, it would entail frictions with the United States and Israel—if not outright conflict with the latter— and, on the other hand, it would always fall short of anything that would satisfy the Arabs. The only safe course clearly lay in neutralizing the Arab-Israeli dispute, shoring up the British position by strengthening Britain's only remaining friends—the ruling Hashemites in Jordan and Iraq—and holding on to the Suez base for as long as possible.

On April 6, 1950, the British Embassy in Washington informally suggested to the State Department that both powers could best contribute to stabilization of the Middle East conflict by issuing a statement that would guarantee the inviolability of frontiers in the Palestine area; the Embassy also suggested that this might be timed to follow the announcement by King Abdullah of the annexation of the West Bank, which was expected later that month. The Department's reaction was lukewarm, mainly because Abdullah's action, while strongly favored by the British, was opposed by the Arab League and by Israel, and the proposed guarantee would constitute a formal acknowledgement of it. The matter was therefore deferred for discussion at the Foreign Ministers' meeting.[34]

32. For texts of the Treaties of Preferential Alliance with Iraq and Egypt, and the Treaty of Alliance with Jordan, see J. C. Hurewitz, *Diplomacy in the Near and Middle East, A Documentary Record: 1914–1956*, reprint edition (New York: Octagon, 1972), pp. 178–181, 203–211, and 296–299.

33. The new dangers first struck home in the waning stages of the Palestine war, when the crossing by Israeli forces of the Egypt-Israel border caused London to warn the Israelis that it would have to come to Egypt's defense under the 1936 Treaty unless they withdrew, and Israeli fighters shot down several R.A.F. reconnaissance planes a few days later. See Kirk, *Middle East 1945–1950*, pp. 293–294.

34. Information provided by staff of the Historical Office at the Department of State.

The British approach was reminiscent of a proposal of Bevin's fourteen months earlier that had included "a retraction of the Israeli-held area, which would be surrounded by a circle of weak Arab states held together by foreign aid, given also to Israel, and the whole result disciplined and restrained by Anglo-American agreement."[35] The plan had been rejected in Washington on grounds of impracticality and because it "would constitute a continuing invitation to Soviet intrigue and intervention in the area,"[36] presumably because of the close resulting association between the United States and British imperialism.

Despite American coolness to the April 6 proposal, State Department thinking was beginning to turn in the same direction.[37] George McGhee, the Assistant Secretary in charge of Middle Eastern affairs, had just returned from visits to the area and participation in the Istanbul and Cairo conferences. Two things in particular had strongly impressed him. One was the degree to which political and social unrest in the Arab countries had proven fertile ground for the growth of pro-Soviet sentiment. Barely two years after Moscow had vied with Washington for first honors in extending recognition to Israel, responsible Arab officials were calling for treaties of friendship with the Soviet Union,[38] the Secretary-General of the Arab League was declaring that these "views express the sentiments of every Arab,"[39] and there was plenty of evidence in the media that the idea had struck a responsive chord in the public mind.[40]

Here, as in other parts of the Third World at the height of the Cold War, however, Americans misread the significance and the roots of pro-Soviet

35. Dean Acheson, *Present at the Creation: My Years at the State Department* (New York: Norton, 1969), p. 259.

36. Ibid.

37. The following discussion is partially based on personal interviews with Raymond Hare, then Deputy Assistant Secretary for Near Eastern and African Affairs, January 25, 1973; Parker Hart, who in 1952–1955 was Director of the Office of Near Eastern Affairs, January 25 and February 6, 1973; and George McGhee, February 1, 1973.

38. For instance, see the statement by Ma'ruf Ad-Dawalibi, Syria's Minister of Economy, in *Al-Misri* (Cairo), April 9, 1950; also quoted in the *New York Times*, April 12, 1950.

39. *New York Times*, April 23, 1950.

40. Ad-Dawalibi's suggestion was widely and approvingly discussed in the Arab press. For a review of this reaction, see the article by Albion Ross, ibid., May 28, 1950, section IV, p. 4. The suggestion also elicited a prompt Soviet response. The Soviet Minister in Damascus, Daniel Solod, held several meetings with Ad-Dawalibi and offered the Syrians a treaty of friendship, commercial agreements, and credits for the purchase of Soviet and Czech armaments. See *Al-Ahram* (Cairo), April 18, May 9, and May 13, 1950.

sentiment. Nationalists sought Soviet support only to counterbalance Western predominance and control, and they were willing to accept the support only on their own terms, not Moscow's.[41] There was, during this period, no noticeable increase in the influence of local Communism. Communist parties were banned in all Arab countries and remained so. In fact, Communists were exhorted to struggle against the nationalists precisely on the grounds that the latter were no more pro-Soviet than they were pro-Western.[42] Nonetheless, the Communist "threat" had been a subject of discussion at both U.S. diplomatic conferences. At Istanbul, McGhee had told the assembled Chiefs of Mission that "to avert the threat of Communism from the inside" was at the basis of American policy in the area, complementing the containment of direct Soviet intervention in Greece and Turkey.[43] The Cairo meeting had been attended by personnel from the U.S. embassy in Moscow, including the Ambassador, who officially was in Egypt "on vacation only."[44] While Moscow's success was publicly attributed to the exploits of "Soviet propagandists,"[45] privately there was serious concern that a vacuum of influence had been produced by the retraction of British power, and there was a growing feeling that the United States should act to fill it without much further delay.

Reinforcing this feeling was the second impression McGhee had gathered from his trips: the extent of the fears expressed by Arab leaders about inter-Arab strife resulting from hegemonic and annexationist ambitions, and the consequent need for some commitment by the Great Powers to the status quo. Pro-Western Arab governments had been pressing Washington for some such move for the better part of a year.[46] Moreover, the shaky Arab-Israeli

41. For representative statements, see, e.g., Ad-Dawalibi's press conference in *Al-Ahram*, May 15, 1950, and the interview with M. Kamel Al-Bandari, a former Egyptian ambassador to Moscow, in ibid., May 22, 1950. More on the state of mind of the nationalists, particularly in Syria, is in Seale, *Struggle for Syria*, pp. 101–105.

42. The leader of the Communist Party in Syria and Lebanon told his followers in a 1951 Report: "We must work constantly also to unmask groups and parties claiming to be 'socialist,' such as the Arab Socialist Party, the Islamic Socialist front, and Al Ba'ath in Syria, for through their seductive propaganda they . . . try to prevent the growth of popular sympathy for the world-wide camp of peace and socialism led by the Soviet Union by calling for a so-called 'third force' or 'neutrality' between the two camps" (English translation by Harold W. Glidden, in *Middle East Journal* 8 [Spring 1953], 206–221).

43. McDonald, *My Mission in Israel*, p. 199.

44. *Al-Ahram*, March 8, 1950; and *New York Times*, March 12, 1950.

45. *New York Times*, April 23, 1950.

46. See, e.g., the lengthy reports by the Lebanese Minister to the U.S., Dr. Charles Malik, to his government on August 5, 1949, and September 9, 1950, published in

armistice structure needed bolstering. Long discussions ensued at the Near East Office, and the conviction grew that a statement guaranteeing frontiers would convey a clear signal to the Russians about the continued Western interest in the Middle East area and would "alla[y] the fears of the Arabs of each other, as well as those between Israel and the Arab States."[47]

Consequently, in preparation for the Foreign Ministers' meetings in May, a paper[48] was prepared in the latter part of April within the NEA Office and fully cleared within the State Department, suggesting that Secretary Acheson propose to his French and British counterparts the issuance by the three governments of separate but similarly worded "reassuring declarations upon the occasion of the Foreign Ministers' meeting." The statements would read as follows:

The Government of ———, deeply interested in the establishment and main-tenance of peace and stability in the Near East, reaffirms its policy of constant support of political independence and territorial integrityof the states in that area. It continues unalterably opposed to the violation of the frontiers of states through external force. The Government of ———, should it receive reliable information that any Near Eastern state was preparing to violate existing fron-tiers or armistice lines, would immediately take action consistent with its obligations as a member of the United Nations, both within and without the United Nations, to prevent such violation.

The State Department anticipated a "probably favorable" British and French response. But the proposed formulation deviated from British thinking in one major way: the guarantee it embodied extended beyond the Palestine area to cover the entire region. This was consistent with the American objective of discouraging Hashemite and other ambitions, but it did not necessarily fit the aims of the British, who were known to favor unity schemes in the Fertile Crescent under Iraqi or Jordanian leadership,[49] and who had

---

Charles Malik, *Charles Malik and the Palestinian Cause* [in Arabic] (Beirut: Badran, 1973), especially p. 167. Lebanon's fears of Syrian motives and the probable attitudes of the Western powers on unification of the two countries are discussed by Malik on pp. 117–121.

47. Personal communication from George McGhee, March 21, 1973.

48. U.S. Department of State Archives, "Near Eastern Security," Top Secret, April 28, 1950.

49. Another State Department paper prepared for Acheson had this to say: "[T]he tenor of British approaches in the past suggests the Government of the United Kingdom is inclined to be sympathetic to a union which would permit the Hashemite family of Iraq, traditional friends of the British, to predominate in a unified government or federation. Mr. Bevin, in somewhat casual and oblique fashion, orally indicated last fall that he was personally inclined in favor of the proposals then being advanced by

moreover made clear to Washington their belief that they were "already exerting a stabilizing influence" beyond the Palestine area through their treaty relationships.[50] On the other hand, the proposed declaration amounted to tacit U.S. concurrence in the Jordanian annexation, which had been announced on April 24 and formally recognized by London on the 27th. The declaration therefore satisfied the British request of April 6 and was acceptable to Bevin.

THE ARMS ISSUE

Thus, as Acheson prepared to meet his two European colleagues in London, his brief included a proposed guarantee of the status quo in the Middle East. As the foregoing analysis indicates, from a Western standpoint one could easily make a case for such a pledge in the spring of 1950. It could serve as a stopgap warning to Moscow not to attempt any militaristic adventures in the area, and could later be replaced by a full-fledged security pact. It could also supplement the unsteady Arab-Israeli armistice, defuse the tense Jordanian situation, and discourage inter-Arab designs. Arab unity schemes could still be brought forth under its umbrella, provided they were advanced by diplomatic and not by military means.

The instrument that was eventually worked out at the tripartite meeting—a much more substantial undertaking than the modest "reassuring" statements originally envisaged—may have indeed fulfilled several of these purposes, though to what degree will never be known with certainty. As it turned out, however, the impelling motive that prompted the major Declaration issued after the May meetings lay elsewhere. It is significant in this context that Secretary Acheson, reminiscing about the Declaration many years later, thought that the document, as a joint guarantee against territorial aggression, was "not easy to explain," and he candidly expressed his doubts that "it had ever lived." For, within a few years, he pointed out, its own sponsors would break its injunctions—the British and French (together with the Israelis, who originally were to be one of the restrained parties) by themselves committing military aggression in Egypt in 1956, and the United States by acting unilaterally in Lebanon in 1958.[51]

Syria and Iraq" (U.S. Department of State Archives, "The Political Union of Syria and Iraq," Top Secret, April 25, 1950; also published in *Foreign Relations 1950*, Vol. V, pp. 1206–1210).

50. U.S. Department of State Archives, "Near Eastern Security," p. 1.

51. Acheson, *Present at the Creation*, p. 396.

· The clue to the principal objective of the Declaration, and the area of its most far-reaching impact, should be sought in its weapons supply aspects. The evidence indicates that the Declaration was conceived by Washington chiefly as a device designed to deal with a number of arms transfer problems that had reached a critical stage at that precise time of April–May 1950. The problems were: the onset of a small-scale but potentially dangerous arms race in the Palestine area, particularly between Israel and Egypt; the need to initiate the politically very sensitive Western provision of arms to Israel; and the need to assuage Israeli and American Jewish anxieties about ongoing British shipments of heavy weapons to Egypt.

The urgency of the matter stemmed from the intense pressure then being applied by pro-Israeli circles in the United States on the Truman Administration to (1) respond favorably to an Israeli request made in February 1950 for a substantial amount of U.S. arms, and (2) exert pressure on London to stop its sale of arms to Arab countries. The United Nations had installed an embargo on weapons transfer to the Middle East on May 29, 1948, at the time of the first truce in the Palestine war. This embargo supplemented an earlier, unilateral one that the United States had imposed on December 5, 1947, shortly after the partition resolution had been adopted.[52] The U.N. restrictions were lifted on August 11, 1949, after the conclusion of the armistice agreements; and on the following day, Britain announced the resumption of its supplies of armaments contracted by Arab governments.

London's treaties with Iraq, Egypt, and Jordan required her to assure, in words of the Iraqi treaty, "the provision of arms, ammunition, equipment, ships and aeroplanes of the latest available pattern."[53] Egypt, in particular, had placed several orders for aircraft, tanks, and ships both prior to and during the Palestine war, which Britain, unwilling to give Cairo any grounds for denunciation of the treaty, now proceeded to fill. New arms agreements were reached as well. In the second half of 1949 and the first few months of 1950, some ten Gloster Meteor F.4 jet fighters, a squadron of Vampire jet

52. The U.S. decision had resulted in the revocation of the approval for sale of sufficient arms and ammunition to Syria to train one hundred pilots for one year, which apparently was the only transaction with Arab parties then in progress. Since the end of World War II, the U.S. had supplied only about $8,000 worth of light arms for internal security to Arab countries; *Foreign Relations 1947*, pp. 1300, 1304. Agents of the Jewish Palestinian community were actively purchasing military equipment from private dealers.

53. Hurewitz, *Diplomacy*, p. 181. There were some differences in wording between the treaties. The Jordanian one did not include the phrase "of the latest available pattern. . . ."

fighter-bombers, several obsolescent propeller-driven fighters, six frigates varying between 1,000 and 1,400 tons and carrying 4-inch guns as their main armament, and a number of Sherman tanks were delivered.[54] British arms in smaller quantities were also supplied to Jordan and Iraq, while France sent armaments to Syria.[55]

The Israeli reaction was not long in coming. Israel had closed the 1948 war not only in victory but in a military position that compared favorably with that of all the Arab states combined. Despite the embargo, she had been able to acquire sufficient heavy armaments abroad to satisfy her immediate needs after the first cease-fire. Her clandestine procurement efforts in Europe, Latin America, and the United States, aided by the efforts of the Jewish communities, and at times with the unofficial support of the local governments, had resulted in an efficient organizational network that continued its work after the armistice, but now openly and in coordination with the Israeli state machinery.[56] In 1949–1950, Israel was able to acquire surplus and phased-out weapons from several governments and private sources in Europe and other parts of the world, including the faraway Philippines,[57] that her technologically proficient local arms shops could turn into useful additions to the country's military inventory.

There was therefore little fear that the British shipments to Egypt would alter the balance of power. In fact, Prime Minister Ben-Gurion claimed in May 1951 that Israel was "the strongest military power in the Middle East apart from Turkey."[58] Nonetheless, substantial Arab acquisitions of arms were cause for serious worry. They would encourage the Arab states to maintain the state of war and their refusal to negotiate a permanent peace settlement; they might tempt the Arabs to launch another war; and they would have to be compensated for by increased Israeli arms purchases at a time of severe economic strains caused by the large influx of Jewish immigrants to the new

54. Details of arms transactions and references are included in Tables 3, 4, and 5 in the next chapter.

55. The British *Sharq Al-Adna* [Near East] radio station reported on December 31, 1949, that Syria had received twenty-three 18-ton tanks and four 105-mm. guns from the French.

56. For an authoritative and very detailed account of these efforts, particularly in the United States, see Leonard Slater, *The Pledge* (New York: Simon and Schuster, 1970). Also very informative are: Col. Benjamin Kagan, *The Secret Battle for Israel* (Cleveland: World, 1966); and Robert Jackson, *The Israeli Air Force Story* (London: Tom Stacey, 1970), chaps. 1 and 2. Kagan's figures on Arab inventories are not reliable.

57. Parker Hart interview; *Parliamentary Debates* (House of Commons), May 16–June 3, 1949, col. 879.

58. *New York Times*, May 28, 1951.

state—which by 1952 would double the size of its population. Moreover, Britain and the United States remained unwilling to sell arms to Israel, in line with the policy of restraint that the major arms suppliers had elected to follow when the United Nations embargo had been lifted. This position had now become vulnerable, however, in view of the British shipments.

Starting in January 1950, a strong Israeli diplomatic and propaganda campaign was unleashed, with the American government as the primary target, for the twin purposes of compelling Britain to stop or at least reduce her arms sales to the Arabs, and bringing about a change in the Anglo-American policy of denying arms to Israel.

Quiet contacts had been carried out in late 1949, but the public campaign opened in earnest with a letter from New York Representative Jacob Javits to Secretary of State Acheson sent on December 28, 1949. Javits stated that, while he was abroad on a mission for the House Foreign Affairs Committee, he had visited Israel, where he had heard vigorous complaints about the British arms supplies. He had checked in London "and was satisfied that the British were shipping heavy arms such as naval frigates and jet fighter planes, armoured cars, heavy tanks, and automatic rifles to Egypt, Iraq, and Jordan." [59] He questioned the use to which the recipients would put these weapons and asked for the Department's views on the American attitude.

Acheson replied on January 12, explaining that the U.S. government was opposed to an arms race in the Middle East, that all arms shipments should be for internal security and self-defense purposes only, and that the U.S. would "be quick to use all of its influence ... within the United Nations and outside" to deter any outbreak of hostilities. At the same time, since the Middle East was "a region the security of which is of great importance to the west[,] it is desirable that the countries in this part of the world obtain from reliable and friendly sources" arms for their security. The British were furnishing arms under binding treaty arrangements, and all information available did not indicate "any serious preparations" for renewed warfare. [60]

Acheson's "frank reply," in Javits' words, "set in train [a] vigorous discussion" on the question of arms supplies to the Arabs and Israel that soon developed into a textbook case in pressure politics that would last until the day the Tripartite Declaration was proclaimed, turning this into the stickiest issue in American Middle East policy during the first half of 1950. On January 25, a spokesman for the Israeli Foreign Ministry said the Secretary's

59. Javits, statement in the U.S. Congress, House of Representatives, *Congressional Record*, Vol. 96, Part 3 (March 15, 1950), p. 3420.

60. Ibid., p. 3430; and *New York Times*, January 16, 1950.

letter to Javits "has caused the Israeli government serious concern" and that events had left his government no choice "but to increase its own defensive capacity to the maximum of its ability."[61] The next day, Javits sent a second letter to Acheson, asking the State Department to act to halt the "Near East arms race" and raising the specter of Communism as the big winner in the area if there were a renewal of hostilities.[62]

The Acheson-Javits exchange set the terms of the ensuing debate; the two sides staked out their respective positions, and there would be no significant change in them as events unfolded. A new dimension was added on January 29, however, when the president of the Zionist Organization of America (Z.O.A.) linked the British arms shipments to U.S. Marshall Plan aid to Britain.[63] On February 27, Senator Lehman of New York sounded the same note in the Senate, warning that he was "not willing to help arm Britain or any other country in order that such a country may arm Egypt to renew warfare against Israel." Speaking in the House on March 15, Javits suggested that some of the arms going to the Arab countries might have been provided to Britain under the Lend-Lease arrangement during the war, a factor, he said, "we certainly have a right to consider ... in assessing" British policy.[64]

In the meantime, Israel had submitted an official request for arms to Washington and had informally approached the British government with a similar solicitation. Included were heavy weapons such as tanks, 155-mm. howitzers, medium-range artillery, and aircraft.[65] The requests had been preceded by the publication of a number of press reports based on Israeli military sources that played up the extent of British shipments to the Arabs,[66] while a similar compilation of "information" on Egyptian arms purchases abroad was transmitted to the State Department by the Israeli Foreign

61. Tel Aviv Radio broadcast, January 25, 1960; and *New York Times*, January 26, 1950.

62. *New York Times*, January 27, 1950.

63. In the same speech, Z.O.A. president D. Frisch asked for an American guarantee of Israel's security; ibid., January 30, 1950.

64. U.S. Congress, *Congressional Record*, Senate, Vol. 96, Part 2, p. 2404; and ibid., House of Representatives, Vol. 96, Part 3, p. 3430. On January 28, a Foreign Office spokesman had stated in London that armaments going to the Arab countries were all British-made; *Al-Ahram*, January 29, 1950.

65. *New York Times*, February 27 and April 6, 1950; *Al-Ahram*, April 7, 1950; and *The New Palestine* (New York), April 1950, p. 13.

66. See, for instance, Francis Ofner, "Mideast Arms Race Brews as Israelis Lash 'Aid to Egypt,'" *Christian Science Monitor*, January 31, 1950; and *New York Times*, February 21, 1950, p. 17. Also see *New York Post*, March 23, 1950.

Ministry.[67] The Department announced that it would require full information on the status of the Israeli arsenal before it could reach a decision.[68]

Throughout February, March, April, and May, while members of both Houses of Congress and other political figures hammered the Administration with calls for intervention in London, on which were now tacked demands for approval of the Israeli arms request,[69] the campaign was taken directly to the White House and the State Department by a series of visiting personalities and delegations. For instance, on February 10, the leaders of the A.F.L. and the C.I.O. called on President Truman, who, complained the Z.O.A. monthly *The New Palestine*, "subsequently transmitted their protest to the Department of State—but exerted no great pressure toward a change in the American view."[70] Truman apparently was more forthcoming with the chairman of the House Committee on Rules, Representative A. J. Sabath of Illinois, who said of his visit to the President:

I obtained the President's assurances and was informed that he was presently looking into this important matter and into the reports that I gave him. He told me that in view of the fact that all the Jews in America are vitally interested and have appealed to me to take this matter up with him, he is going to reinforce his efforts in stopping this supplying of arms by Great Britain to the Arab Nations.[71]

The American labor leaders also paid a visit to the State Department, and so did—among others—a delegation of top leaders of all U.S. Zionist groups, another composed of thirty-two congressmen, and, on March 10, Senator Herbert Lehman.

The conversation between Lehman and Acheson is particularly revealing. The Secretary assured his visitor that on the basis of all available reports, including those of the chief United Nations observer in the area, who was an American Marine Corps General (Brig. General William E. Riley), the Department "sincerely did not believe that Egypt was planning to attack Israel" or that "the present situation was leading to a renewal of the conflict."

---

67. *New York Times*, February 13, 1950.

68. Ibid., February 27, 1950.

69. See, e.g., in addition to items cited in other footnotes in this section: *New York Times*, February 19 and 28, March 11 and 29, and May 9, 12, 14, and 23, 1950; *Congressional Record* (House), Vol. 96, Part 13, p. A1076; and ibid., Part 15, p. A3719.

70. "State Department Pursues Stubborn Policy in Rearming of Arabs," *The New Palestine*, March 1950, p. 17. The article concluded with the statement that "the situation in Washington and the attitude here toward Arab rearmament should be brought home to American Jews all over the country."

71. Ibid., p. 25. These remarks were also quoted in *Al-Ahram*, April 2, 1950, indicating the attention with which the situation was being followed in Cairo.

He pointed out that the Middle East was a strategically vital area, and that "the military situation vis-à-vis the Soviet Union made it desirable for us to rely as much as possible and wherever possible upon the military strength of friendly nations, such as this strength was." Finally, he assured the Senator that Britain was not sending to the Arabs any armaments that were of American origin or for which the United States was furnishing replacements. For his part, Lehman reiterated Israeli fears that the Arab countries might use their new arms for a second round, and he warned Acheson that "there were a number of people in Congress who would oppose" arms aid to Britain under the Mutual Defense Assistance Pact if the latter continued to rearm the Arabs.[72]

Despite the intensive lobbying, Israel's arms requests did not fall on sympathetic ears in either Washington or London. The British reply was straightforward and negative: the Israelis were told that they would be allowed to purchase arms in Britain once they had reached a peace settlement with their neighbors.[73] The American response was equally negative, but much less definitive. On April 6, it was reported that, owing to the heavy demand for U.S. weapons in the NATO countries of Europe, the Department of Defense had vetoed the supply of tanks and artillery to Israel, but that surplus jet fighters might be supplied.[74] On the following day, however, the State Department said that the request was under continuing review and that no final decisions had been made.[75] There the matter rested.

While no documentation has become available, several reasons for British and American coolness towards Israel's bids can be surmised. One was fear of the repercussions in the Arab world, then seething with resentment at the loss of Palestine and Western responsibility for this outcome.[76] Despite the crisis in Arab-American relations, the United States was hopeful of mending the situation, primarily through economic and technical aid. The Point Four program was getting under way, and the coordination of its application in the Middle East had been one of the main tasks of the just completed diplomatic conference in Cairo. In fact, some news reports at the time of the conference had suggested that the emerging policy of economic aid would be combined with political withdrawal from the Palestine question, so as to minimize the

72. U.S. Department of State Archives, "Memorandum of Conversation on the Near Eastern Armaments Situation," Secret, March 10, 1950.

73. *New York Times*, April 20 and June 1, 1950.

74. Ibid., April 7, 1950.

75. Ibid., April 8, 1950; see also the Acheson statement on May 3, ibid., May 4, 1950.

76. Interview with Alfred L. Atherton, January 29, 1973.

latter's nefarious effects on the American position in the area.[77] There was no surer way of further antagonizing the Arabs than supplying arms to Israel. Moreover, there were Arab requests for U.S. arms pending as well,[78] and satisfying only the Israeli demands would make matters even worse, while giving weapons to both sides would add fuel to the incipient arms race and would domestically open a political "can of worms."

A second consideration was some anxiety over the unlikely but not altogether dismissible possibility that the Arab countries, particularly Egypt and Syria, might seek arms from the Soviet bloc.[79] The spontaneous and widespread approval that Ad-Dawalibi's suggestion for an opening to the East elicited has already been mentioned. In the first week of May, the diplomatic correspondent of *Al-Ahram* reported, in what seemed an officially inspired—and prophetic—story, that the Egyptian government saw no particular impediment to its purchase of weapons needed for defense from Russia or other arms producers, such as the Skoda works in Czechoslovakia. The report added that the difficulties raised by Britain and the United States in the face of Egyptian arms requests might impel Cairo to accept the "generous offers" made by the Soviet Union of "all types of armaments" in exchange for cotton.[80]

A third, and probably overriding, factor was the confidence that Israel's security would not be jeopardized by the refusal to honor her requests. Current shipments to Arab states by Britain would actually tend to establish a military balance between Israel and her opponents rather than upset an existing balance to the disadvantage of the Jewish state. When challenged in the Commons, the Under-Secretary of State for Foreign Affairs justified Britain's decision by stating that, "according to the best information available to us, Israel already has sufficient war material for her internal security and defence."[81] Similarly, a few weeks earlier, Secretary Acheson had told protesting congressmen that British sales to the Arabs were designed to "maintain the balance of power," and that he had expressed his approval of London's policy on that basis.[82] Available figures attest to Israeli armed superiority at the time, even when the British shipments to Egypt in 1949–1950 are included—as the tables and discussion in the next chapter will

77. See Albion Ross, "Envoys in Mid-East Scan New Policies," *New York Times*, February 27, 1950.

78. An Egyptian spokesman said on March 26 that his government had made several such requests; ibid., March 26, 1950.

79. George McGhee interview.

80. *Al-Ahram*, May 5, 1950.

81. *Parliamentary Debates* (oral answers), April 19, 1950, col. 114.

82. *New York Times*, March 29, 1950.

show—and bear out the Western Powers' assessment.[83] This conclusion was probably reinforced by Israel's refusal to accede to Washington's request for full information on her military potential.

The pressure was mounting, however. As the ministerial meetings of May 1950 approached, there was a marked escalation in the rhetoric of the campaign, particularly on the part of Israeli officials. On April 25, an Israeli Foreign Ministry spokesman accused Britain of "provoking an arms race which is creating an explosive situation" in the Middle East.[84] On May 4, fifty-one U.S. Members of Congress of both parties petitioned the Secretary of State to intercede in London for a cessation of arms shipments, while the American Zionist Council announced a series of protest meetings.[85] In the following weeks, at these and several other mass rallies—some of which were held to celebrate the anniversary of Israel's establishment—repeated calls for action were made by influential public figures, including Governor Dewey of New York.[86] The attacks on the State Department were particularly bitter, rivalled only by those against Bevin. In a typical statement, Rabbi Abba Hillel Silver, one of the most prominent American Zionist leaders, charged that "[t]here are forces in the State Department which have not reconciled themselves to the establishment of the State of Israel. . . . It is these same forces which are now supporting and justifying the supply of arms by Britain to the Arab States."[87] Bevin's policy he branded as "stupid and bloody."[88] On May 17, the Israeli representative at the U.N., Abba Eban, acidly warned that "the Powers most intimately concerned with the maintenance of stability in the Near East will be destroying that stability with their own hands so long as they persist in concerting this extraordinary policy of one-sided rearmament."[89]

THE DECLARATION TAKES SHAPE

In fact, it was a sufficient "concerting of policy" between London and Washington on arms supplies that American officials felt was lacking. They also felt that some such "concerting" was urgently needed if a way out of the uncomfortable position in which the Administration—and the State Depart-

---

83. For confirmation from an Israeli source, see *Palestine Post* (Jerusalem), April 6, 1950.

84. *New York Times*, April 26, 1950.   85. Ibid., May 4, 1950.

86. Ibid., May 13, 1950.

87. The full text was inserted in the *Congressional Record*, Vol. 96, Part 15, p. A3719. For a direct attack on Acheson, see the speech by New York Representative A. Tauriello at a Madison Square Garden rally on March 24, 1950, on the eve of the issuance of the Tripartite Declaration; in ibid., p. A4243.

88. *New York Times*, May 13, 1950.   89. Ibid., May 18, 1950.

ment in particular—had been placed by the pro-Israel campaign was to be found that would satisfy the Israelis while preserving those elements of current policy deemed necessary for the safeguarding of the Western position in the region. Secretary Acheson had told Senator Lehman that he would raise the arms question with Bevin at the May meetings,[90] and, while in public he continued to defend the British position and to refuse all demands to seek a change in British policy, the Near East Office at the State Department proceeded to chart a course of action.

In preparation of the U.S. position at the London meetings, two documents were drafted. One was a State Department paper which addressed itself directly to the question of securing British and French cooperation in a joint approach that would minimize the political and military problems arising from the supply of arms to the Arab states and Israel.[91] This was a brief but significant paper, for it appears to have reflected candidly and accurately the thinking that eventually produced the Tripartite Declaration, and therefore it deserves some detailed attention.[92]

In discussing the background of the problem, the paper laid out the factors that had to be taken into account. U.S. policy was to permit the supply of reasonable amounts of military material to both sides, provided this did not encourage an arms race. Britain followed a similar policy, and in the case of Egypt was guided by her plans for Anglo-Egyptian partnership in defending the area against Soviet aggression. The United States supported these plans, and, since the trend in the area seemed to be away from war, "interposed no objection to the principle" of British arms shipments to the Arabs "within the framework of the plans for Anglo-Egyptian and other Anglo-Arab cooperation." France apparently was supplying arms to Syria, but adequate information on French policy and on actual shipments was lacking. Israel had strongly criticized the United States for not pressuring the British, and Israel's American sympathizers—an element, said the paper, that "figures prominently in the American domestic scene"—were accusing the State Department of encouraging Arab war aims. Finally, the Israeli government

90. U.S. Department of State Archives, "Memorandum of Conversation," p. 3.

91. U.S. Department of State Archives, "Arms Shipments to Arab States and Israel," Top Secret, April 20, 1950; also published in *Foreign Relations 1950*, Vol. V, pp. 135–138.

92. This was ascertained by the author in interviews carried out with several of the American—and some British—officials who were involved in the decision-making process at the time, particularly those with George McGhee and Raymond Hare, who were mainly responsible for the drafting of the papers emanating from the Near East Office.

had requested "a considerable amount of heavy military equipment," in support of which request a public campaign was being actively conducted.

The paper concluded with the following set of recommendations:

A. *Tripartite Discussions*
   1. The Secretary might wish to impress upon Messrs. Bevin and Schuman the latent danger of the renewal of hostilities in Palestine and the explosive nature of the Near Eastern situation in general.
   2. He might also suggest to Messrs. Schuman and Bevin that the US, UK and France might make public declarations that they will not permit the shipment of arms to any Near Eastern country unless the purchasing country give to the supplying country formal assurance to undertake no aggression against any other Near Eastern state.

B. *Discussions with Mr. Bevin*
   1. The Secretary might wish to suggest to Mr. Bevin the desirability of a review of the arms program planned for Egypt in order to make absolutely certain that it does not exceed that required for the attainment of the UK's political and military objectives.

C. *Discussions with Mr. Schuman*
   1. The Secretary might wish to point out to Mr. Schuman the desirability of a US-French exchange of information on the quantities of arms both nations have permitted to go to the Near East since the UN Palestine arms embargo was lifted on August 11, 1949, and which they may subsequently permit to go. We have the impression that the French reaction is not favorable. We already have a reasonably satisfactory arrangement for exchanging information with the British on this subject.

Acheson's basic dilemma was clearly reflected in these carefully phrased recommendations. On the one hand, he was determined to stick to a policy of maximum feasible evenhandedness towards Arabs and Israelis, which he favored and felt was necessary both to protect the American position from further deterioration and to avoid giving the Russians an entry into the area. As Under-Secretary of State in 1945–1947, Acheson had disapproved of Truman's support for Jewish national aspirations in Palestine. If fulfilled, he believed, they would set off a reaction that would "imperil not only American but all Western interests in the Near East." In his view, those Americans who were committed to the Zionist cause had lost sight of "the totality of American interests."[93] He had returned to the State Department as Secretary in early 1949, just as the first Arab-Israeli war came to an end and the perceived Soviet challenge to the "Free World" was fast becoming the preeminent

93. Acheson, *Present at the Creation*, p. 169.

obsession of American policymakers, including himself. To protect the national security on the Middle East flank, he believed, the maintenance of good relations with the Arabs was essential and domestic politics could not be allowed to take precedence.[94] On the other hand, the intensity of the pressures on the State Department from the pro-Israeli forces, reinforced by the President's known sympathies, as well as Acheson's own "evenhandedness" approach, required some show of action on the arms issue. Furthermore, uncontrolled and cumulative British weapons supplies would eventually become a truly destabilizing factor. And continued dearth of information on French policy and supplies could throw out of joint any attempt to maintain a rough armaments equilibrium between the regional opponents. Thus, in the opinion of Acheson and his State Department aides, what was needed was: caution and better consultation on the part of the suppliers; more British restraint in arming the Arabs but keeping them moderately satisfied; and a formula which would reassure the Israelis that these arms would not be used to attack them and that there would be no discrimination against them in Western policy.

The second document bearing on the arms issue was a National Security Council memorandum, NSC-65, which also dealt with other Near East matters to be discussed in London, particularly the guarantee of the territorial status quo.[95] At the time, the NSC, which was created in 1947, had not yet acquired the large staff and independent power and resources that it would develop later on. It served mainly as a forum for the reconciliation of divergent views among the several departments and agencies concerned with defense and foreign policy issues. Most of its papers originated in the Policy Planning Staff at the State Department and were then circulated for comment and revisions before submission to the President. NSC-65 went through three drafts before it was finally approved. Originally prepared in March, it was commented on by President Truman at an NSC meeting on April 14, and underwent substantial revisions in the second half of April. Essentially, Truman insisted on a formula that would permit the Israelis to get armaments from the West. At his behest, a clause was added to the effect that the United States would "give sympathetic consideration to Israel's application for

94. Gaddis Smith, *Dean Acheson* (New York: Cooper Square, 1972), p. 332. This volume in a series on American Secretaries of State and their Diplomacy is a very perceptive account of Acheson, based largely on unpublished material and still restricted government documents.

95. The text and related information are in *Foreign Relations 1950*, Vol. VI, pp. 131–135 and 162–166.

export licenses for defensive military equipment sufficient to discourage attack from beyond its borders." [96]

Further recommendations inserted in the second draft called for the issuance, in concert with Britain and France, of a commitment to "take vigorous action both within and without the United Nations should it appear that an attempt to renew hostilities will be made." This drew strong opposition from the Defense Department and the Joint Chiefs of Staff (JCS), who objected to the idea of an intervention of any sort in the Middle East. Heretofore, the argument went, the United States had totally relied on Britain for the maintenance of regional stability. True, the State Department was advocating a policy of balanced shipments of arms to both Arabs and Israelis only in the context of a security arrangement of some sort and subject to a pledge by the recipients not to use these weapons against one another. These safeguards could break down, however, and the military were opposed to any initiative that might directly involve U.S. forces in future local conflicts. The Pentagon's opposition was further detailed in a memorandum that the Chairman of the JCS, General Omar Bradley, addressed to the President. Truman apparently objected to the military's extreme position. A third and final version met the Pentagon's objections to some extent by inserting the proviso that "such action would not involve the use of U.S. military forces," but this version was otherwise identical to the second draft. [97] The final version of NSC-65 did not diverge in the substance of its recommendations from the briefs prepared for Acheson within the State Department; it explicitly allowed the Administration to bring the Middle East, for the first time, within the orbit of American foreign commitments.

The NSC decision, carrying the approval of the President, gave the green light to the U.S. delegation at the London talks to negotiate a document of a substantially different magnitude, both in its weight as an instrument of policy and in its implications, than the separate and unilateral statements on arms supplies and the political status quo that the State Department had earlier proposed to suggest. It seems that just prior to the start of the London meetings, a decision was reached within the Near East Office, which Acheson approved, to lump the two statements together into one declaration that would be issued jointly by the three Western governments. [98] The principal reason

96. Ibid., p. 166.   97. Ibid., p. 162.

98. Secretary Acheson proposed the idea of such a joint declaration to President Truman on April 24th. Truman welcomed the idea, stating that such a declaration would remove the objections he had to the first draft of NSC-65, which he felt was "much too one-sided and would cause trouble" with pro-Israeli circles; ibid., pp. 132 and 138.

for this major step apparently was the desire to ensure coordination among the arms suppliers so as to keep the Arab-Israeli military balance under control. The main objective was "to legitimize arms shipments both to Israel and the Arab states, and provide just enough arms to both sides to keep them reasonably happy, but balanced and controlled by the three powers."[99] Given, however, the generally uncooperative French attitude and the suspiciousness that permeated Franco-British relations in matters affecting the Middle East, no such tight control was likely to materialize unless the suppliers undertook to coordinate their arms transfer policies not only vis-à-vis their respective clients but also vis-à-vis one another.

Secretary Acheson arrived in London on May 9, and he met with Bevin and Schuman on several occasions between the 9th and the 18th. The staff talks had started earlier.[100] A subcommittee had been formed to discuss Middle Eastern affairs, and its meetings had begun on May 1st. This was a bipartite body, in which the French did not participate. The American side was led by Raymond Hare of the Near East Bureau, and Joseph Palmer, who was First Secretary at the London Embassy; while the British side was led by Michael Wright, who had been present at the 1947 talks, and by Geoffrey Furlonge, the Head of the Eastern Department at the Foreign Office. On May 3, the Americans submitted a draft of the proposed Declaration, which was only one of several topics on the subcommittee's agenda. This was discussed, revised, and sent back to the two governments for further comment.

At the meetings, the British initially expressed opposition to French co-sponsorship of a Middle East declaration. Furthermore, their main interest lay, not in arms control, but in extending an Anglo-American political guarantee that would have a stabilizing effect on the local situation and expedite their own efforts to organize regional defense. In turn, the success of these efforts depended largely on their ability to continue to supply arms to their clients. For Washington, first priority went to defusing the situation created by the British arms shipments; the quieting of domestic opposition and the prevention of an arms race were the major objectives. There was insistence on participation by the French, both to keep tabs on their arms

99. Personal communication from George McGhee, March 21, 1973.

100. The following description of the London talks is based on: documentary material in *Foreign Relations 1950*; an interview on January 27, 1973, with Loy Henderson, who was Director of the Office of Near Eastern Affairs in 1947–1948 and in 1953 became Deputy Under-Secretary of State for Administration; an interview on June 15, 1973, with Anthony Nutting, who became Britain's Under-Secretary of State for Foreign Affairs in 1951; and on other interviews with Raymond Hare, Parker Hart, and George McGhee.

transfers and to still their constant complaints about being left out of matters concerned with the Middle East. The Americans maintained that a declared readiness to supply armaments to all Middle East parties, within a system for exchange of information and for coordination of policies between the three major suppliers, was an approach that would satisfy everybody. The United States, they argued, certainly shared Britain's concern for the political stability of the region, and the proof of this was the proposed trilateral pledge to uphold the current status quo against changes by force.

The British eventually went along with American desires, but not without introducing a direct reference in the text to regional defense. This would explicitly and publicly line up the co-sponsors of the Declaration behind British plans for Anglo-Arab cooperation, which London knew would be strongly resisted by the nationalists.[101] It would also provide an added justification—which the U.S. supported—for the supply of arms to the countries of the region.

On May 12, a joint draft was accepted in substance by both sides. Discussions at the subcommittee level and between Acheson and Bevin continued on problems of language, which the two Secretaries dealt with only perfunctorily, preoccupied as they were with problems of European economics and defense.[102] The British, mindful of their problems with Iraq and Egypt, wanted the statement to be couched in a neutral language that would not produce too negative an impression in these countries. On May 18, the last day of meetings, Acheson and Bevin submitted their agreed-upon draft to Schuman and asked him to join in issuing the Declaration.

Schuman was "furious" at not being consulted earlier in the process, but finally said he was not opposed in principle and would study the proposal.[103] The French soon realized that the document provided, at no political cost to themselves, an opportunity for reasserting France's prominent role, and abiding interest, in the politics of the Middle East. In fact, it gave them some voice in the affairs of an area much larger than their remaining sphere of

101. Anglo-Egyptian talks to renegotiate the 1936 Treaty on this basis began immediately following the issuance of the Declaration, lasted until October 1951, and ended in failure. The minutes are in Egypt, Ministry of Foreign Affairs, *Records of Conversation.*

102. The Schuman Plan for a West European coal and steel community, alliance defense problems, the Communist peace offensive, and Indochina were the problems upon which the three Ministers focused most of their attention, according to Acheson. It is significant that in an extensive two-chapter discussion of the London meetings in Acheson's memoirs, the Tripartite Declaration merited only three paragraphs; *Present at the Creation,* pp. 382–401.

103. Raymond Hare interview.

influence in Syria and Lebanon. The continued importance of the region for French interests would later be underlined by the senior French ambassador in the Middle East, Maurice Couve de Murville—who was posted in Cairo— at a regional conference of French envoys held in Beirut in April 1951. "France is particularly interested in the defense of the Middle East," he would declare, "because this region is the essential source for her petroleum supplies, the nub of her lines of communication with Indochina, and one of the important points of French policy in the Mediterranean." [104]

Paris having signalled its approval, the three powers joined in issuing the following Declaration on May 25, 1950:

The Governments of the United Kingdom, France and the United States, having had occasion during the recent Foreign Ministers meeting in London to review certain questions affecting the peace and stability of the Arab States and of Israel, and particularly that of the supply of arms and war material to these states, have resolved to make the following statements:

1. The three Governments recognize that the Arab States and Israel all need to maintain a certain level of armed forces for the purposes of assuring their internal security and their legitimate self-defense and to permit them to play their part in the defense of the area as a whole. All applications for arms or war material for these countries will be considered in the light of these principles. In this connection the three Governments wish to recall and reaffirm the terms of the statements made by their representatives on the Security Council on August 4, 1949, in which they declared their opposition to the development of an arms race between the Arab States and Israel.

2. The three Governments declare that assurances have been received from all the states in question, to which they permit arms to be supplied from their countries, that the purchasing state does not intend to undertake any act of aggression against any other state. Similar assurances will be requested from any other site in the area to which they permit arms to be supplied in the future.

3. The three Governments take this opportunity of declaring their deep interest in and their desire to promote the establishment and maintenance of peace and stability in the area and their unalterable opposition to the use of force or threat of force between any of the states in that area. The three Governments, should they find that any of these states was preparing to violate frontiers or armistice lines, would, consistently with their obligations as members of the United Nations, immediately take action, both within and outside the United Nations, to prevent such violation.

104. *Cahiers de l'Orient Contemporain* (Paris) 8 (1st semester, 1951), 45–46.

CHAPTER 5 OPERATIONAL ASPECTS OF THE ARMS CONTROL SYSTEM

Quis custodiet ipsos custodes?
Juvenal

The rather lengthy analysis in the previous chapter of the genesis of the Tripartite Declaration serves more than an historical purpose. It reveals the objectives and the attitudes that the three Western sponsors brought to bear on the question of arms to the Middle East and that would govern their manipulation of the arms transfer process while their near-monopoly on arms supplies lasted. These objectives and attitudes would in fact remain fairly constant throughout most of the five-year life span of the control regime instituted under the 1950 Declaration. They were by no means uniform, however. There was considerable distance between the position of the British and the Americans, on the one hand, and that of the French on the other.

WESTERN ARMS SUPPLY POLICIES, 1950–1955

The principal Anglo-American objectives were dictated first and foremost by the global requirements of the Cold War, and only secondarily—though importantly—by regional conditions. These objectives were: (1) stabilization of the Arab-Israeli conflict by controlling the local military balance; and (2) the creation of a regional defense grouping around Western military assistance, which would secure the area against Communist encroachment, preempt the possible spread of Soviet influence, and provide some form of continued Western military presence in the Arab Middle East. Together with economic assistance, the ministration of armaments was the main lever the West possessed to influence the policies of local regimes.

The French attitude had a narrower regional focus. Their primary aim was to regain some of their lost influence in the Levant, and insofar as association with the Anglo-Saxons helped this by restoring to France the role of co-overseer and guarantor of the regional political configuration of power, the joint approach laid out in the Tripartite Declaration was welcome. Should arms sales become more useful than arms control in the quest for influence, however, Paris was ready to disregard the injunctions of an undertaking it had joined by last-minute invitation, and in the shaping of which it had played no part.

For the Europeans there was another aspect of no mean importance, namely, the economic one. However limited in their scope, arms sales to Middle Eastern governments helped to keep British workers in the troubled defense industries on the payroll, and were a welcome boost to the renascent French industry, then struggling to recover from the almost total destruction it had suffered in the Second World War.

Finally, Britain felt that she had to balance the benefits of arms control against a prudent observance of her arms supply obligations towards her restive Arab "allies" if she was to preserve her shaky treaty relationships.

Operating in concert, these various incentives and constraints produced the following policy pattern as the three Western powers prepared to co-ordinate their arms transfers in 1950: The United States was least willing to provide military equipment to any of the countries directly involved in the Palestine conflict—meaning Israel and the immediately contiguous Arab states—save under strict safeguards as to its use, such as might be afforded by a regional pact under Western command. Britain was equally chary of provoking another round of fighting in the area, but felt that the maintenance of her position there required a limited but continuing supply of arms. France, less concerned than her partners about the political consequences of renewed conflict between the Arabs and Israel, and anxious to break into the pre-dominantly British arms market, was willing to take a much more flexible stance toward the limitations embodied in the Declaration.

Table 5. Major Weapon Exports to the Middle East, *1950–1955 (in U.S. $ millions at constant 1968 prices)*

Supplier	1950	1951	1952	1953	1954	1955
U.K.	25	6	5	30	37	26
U.S.A.	3	2	2	10	16	15
France	2	1	1	2	14	35

SOURCE: Stockholm International Peace Research Institute (SIPRI), *Arms Trade with the Third World* (New York: Humanities Press, 1971). Iran is included but not Turkey or North Africa, except for Egypt.

The manner in which this pattern was translated into actual arms transfers during this period is reflected in Table 5, above.[1] A brief description of the performance of each of the tripartite suppliers is in order before analyzing the manner in which the arms rationing was implemented.

Great Britain

In absolute amounts, the largest provider of arms during this period was Great Britain, and Egypt was her main recipient.[2] While the large arms sales to Cairo in 1949–1950 had provided the main impetus for the rationing policy, there was a substantial decrease in the flow to Egypt in 1951 and 1952. This was due to the crisis over the Suez Canal base, which came to a head in October 1951 with Cairo's denunciation of the 1936 Treaty. An embargo on arms supplies was immediately clamped by London that included a suspension of all outstanding licenses for the export of weapons, ammunition, munition-making machinery, and other military equipment.[3] The total amount of British heavy arms going to the Middle East was thereby radically reduced.

Arms deliveries to Egypt had in fact already slowed down to an almost complete halt starting in September 1950, as Britain sought to induce a more cooperative Egyptian attitude in the negotiations then under way over the future status of Suez and the Sudan by alternatively restricting and relaxing the arms flow. On September 12, the British ambassador had informed Cairo that the delivery of Centurion tanks and jet aircraft would be suspended because of the Korean emergency, which required that all production be diverted to the war in the Far East.[4] This brought immediate protests from the Egyptians. Foreign Minister Muhammad Salaheddin was reported to have made strong personal representations before Foreign Secretary Bevin;[5] and *Al-Muqattam*, a leading Cairo paper close to the Palace, expressed an opinion current in the rest of the Egyptian press when it observed that "at the stroke of a pen this decision abolishes the official and obligatory character

1. Although Iran is included in Table 5, arms transfers to this country in 1950–1954 were minimal, due to the crisis in Western-Iranian relations brought about by Premier Mussaddiq's nationalist oil policy. Relations would pick up again only in 1955, with Iran's adherence to the newly formed Baghdad Pact. For details see SIPRI, *Arms Trade with the Third World* (New York: Humanities Press, 1971), p. 840.

2. Details of heavy-arms acquisitions by Egypt in 1950–1955 are in Table 6.

3. *New York Times*, October 23, 1951.

4. Royal Institute of International Affairs (R.I.I.A.), *Great Britain and Egypt, 1914–1951*, Information Paper No. 19, 3d edition (London: R.I.I.A., 1952), p. 129.

5. *Al-Ahram*, October 3, 1950. Bevin and Salaheddin met at the United Nations on September 28.

of the 1936 Treaty."[6] On October 1, the Egyptian Cabinet approved the allocation of $8.6 million to arms purchases from other sources;[7] and later that month, Salaheddin met with the U.S. Secretaries of State and Defense and formally requested American military aid.[8]

As the opening of the Egyptian parliamentary session in November approached, Whitehall relented, fearful that the Wafdist government would go through with its threatened denunciation of the Treaty of Alliance. In early November, a lifting of the suspension was announced. In practice, however, shipments were not resumed. British parliamentary opposition and the government's increasing reluctance to provide arms that might be used against its own troops in the Canal zone held up arms transfers until a total embargo was announced in October of the following year.[9]

Another relaxation of the embargo occurred in the latter part of 1952, following the July coup d'etat in Egypt and the installation of the military regime. On September 19, the new Nagib government formally requested the fulfillment of existing contracts for tanks and aircraft, which, the new Prime Minister said, had already been 80 percent paid for.[10] The advent of military rule in Egypt had been initially greeted with great suspicion by the British, though they privately acknowledged that any strong successor to the Wafd would probably be an improvement, both domestically and in terms of Anglo-Egyptian relations. Realizing that Sudanese opinion favored independence, and with their freedom of action no longer shackled by Faruq's ambition to rule over a "united Nile Valley," the Free Officers moved swiftly to resolve the long-standing stalemate over the Sudan Condominium.[11] This broke the ice. To encourage the new trend, London agreed in November to transfer to Egypt a number of Gloster-Meteor jet fighters.[12]

6. Quoted in R.I.I.A., *Great Britain and Egypt*, p. 129.

7. *Al-Ahram*, October 1, 1950.

8. Ibid., October 18 and 19, 1950. At a press conference in Washington, the Egyptian Foreign Minister deplored the British suspension and threatened to apply for arms from "other sources," meaning the Eastern bloc, unless Egypt received military equipment from the Western powers; ibid., October 20, 1950.

9. On November 22, 1950, the shipment of sixteen Centurion tanks that were part of a deal concluded in 1949 and were already partly paid for was postponed under pressure from Parliament; *New York Times*, November 23, 1950. On October 10, 1951, *Al-Ahram* reported authoritative Egyptian sources as saying that only spare parts had been received from the U.K. since September 1950.

10. *Al-Ahram*, September 18, 19, and 25, 1952.

11. Anglo-Egyptian agreement on the Sudan was reached in February 1953. For a succinct account of this matter, see John Marlowe, *A History of Modern Egypt and Anglo-Egyptian Relations, 1800–1956* (Hamden, Conn.: Archon 1965), pp. 381–397.

12. *Parliamentary Debates* (Commons), February 2, 1953, cols. 1466–1469.

The honeymoon proved short-lived, however. Although a full squadron of twelve aircraft was to be provided, only four had reached their destination in February 1953 when political relations began to deteriorate precipitously over the issue of the Canal base, and further deliveries were suspended.[13] No more British arms would go to Egypt until the conclusion of the Suez Agreement in July 1954. The negative effect of this behavior on the Egyptians' assessment of the intentions and reliability of their major Western arms supplier can be imagined.[14]

The renewed sale of jets to Egypt provided the opportunity for the first major British arms transfer to Israel.[15] In the fall of 1952, London informed Tel Aviv of its readiness to furnish a squadron of similar jet aircraft to the Israelis, who were known to be shopping for their first jet aircraft.[16] Syria, Lebanon, and Iraq would also be permitted to acquire jet aircraft, however, and this made the whole proposition much less attractive to the Israelis. They formally protested the arms sales to the Arabs both in London and Washington; but on January 7, 1953, it was announced that the American government did not object to the transactions; and on the next day, an official Foreign Office spokesman stated that in the British view the sales did not violate the Tripartite Declaration.[17] This meant that the Western powers saw no jeopardy to Israel's overall military superiority in the air resulting from a larger number of jets going to the Arabs than to Israel. In fact, Minister of State for Foreign Affairs Selwyn Lloyd told his parliamentary critics that Israel would stand to lose from a cancellation of the multiple sale, for she would be deprived of jet warplanes, of which she currently had none, while her opponents already possessed such aircraft; moreover, the new shipments would not "affect the

13. Robert Jackson, *The Israeli Air Force Story* (London: Tom Stacey, 1970), p. 53.

14. The failure of Nasser's first major effort to obtain U.S. arms came at about the same time. "Everyone should understand that I had no freedom of choice," he said after announcing the Soviet arms deal in 1955. The deal would not have been concluded "if I had found that Britain would supply me with arms without using this as a means to pressure me . . ." (Interview with Tom Little, Arab News Agency, October 1, 1955; in United Arab Republic, Ministry of National Guidance, *Collected Speeches, Declarations and Statements of President Gamal Abdel Nasser [in Arabic], Part I: 23 July 1952–January 1958* [Cairo, n.d.], pp. 414–416).

15. Details of Israeli heavy-arms acquisitions in 1950–1955 are in Table 7.

16. Benjamin Kagan, *The Secret Battle for Israel* (Cleveland: World, 1966), pp. 192–194.

17. *New York Times*, December 29, 1952, January 8, 1953; *Al-Ahram*, January 9, 1953; and *Parliamentary Debates* (Lords), January 20, 1953, cols. 1081–1083. Israeli Foreign Minister Moshe Sharett submitted a formal note of protest to the British Foreign Office on January 7, 1953.

balance of air power," which was determined by many factors other than simple numerical parity.[18]

In the end, Israel was allowed to purchase twenty-eight Gloster-Meteors in Britain in 1952–1953, instead of the original fourteen, though seven of these apparently were quietly transferred through a private firm.[19] Syria received Meteors too, while Iraq and Lebanon were provided with Vampire fighter-bombers.[20] Egypt acquired only four aircraft, pending resolution of the Suez dispute.[21]

While political motives were partially responsible for these substantial British military transfers to the Arab-Israeli area, the economic incentive was clearly present too, and so was the related motive of market protection or "preemptive salesmanship." At the time when the British made their offer, the two major local powers, Egypt and Israel, were actively seeking arms abroad. The new Egyptian regime was making a strong bid for American arms—which, as will be seen, Washington appears to have encouraged—and a military purchasing mission was on its way to the United States. Israel was shopping for jet warplanes in France, and she had earlier in the year requested to buy Ouragan fighters, a request the French had reluctantly turned down after consultations with Britain and the U.S.[22] The Israelis had then turned to Italy, where Vampire planes were being produced under a British license. London's approval was necessary for the sale of these aircraft, and the Italians were pressing for the required permission.[23] Since in military procurement there is a strong premium on standardization, and consequently on avoiding supplier diversification, there was an obvious British interest both in capturing the new Israeli market before other European suppliers did—as Israel would thenceforth be expected to give preference to British products—and in protecting her traditional outlets in the Arab countries against American intrusion.

In addition to political and prestige benefits attendent on such cornering of recipient markets, economic considerations made this highly advantageous

18. *Parliamentary Debates* (Commons), February 17, 1953, cols. 1079–1080.

19. Edward Luttwak and Dan Horowitz, *The Israeli Army* (New York: Harper & Row, 1975), p. 123; and Jackson, *Israeli Air Force*, pp. 63 and 251. Colonel Kagan, who was personally in charge of aircraft purchases in Europe for the Israeli Ministry of Defense, says the sale of these additional Meteors was not only approved by the British government but also suggested by it; *Secret Battle*, p. 194.

20. SIPRI, *Arms Trade with the Third World*, pp. 842–850.

21. *Parliamentary Debates* (Commons), February 17, 1954, col. 1960.

22. Kagan, *Secret Battle*, pp. 191–192.

23. Ibid., pp. 192–193.

for several reasons. As Selwyn Lloyd told the House of Commons in support of the Meteor sales:

> These aircraft are not required at home, nor are they required for other N.A.T.O. countries.
>
> [Furthermore,] a modern jet fighter costs a great deal of money. . . . The labour element is very high indeed, and it is extremely important that we should get into these markets if we are to earn our living in the world. From the point of view of a worth-while export, it is very much to the economic advantage of this country to succeed in getting into these markets.
>
> Thirdly, these sales will help to maintain our productive capacity at home. . . . The only way to make [the Defense] burden tolerable and, at the same time, to maintain productive capacity and a skilled labour force which will be adequate for an emergency if it comes is to sell part of our arms production abroad. . . . [T]he sale of 70 aircraft . . . would prevent 2,000 men being stood off for a period of six months.
>
> On the three points which I have put so far, I submit that the case for continuing with these sales is overwhelming upon economic grounds.[24]

Symbolic of the arms transfer policy that Britain followed in 1950–1955 was the other major "package" transaction concluded during this period: in July 1955, she simultaneously sold Egypt and Israel two destroyers each. Thus, the economic imperative was satisfied, while at least the semblance of balanced supplies was preserved.

United States

As Table 5 indicates, the United States remained reluctant to become a major supplier of arms to the Middle East throughout this period, preferring to leave this role to her European partners. The slight increase in the total flow starting in 1953 is mainly attributable to a gradual resumption of military aid to Iran after the overthrow of the Mussaddiq regime in July of that year, and to arms transfers to Iraq beginning in the second half of 1954, after Baghdad and Washington signed a military assistance agreement in April. In following this standoffish path, Washington had to turn down arms requests from all the countries of the area—with the exception of Jordan, whose Arab Legion was led by British officers and equipped with British arms under a British subsidy.

Nonetheless, there was an oft-stated American willingness to supply arms, provided the recipients organized themselves for regional defense against Communism under Western leadership. This, or in its default a bilateral military aid agreement providing for the stationing of a U.S. military mission

24. *Parliamentary Debates* (Commons), February 17, 1953, cols. 1080–1081.

in the recipient country, was held to be a necessary prerequisite in view of the domestic political constraints on the supply of arms without adequate safeguards to any Arab regime likely to use them against Israel.[25] Moreover, the formation of a regional defense pact was in itself a major objective of American policy. Indeed, under Secretary of State John Foster Dulles it became *the* primary objective, as the American relationship with the Nasser regime would demonstrate. Military assistance was the "bait," the only quid pro quo Washington could offer to entice the countries of the area into an anti-Soviet partnership that was neither directed at the party (Israel) held by those countries to present the greater danger to their security, nor politically popular in a region seething with anti-Western animosity. "[W]e want to work for a regional-defense arrangement. That is our objective," the Deputy Assistant Secretary of State for the Near East, John Jernegan, told the Senate Foreign Relations Committee in 1953,

and we believe that one of the ways of reaching it is to be able to offer this inducement of military aid to show the Arab countries that in joining up with such an organization, they are not merely adding weakness to weakness, adding zero to zero and producing zero. . . . If we merely ask them to join an organization with no assistance, their answer is likely to be "We already have an organization through the Arab League. If you are not going to help make our countries stronger, there is no use joining another organization."

Senator SMITH: Have they taken the initiative and come after us for military aid or are we offering it as an inducement to play ball with us or is it a combination of both?

Mr. JERNEGAN: A combination of both.[26]

Eventually, only one Arab country, Iraq, would join a Western defense pact, and it was mainly in expectation of this that military aid to Baghdad was made available in 1954.[27] Devoid of wider Arab support, the Baghdad Pact was a nonstarter and never lived up to Western expectations. In fact the American failure to secure Egyptian acquiescence in Western plans turned the Pact into a major liability, for it placed Nasser in an unequivocally adversary relationship to American policies in the area, ending the close and friendly relationship that had grown up between Cairo and Washington since the 1952 coup.

25. Alfred Atherton and Raymond Hare interviews.

26. U.S. Congress, Senate, Committee on Foreign Relations, *Mutual Security Act of 1953, Hearings,* 83d Congress, 2d session, 1953, p. 274.

27. Interview on January 29, 1973, with Waldemar Gallman, who was U.S. Ambassador to Iraq in 1954–1958.

Ironically, the failure of the Baghdad Pact saved Washington from the horns of a fundamental dilemma that was implicit in the American approach to the Middle East during this period and strongly affected arms supply policy: how to build a viable regional defense organization based on substantial military aid to a number of Arab countries without precipitating an Arab-Israeli arms race, and without jeopardizing Israel's security. Inherent in the approach were several contradictory strands that could not be reconciled; in this situation, to balance the supply of arms to the area was extremely difficult, and the safest course was to deny arms to everybody. Policy was reduced to a day-to-day attempt to harmonize these different strands, a task that often resulted in sheer inaction. Immobilism in fact eventually led to failure. In 1955, Nasser's various requests for U.S. arms went unheeded, and he proceeded to do away with the tripartite rationing policy in one blow by turning East for the arms he needed.[28]

France

Aside from a small amount of equipment to Syria in 1949–1950, and the sale of sixty war-surplus Mosquito planes to Israel in 1950, no major transfers of heavy arms by France to the Middle East—or any other foreign customers— took place until 1954.[29] In that year, Israel became France's largest arms recipient, both regional and globally, accounting in 1955–1965 for over half of total French weapons exports.[30]

At the beginning of the fifties, the French armaments industry was still recovering from the ravages of the Second World War and had to cope with the requirements of the conflict in Indochina. The French arms export potential was very limited. Work was under way on the prototypes of several new jet aircraft, however; and as early as June 1950, the Israelis obtained initial authorization from the French government for the purchase of the Ouragan jet fighter.[31] This plane was still in the development stage at the Dassault factories at that time, and the French action merely meant that the Israelis could take a close look at the product preliminary to a possible formal purchase request. Coming only weeks after the issuance of the Tripartite

28. The particulars of American arms-transfer policy toward Egypt form the subject of Chapter 6, below.

29. Shortly after the Tripartite Declaration was issued, a French government spokesman announced that, with Anglo-American approval, France was willing to sell light weapons and ammunition to the Arab countries and Israel, but that no heavy arms could be spared for export; *Al-Ahram*, June 9, 1950.

30. SIPRI, *Arms Trade with the Third World*, pp. 250–251.

31. Kagan, *Secret Battle*, p. 165.

Declaration, this was indicative of the general attitude that the French took on the issue of arms supplies. Paris wanted to break into the arms export field again; and in the Middle East, Israel appeared as the most eager and potentially the biggest customer, since the major Arab countries were traditional British clients. The Franco-Israeli arms connection did not come into its own until 1954, but this was due more to France's inability to satisfy Israel's needs immediately than to any reluctance to do so.[32]

In effect, two trends of opinion were discernible in those governmental circles that had an input into arms transfer policy. One, mostly represented by the Foreign Ministry, advocated strict respect for the tripartite policy of arms equilibrium, for this was held necessary to minimize Arab nationalist pressure against the remaining French interests in Syria and Lebanon. Cairo in particular had long been a haven for Tunisian, Moroccan, and Algerian political leaders fighting against French rule, and Egyptian support for the rebel movements in North Africa increased after the Officers' coup. Until the Algerian revolution formally began in November 1954 and Nasser's active support for it both politically and with military aid became evident, the Foreign Ministry acted as a restraining force against substantial arms shipments to Israel, though in some instances it was overruled or simply ignored. There was no objection to balanced supplies going to both sides, but this was precluded by the Anglo-American desire to keep the arms flow to a minimum and by British unwillingness to foster French competition with her own products.

This all began to change with the deterioration of the situation in Algeria and the emergence of Israel as a potentially useful ally of France in the Arab East against a common adversary in Egypt. By December 1954, Pierre Maillard, who was in charge of the Levant section at the Quai d'Orsay, had this to say to Israeli diplomats who suggested the need to strengthen the Tripartite Declaration now that the British were leaving Suez: "The Declaration is already obsolete. It is no longer binding on anyone, not even the three Western Powers which signed it. Washington and London are outbidding one another and a united Western policy exists only in the imagination of some

32. On this subject, see Kagan, *Secret Battle*, chaps. 21, 24, and 27; Shimon Peres, *David's Sling* (London: Weidenfeld & Nicolson, 1970), chap. 3; Michel Bar-Zohar, *Suez: Ultra Secret* (Paris: Fayard, 1964), passim; Jacob Tsur, *Prélude à Suez, Journal d'une ambassade, 1953–1956* (Paris: Presses de la Cité, 1968), passim; and Sylvia K. Crosbie, *A Tacit Alliance: France and Israel from Suez to the Six Day War* (Princeton, N.J.: Princeton University Press, 1974). Kagan, Peres, and Tsur were directly involved in the Israeli arms purchasing effort in France.

officials. If this Declaration is taken seriously, the only result will be to tie France's hands, notably in the field of arms supplies." [33]

The change of heart among the diplomats—though only tentative at this stage, as French attempts to reach an accommodation with Nasser continued until the fall of 1955 and included the sale of some arms to Egypt—brought them closer to the school of those who argued for large-scale arms sales to Israel. This group was composed mainly of military people, officials at the Ministry of Defense and the service ministries, leading political figures of the Socialist left who were sympathetic to Israel, and representatives of the armaments industry. It was through these circles that Israeli envoys made their initial contacts and worked out the specifics of individual arms purchases, leaving the approach to the Foreign Ministry for political approval to a later stage, when support for their arms requests had already gathered momentum in other parts of the French bureaucracy.

For this strategy to succeed, the initial assistance of key political figures was neccessary, and the friendship and support of several of these individuals, including Defense Minister General Pierre Koenig, Air Secretary Diomede Catroux, and Interior Minister—later Defense Minister—Maurice Bourges-Maunoury, was assiduously cultivated. The method paid off. In mid-1952, agreement was reached between Israel and the French Defense Ministry on the transfer of twenty-five Ouragan jet fighters and three Nord-2500 transports, but the sale was vetoed by the tripartite powers under the terms of the 1950 Declaration.[34] In August 1954, the first large arms transfer agreements between the two countries were concluded. They covered mainly the sale of a squadron of the new Mystère-II jet fighters, two squadrons of Ouragan jets, one hundred AMX-13 tanks, and a large number of heavy artillery guns.[35] Soon afterwards, in the early part of 1955, David Ben-Gurion, who had become Defense Minister in February, wrote to Premier Edgar Faure that Israel had decided to equip her army entirely with French weapons, and four different purchasing missions were sent to Paris.[36] Several more agreements were reached before the end of 1955, including one that replaced the

33. As paraphrased by Tsur, who was Israel's ambassador in Paris at the time; *Prélude à Suez*, pp. 142–143.

34. Crosbie, *A Tacit Alliance*, p. 42.

35. The most detailed accounts are in Bar-Zohar, particularly pp. 76 and 81, and in Michael Brecher, *Decisions in Israel's Foreign Policy* (New Haven, Conn.: Yale University Press, 1975), pp. 162–163.

36. Kennett Love, *Suez: The Twice-Fought War* (New York: McGraw-Hill, 1969), p. 140. A more extended discussion of this period in French-Israeli relations can be found on pp. 129–164 of this comprehensive and well-researched book.

Mystère-IIs on order with the more advanced Mystère-IV, a fighter and interceptor that remained operational with the Israeli air force into the 1970s.

Apart from signalling the beginning of a long Franco-Israeli relationship in the arms field, turning France into a major regional arms supplier, the 1954 agreements were highly significant in two main respects. First, they were reached in secret. France acted unilaterally and without consultation with her tripartite partners, thereby dealing a serious blow to the policy of coordinated arms balance. Admittedly, the rationale that underlay the tripartite approach was primarily an Anglo-American rationale, and from the outset it was unavoidable that the French would go their own way as soon as the opportunity presented itself, despite the reservations of the Middle East specialists in the Foreign Ministry. Be that as it may, the supply of modern weapons in such large quantities to the country that was already regarded as the strongest military force in the area made the further preservation of a low-level equilibrium in arms transfers to the Arab-Israeli area an impossible task. Furthermore, the news of the French arms deal, which leaked out in March 1955, just as Nasser was beginning to turn his attention seriously to rearmament in the wake of the large Israeli raid on Egyptian army camps in Gaza in February, made it imperative for Egypt to seek to redress the arms balance as a matter of the first priority.[37] The French action was the first large step that would soon turn what had so far been an arms "crawl" into a full-fledged arms race.

THE NEAR EAST ARMS COORDINATING COMMITTEE

The United States, Britain, and France administered the rationing of arms to the Middle East, from May 1950 until the collapse of this policy in 1955, through the instrumentality of an intergovernmental body that was known as the Near East Arms Coordinating Committee (NEACC). This is generally considered to have been the only relatively successful endeavor in the sphere of control and limitation of arms transfers to conflict regions.[38] In fact, two distinctive aspects render it a unique experiment in the area of conventional arms control. The tripartite rationing regime (1) was multinational rather than unilateral as in the case of individual countries that decide to ration or deny

37. See Chapter 6, below.
38. John Stanley and Maurice Pearton, *The International Trade in Arms* (London: Chatto & Windus, 1972), p. 197; Geoffrey Kemp, *Arms and Security: The Egypt-Israel Case*, Adelphi Paper, No. 52 (London: Institute for Strategic Studies, October 1968), p. 19; and François Duchêne, "The Arms Trade and the Middle East," *Political Quarterly* 44 (October–December 1973), 455.

arms to governments or regions involved in disputes;[39] and (2) was implemented during a period of relative peace between the parties to the regional conflict rather than in the context of a hot war and for the duration of that war, as has been the case on several occasions.[40] Yet, little has become known about the manner in which this body generally conducted its work and fulfilled its assigned functions. Indeed, these functions themselves have remained unclear, as the Committee's specific mandate was never made a matter of public record. The tripartite powers intended it to remain a secret administrative organ, and knowledge of its very existence was shielded from Middle Eastern governments.[41]

Three aspects of the NEACC's work are worthy of examination: its purpose, its modus operandi, and the guidelines by which it reached its decisions—particularly its conception of the meaning of "arms balance."[42]

The NEACC was assigned the task of reviewing all applications for arms purchases or grants emanating from the Arab and Israeli governments, in order to ensure that fulfillment of any one such request did not (1) affect the regional arms balance in a destabilizing manner, and (2) encourage a speeded-up weapons competition. The rationing system aimed at *controlling the*

39. Examples of such individual policies abound: Sweden's refusal since 1956 to sell arms to the Middle East, France's 1967–1974 embargo on arms to the countries involved in the 1967 war, and the refusal of most arms suppliers to trade with South Africa or Rhodesia. While the last case can be called multinational, it differs from the 1950–1955 tripartite policy in that this was jointly carried out within a framework of intergovernmental coordination.

40. Practically all other embargoes imposed on conflict areas have been implemented while hostilities were in progress, and in most cases they did not survive the cessation of active warfare. The prime example was the embargo imposed on India and Pakistan at the time of the 1965 war in the Asian subcontinent.

41. The Israelis came to know of the NEACC through their French contacts, but, as far as is ascertainable from interviews with Egyptian officers who were at the time in charge of arms procurement, the Arab governments were not acquainted with the existence of the Committee. Awareness of the NEACC apparently first came in May 1956, during the buildup to the Suez crisis, when news of Anglo-French-U.S. meetings to discuss Middle East arms shipments were prominently reported in the Arab press; *Egyptian Gazette*, May 10, 1956. Egypt's recognition of the People's Republic of China came a few days later, and, on May 18, the Cairo daily *Al-Gumhuriyya* linked this diplomatic move to the disclosure that the Western powers were conspiring to ship arms to Israel "on pretext of establishing a balance of power in the area" (Editorial, May 17, 1956, cited in Oles M. Smolansky, *The Soviet Union and the Arab East under Khrushchev* [Lewisburg, Penn.: Bucknell University Press, 1974], p. 38).

42. Unless otherwise indicated, the information on which the following analysis is based was obtained in personal interviews, particularly those with Parker Hart, Raymond Hare, Loy Henderson, Alfred Atherton, and Sir Harold Beeley, who was then at the British Embassy in Washington and later became ambassador to Egypt.

direction of the arms flow to the region so that the spread would be "even" between potential antagonists, and at *limiting the magnitude* of the flow so as to discourage an arms race that would increase the danger of renewed warfare even in the absence of a clear military superiority for either side. That arms races almost inevitably lead to armed conflict was a notion widely accepted among the decision-makers.

Within these parameters, there was no intention to drastically curtail the supply of armaments, for reasons already discussed: the desire to build up local military strength for regional defense against the Soviet threat; the wish to preserve Western influence and treaty arrangements; the need to forestall an Arab resort to the Soviet bloc for arms; and, lastly, the wish to reap the economic benefits of an active arms trade. These motives were not equally shared by the three powers. Nonetheless, singly and in conjunction, they were stronger, more palpable, and had more immediately interested advocates than the nebulous, never operationally well defined, long-term goal of preserving an abstract "arms balance" or preventing a future "arms race." The will to provide arms was made explicit in the text itself of the 1950 Declaration, whereas the keeping of a military balance was an implied notion that gained its authority from statements by Western leaders rather than from the Declaration.[43] Right from the outset, the arms-limitation duties of the NEACC were vitiated by the need to respond to these incentives to maintain a substantial flow of armaments to the Middle East.

A further and equally important function of the Committee was to act as a watchdog over the individual arms transfer practices of its members. It was a forum for the reconciliation of divergent views regarding the size and timing of particular arms sales, for bargaining over who would supply which arms to whom, and for keeping tabs on whether the three suppliers were respecting each other's markets. These had been "allocated" at the time of the issuance of the Declaration, both by virtue of previous supplier-recipient ties and by a tacit understanding on political spheres of influence. Thus, in seeking assurances from the Middle Eastern governments of their readiness to comply with the nonaggression condition laid out in paragraph 2 of the Declaration, London had dealt with Egypt, Jordan, Iraq, and Saudi Arabia; Washington with Saudi Arabia, Egypt, Israel, and Syria; and France with Syria and Lebanon.[44]

43. See the opening pages of Chapter 6 for a sample of such statements.
44. Anthony Nutting, *No End of a Lesson* (New York: Potter, 1967), p. 179. *Al-Ahram* noted on May 29, 1950, that this peculiar division of responsibilities had

Most meetings of the NEACC took place in Washington. While the Truman Administration remained in office, the Committee was largely inactive. The British wanted close consultations in order to keep informed on arms requests from the area, but Secretary Acheson reportedly insisted that local governments should not be given the impression that the Western powers were ganging up on them.[45] Moreover, this was a period when the arms flow had slackened considerably as the Anglo-Egyptian dispute intensified and the Korean War siphoned off available arms stocks in the West. By mid-1952, however, the Committee began to meet more regularly, eventually reaching a rate of a meeting every three weeks. Each member country was usually represented by one delegate, who was seconded by military or civilian experts according to need. Parker Hart, the Director of the Bureau of Near Eastern and African Affairs in the State Department, regularly represented the American side from the summer of 1952 to the summer of 1955. The U.K. and France were represented by embassy officials, routinely at the First Secretary level.

No country had veto power over the arms supply decisions of the other two, and the Committee was in no way a body that made final determinations as to which arms would be shipped to the Middle East. Its rulings were recommendations that each side made to its own government in light of the exchange of views and information at the Committee meetings. As a rule, relations within the NEACC have been described as cooperative, although disagreements occurred at times and no consensus could be reached, particularly whenever one of the three governments felt that it had to make a particular sale. On particular issues of policy, the French often found themselves ranged against the British and the Americans. On the other hand, in terms of the thrust of the Committee's work, the Europeans tended to be more eager to supply than to restrict arms, while pressure for restraint often had to come from the American side.

As the primary advocate of arms control, the U.S. regularly sought to discourage the sale of offensive weapons in particular and of all major weapons in general. American representatives resisted the sale of fighter aircraft, bombers, heavy artillery, and tanks. No objections were raised regarding small arms, communications equipment, and other material that was partic-

---

been a matter of concern for the Lebanese Council of Ministers, presumably because it appeared to limit Lebanon's sources of arms to only one country.

45. This information was provided by the Intelligence and Research Office, Department of State. Apparently, Acheson feared that the existence of the Committee would sooner or later be revealed.

Table 6. Egypt: Identifiable Heavy-Arms Acquisitions, May 1950–
August 1955

Source	Weapon	Number	Agreement	Delivery
U.K.	Frigate	8	1948, 1949	1949–1950
U.K.	Fleet minesweeper	3	1949	1949–1950
U.K.	Motor torpedo boat	6	1949	1950
U.K.	Gloster-Meteor jet fighter	15	1948, 1949	1949–1950
U.K.	Vampire jet fighter-bomber	15	1949	1950
U.K.	Centurion heavy tank	41	1949	1950, 1955
U.K.	Halifax heavy bomber ⎫	20	1949(?)	1954–1955
U.K.	Lancaster heavy bomber ⎭			
Belgium	Sherman Mark-3 medium tank	150	1949	1949–1950
U.K.	Spitfire-22 fighter	20	1950	1950
U.K.	Gloster-Meteor jet fighter	27	1950	1953, 1955
U.K.	Vampire jet fighter	18	1954	1954–1956
Italy*	Vampire jet fighter	30	—	1953
France	AMX-13 light tank	20	1954	1955, 1956
France	155-mm. self-propelled gun	20	1955	1956
U.K.†	Self-propelled Valentine gun mounting	151	1955	1955
U.K.	Destroyer "Z" class	2	1955	1955

NOTE: Only those acquisitions for which some concrete data have been obtained are shown in this table, which is therefore not exhaustive.

* Acquired indirectly through the Syrian government.

† Purchased indirectly through private dealer.

ularly useful for internal security purposes or that was of a strictly defensive nature.[46] Aircraft that were considered no longer fit for effective military use, such as old C-47s to be used as transports, were also sanctioned. While, with the exception of a few sales to Israel, the U.S. did limit her own arms transfers in this manner, she was not overly successful in convincing her partners to follow a similar path, judging from the types and quantities of heavy arms that were provided to Egypt and Israel during the first half of the 1950s (see Tables 6 and 7).

The NEACC's effectiveness was also undercut by its members' occasional failure to bring intended arms sales before it. Under John Foster Dulles, Washington appears to have restricted the relevance of the Committee's work

46. Which arms are offensive and which are defensive was, then as now, a tricky question that was ultimately determined by the need to deny or justify a sale rather than on its strict merits. See the congressional testimony of Admiral Duncan, Deputy Chief of Naval Operations, for statements to the effect that the funds allocated to military aid for the Arab states and Israel under the Mutual Security Program were to be only for "small arms, light equipment, advice and training" (U.S. House of Representatives, Committee on Foreign Affairs, *The Mutual Security Program, Hearings,* 82d Congress, 1st session, June–July 1951, pp. 869–870).

Table 7. Israel: Identifiable Heavy-Arms Acquisitions, May 1950–
August 1955

Source	Weapon	Number	Agreement	Delivery
Private	Sherman Mark-3 tank	120	n.a.†	1948–1951
U.S.*	Harvard T.6 trainer	20	n.a.†	1948–1950
U.K.*	Cromwell heavy tank	25	n.a.†	1950–1951
France	Mosquito light bomber	60	1950	1950–1951
U.S.	Escort vessel	3	1950	1950
Canada	Frigate	5	1949	1950–1951
U.S.	Mustang P-51 fighter	25	1952	1952
Sweden	Mustang P-51 fighter	25	1952	1952–1953
Italy	Spitfire Mark-9 fighter	30	1952	1953
U.K.	Motor torpedo boat	9	1951	1952
U.K.	Gloster-Meteor jet fighter	28	1952–1954	1953–1955
U.S.	75-mm. antitank gun	n.a.†	n.a.†	1953
Belgium	Gloster-Meteor jet fighter	3	1953	1953
France	Motor torpedo boat	9	n.a.†	1952–1954
U.K.*	Mosquito light bomber	20	1953	1953
U.K.*	Sherman Mark-3 tank	109	1954	1954–1955
France	75-mm. tank gun	150	1954	1954
France	AMX-13 light tank	100	1954	1955
France	Ouragan jet fighter	24	1954	1955
France	Mystère-II jet fighter	15	1954	‡
France	155-mm. self-propelled gun	60	1954	1955
U.K.	Destroyer "Z" class	2	1955	1955

NOTE: Only those acquisitions for which some concrete data have been obtained are listed in this table, which is therefore not exhaustive.
  * Purchased indirectly, through private dealers.
  † Not available.
  ‡ Replaced by Mystère-IV fighters prior to delivery in an agreement concluded in November 1955.

to the immediate Arab-Israeli area, and did not consult with the British and French on, for example, its intended arms aid to Iraq under the April 1954 Mutual Security agreement. According to a British source, all three suppliers sent arms secretly to the area at one time or another during this period.[47] The Franco-Israeli contracts in 1954 have already been mentioned. Later, France's Foreign Minister during the Suez war, Christian Pineau, would justify the large clandestine shipments to Israel by saying: "The U.S. didn't consult with France about sending arms to Iran and Pakistan and Iraq; why should France ask about sending arms to Israel?"[48]

The tripartite powers were also unsuccessful in preventing other suppliers from shipping arms to the Middle East during this period. Sweden, Belgium,

47. Harold Beeley interview.
48. Love, *Twice-Fought War*, p. 141. The American ambassador to Iraq at the time, Waldemar Gallman, confirmed to this author that, as far as he knew, the NEACC did not figure at all in the matter of arms to Baghdad.

and Italy are among those who supplied limited but significant amounts of heavy weaponry, while the trade in small arms and ammunition remained largely uncontrolled. Switzerland, for instance, is held to have exported light weapons to the Middle East to the tune of some $5–7 million per year during 1950–1955, which made up over one third of her total exports to Third World countries.[49] A number of Swedish companies set up arms factories in Egypt in 1952 for the production of submachine guns and rifles.[50] On the other hand, in the absence of a common policy of arms limitation by the three major Western arms-producing countries, the flow of arms from other suppliers would have been larger, judging from the success with which both Israel and the Arabs were able to procure arms in 1949–1950, before the rationing system came into effect.

The joint policy also allowed the tripartite powers to present a stronger common front and prevent arms transfers by other parties in some instances. In July 1954, while the Anglo-Egyptian talks over Suez had reached a critical stage, Washington and London were able to pressure Spain into cancelling a $3.5 million sale of small arms to Egypt. Consisting mainly of mortars and ammunition, the transaction aroused the opposition of the British, who felt the arms would strengthen the Egyptian capability to wage guerrilla warfare against their forces in the Canal zone, were the negotiations to break down.[51]

As for the Soviet bloc, the desirability of purchasing arms from the East was broached at various times by Arab leaders and in the Middle Eastern press during this period.[52] In 1954, a small step in this direction was actually taken by Syria, with the purchase of about thirty German tanks of World War II vintage from Czechoslovakia.[53] Yet, despite the fact that Western willingness

49. SIPRI, *Arms Trade with the Third World*, p. 349.

50. Ibid., pp. 330–331.

51. *New York Times*, July 18, 19, and 22, 1954.

52. Apart from the Syrian flirtation with the idea of accepting Soviet aid in 1950, which has been already discussed, one might mention: (1) Egyptian Foreign Minister Salaheddin's statement to Parliament in May 1951 that Egypt was prepared to "procure arms from either East or West" if the British continued their embargo (ibid., May 2, 1951); (2) similar statements by the President of the Egyptian Chamber of Deputies, in which he explicitly called for arms purchases from Russia (ibid., September 4, 1951); (3) the commercial agreements concluded between the U.S.S.R. and Egypt, and Czechoslovakia and Egypt, in mid-1953, which, according to an official Egyptian spokesman, covered the possible purchase of armaments at a future date if Egypt so desired; and (4) the simultaneous announcement of Czech-Egyptian talks for the purchase of arms from the Skoda factories (ibid., August 18, 1953).

53. Statement by the Syrian Army Chief of Staff, quoted by Patrick Seale, *The Struggle for Syria* (London: Oxford University Press, 1965), p. 233.

to supply arms stemmed partly from the desire to foreclose this option,[54] the NEACC apparently considered the political constraints on Middle Eastern governments against turning to the Soviets so overwhelming that in practice it acted as if these governments had nowhere else to go for their arms but to the West. While this assumption was probably correct in the early part of the decade, eventually it led to the undoing of the rationing system. The cavalier manner in which Egyptian arms requests were handled, even after the first news of a possible deal with Moscow was reported by the U.S. embassy in Cairo in June 1955,[55] suggests that the NEACC acted throughout on the assumption that practically under no circumstances would Middle East capitals shift their arms acquisition efforts toward the Communist bloc.[56]

In general, however, there is little doubt that the tripartite regime succeeded in limiting the quantities of arms that entered the Middle East in 1950–1955. The exact extent of this success cannot be determined without benefit of the Committee's records, for only by comparing actual shipments completed by approval of the Committee with requests that were turned down, deals involving other suppliers that were stopped or otherwise influenced by NEACC action, and transactions by suppliers that took place without knowledge of the Committee can such evaluation be made.[57] But it is clear that, without tripartite coordination, commercial competition between Britain and France alone would have accelerated the local arms race and would have obliged the United States to become a much more active supplier. The amount of weapons made available to Israel by the French in 1953–1955 would have been considerably larger in the absence of the NEACC's restraining effect. The French Foreign Ministry was able to use the Committee as an ally in the bureaucratic infighting with the Ministry of Defense and the military, not only by insisting that transactions be subject to tripartite approval, but also by alerting the Committee in some instances when the Ministry of Defense was determined to complete arms sales without consultation. In the second half of 1954 and in 1955, this forced the Ministry of Defense into the unusual practice of selling weapons systems to a foreign state without informing

54. See above, and also see Dwight D. Eisenhower, *The White House Years: Waging Peace, 1956–1961* (New York: Doubleday, 1965), p. 22.

55. See Chapter 6, below.

56. A similar conclusion is reached by Keith Wheelock in *Nasser's New Egypt* (New York: Praeger, 1960), p. 230.

57. I attempted without success to obtain the NEACC records from the U.S. government. Their release, I was told, requires the explicit permission of the three Western governments and of those Middle East governments whose arms requests form part of the Committee's files, which means that these records may not become available for decades.

the Foreign Ministry, and even of establishing special bookkeeping arrangements to bypass the NEACC.[58]

The rationing system was most effective while the concordance of purposes which initially existed and was expressed in the Tripartite Declaration lasted. The performance of the NEACC could only be a reflection of the larger political interests of its members, and when these began to diverge drastically in the mid-1950s, with the growth of the Franco-Israeli alliance and the increasing involvement of the British and the Americans in regional defense schemes based on the Arab countries, tripartite cooperation rapidly began to dissolve. The Soviet-Egyptian arms deal announced in September 1955 dealt it the final *coup de grace*, and the 1956 Suez crisis buried it. Testifying before the Senate Foreign Relations Committee in February 1956, Secretary Dulles intimated that the "loose cooperation that had been in effect in earlier years was at an end."[59] France reportedly cleared the sale of twelve Mystère-IV aircraft to Israel shortly afterwards with both London and Washington "in accordance with the established procedures for consultation about arms deliveries."[60] This, however, was necessary because the aircraft involved were being manufactured by France to fulfill a NATO allocation.[61] The Committee continued in existence until the 1967 war, but only as an occasionally useful forum for sporadic exchange of information among Western arms suppliers, including at times other governments, such as Italy.[62]

THE "ARMS BALANCE"

A key issue for the appreciation of the NEACC experience from the standpoint of arms control is the manner in which the Committee went about deciding which arms shipments conformed to the broad principle of "low-level arms balance" that it sought to implement.

Theoretically, two complementary methods can be used to investigate how this principle was operationalized. One is to look at the actual arms transfers

58. The Israeli request to purchase Mystère aircraft was communicated by the Quai d'Orsay to the NEACC in the fall of 1954. On October 23, the Israeli Ambassador was informed that London was opposed to the sale, on the grounds that even Britain did not possess such advanced aircraft in the Middle East; Tsur, *Prèlude á Suez*, p. 123. Nonetheless, the French went ahead with the transaction. See Love, *Twice-Fought War*, p. 141; Bar-Zohar, *Suez: Ultra Secret*, pp. 77, 78, and 120; and Crosbie, *Tacit Alliance*, chap. 2.

59. U.S. Congress, Senate, Committee on Foreign Relations, *The Situation in the Middle East, Hearing*, 84th Congress, 2d Session, February 24, 1956, p. 49.

60. Nutting, *No End of a Lesson*, p. 88; Eisenhower, *Waging Peace*, p. 29.

61. Peres, *David's Sling*, pp. 50–53; Kagan, *Secret Battle*, p. 228.

62. Alfred Atherton interview.

made under the aegis of the NEACC, in combination with already available local military power, and attempt to interpret these figures. The other is to ascertain how the decision-makers themselves perceived the regional relationships of armed strength that obtained at the time and the manner in which they should act to affect these relationships in the desired directions.

In practice, unfortunately, the first method proves well-nigh unfeasible, because of the paucity and unreliability of the relevant data. Even if a comprehensive listing of the major-weapons transfers to the region can be compiled—and Tables 6 and 7 on purchases by Israel and Egypt approximate this goal[63]—it would be highly misleading to gauge the Committee's performance by these lights except in the most general terms, simply because the circumstances surrounding each individual transaction remain unknown without the benefit of NEACC records. Many of the transfers listed were made through private arms dealers, by governments not party to the rationing regime, and by NEACC members without consultation with the Committee. In some instances, as with the Mystère-II contract in 1954, France made the sale in secret after having unsuccessfully sought NEACC approval. The matter of "secret" deals must be handled carefully for another reason that further muddies the waters: in an undetermined number of cases, NEACC members knew of such transactions through their individual intelligence services but chose not to raise the issue on a tripartite level.[64] Add to this the unrevealed instances in which the Western powers intervened together or singlehandedly to prevent arms sales by other suppliers,[65] and also those cases which they chose to ignore or where their intervention was unsuccessful, and it becomes readily apparent that only highly imperfect and broad generalizations can be deduced from concrete arms transfer figures.

These figures[66] suggest that Israel received considerably larger quantities

63. Heavy-weapons acquisitions by the other Arab countries directly involved in the Palestine conflict during 1950–1955 were very limited in comparison. For details, see SIPRI, *Arms Trade with the Third World*, pp. 842–850, although the figures in this source, while the most complete of any presently available, are not totally reliable.

64. For example, according to Sir Harold Beeley, London knew of the French plans to sell AMX-13 tanks to Israel in 1954. See also Love, *Twice-Fought War*, p. 95, on Anglo-French frictions over secret arms to Israel in 1954–1955.

65. It is known that in July 1954 the United States withheld permission for Canada to sell Israel any F-86 Sabre jet fighters manufactured under U.S. license; Kagan, *Secret Battle*, pp. 197–201. The Anglo-American intervention in Madrid has already been mentioned. How many of these instances have yet to come to light?

66. Data appearing in Tables 6 and 7 were derived from newspaper reports and from textual analysis of the following sources: Bar-Zohar, *Suez: Ultra Secret*; Jackson, *Israeli Air Force*; Kagan, *Secret Battle*; Peres, *David's Sling*; SIPRI, *Arms Trade with*

of air and ground equipment than Egypt, but slightly fewer naval units. Israel obtained from abroad some 160 piston-engined combat aircraft, as compared to some 40 acquired by Egypt. The Egyptians had the edge in jet warplanes, obtaining about 105 to Israel's 60, but the Israeli Mystère was a recently developed plane, far superior in performance to the obsolescent Gloster-Meteors and Vampires. During the NEACC period, Israel received upwards of 250 tanks, while the Egyptians got about two-thirds that number. But the Anglo-Egyptian dispute seriously constricted Cairo's ability to keep its air force and armor operational, as the British often withheld spare parts and ammunition.[67]

When the small transfers to Syria, Iraq, and Jordan during this five-year period are included, it would appear that only a slight numerical edge in military inventories was allowed the Arab countries vis-à-vis Israel under the tripartite rationing system. If the large French supplies made without NEACC clearance are disregarded, a rough numerical parity is observed in weapons going to Egypt and Israel, with an Arab quantitative advantage when acquisitions by Fertile Crescent countries are included.[68] If weapons already in the area are taken into account, this advantage was offset by the much better shape in which the Israelis emerged from the 1948 war, and the lead they maintained before the rationing came into effect.[69] Furthermore, qualitative

---

the Third World; Slater, *The Pledge*; Love, *Twice-Fought War*; *Brassey's Annual: The Armed Forces Yearbook* (New York: MacMillan, 1951–1953); *Jane's Fighting Ships* (London: Sampson Low, Marston, 1951–1956); Jack Gee, *Mirage: Warplane for the World* (London: Macdonald, 1971); Robert Henriquez, *A Hundred Hours to Suez* (New York: Viking, 1957); Massachusetts Institute of Technology, Center for International Studies, *The Control of Local Conflict*, ACDA/WEC-98, Vol. 3; John L. Sutton and Geoffrey Kemp, *Arms to Developing Countries*, Adelphi Paper, No. 28 (London: Institute for Strategic Studies, October 1966); George Thayer, *The War Business* (New York: Simon and Schuster, 1969); United Kingdom, Foreign Office, cmd 9676, *Export of Surplus War Material*, January 1956; Edward Luttwak and Dan Horowitz, *The Israeli Army* (New York: Harper & Row, 1975); Crosbie, *A Tacit Alliance*; Brecher, *Decisions in Israel's Foreign Policy*; and Zeev Schiff, *A History of the Israeli Army* (San Francisco: Straight Arrow, 1974).

67. Interview with Brigadier General Hassan Al-Badri, Chief of Staff of Egyptian forces in the Sinai in the 1950s, and later military advisor to President Nasser. The Centurion tanks sold by Britain were delivered without ammunition, and only after repeated Egyptian protests did London send a token ten rounds per tank in 1955; Erskine B. Childers, *The Road to Suez* (London: MacGibbon and Kee, 1962), p. 133. This was confirmed to the author by General Al-Badri.

68. But see Dulles's statement below to the effect that Israel had acquired more arms than all the Arabs combined.

69. When, in early 1950, Egypt appeared to be rearming at a fast rate with British assistance and Israel applied to Washington for arms, the Israelis were told by the

factors were considered by the NEACC as well. Differences in training and expected battle performance, technological know-how for the maintenance of equipment and the handling of modern weaponry, and organizational skill must have been weighed in some form by the Committee.

The picture that emerges from this guarded analysis of actual arms transfers is that of an NEACC policy of rough quantitative balance between Israel and the Arabs, a balance slightly tipped to the Arab side only if all of Israel's neighbors are included in the equation, but frankly tipped toward Israel against any one potential Arab adversary, including Egypt. When the element of Israeli qualitative advantage in both equipment maintenance and military skills is added to the picture, the data show that, under the rationing system, Israel was able to acquire sufficient military superiority to defeat any likely combination of Arab opponents.

That this may have been the intention of the Tripartite Powers, as well as the actual outcome of their policies—i.e., that the decision-makers' conception of arms balance and military stability was one in which Israel maintained a margin of absolute regional superiority over the Arab world—is a conclusion shared by several observers.[70] Furthermore, and here we move into the area of individual and "governmental" perception, the exploration of which makes up the second method of inquiry outlined above, this was the notion held by those who actually participated in framing arms supply policy at the time. Such perceptions are a better indicator of the way in which the arms rationing system was implemented than actual arms supply figures, both for reasons of incomplete knowledge already mentioned and because, by definition, they reflect how those who controlled the arms flow understood the situation and the goals they wanted to achieve. On the other hand, these perceptions suffer the drawbacks of vagueness and, in some instances, inconsistency between different individual views. They do not offer a tidy picture of a set of clear guidelines applied by the NEACC to all the cases brought before it. But this is largely a fault of the arms control system itself: as far as can be established from available evidence, the NEACC did not evolve such a set of guidelines but dealt with each individual issue on an ad hoc basis and on its merits,

---

State Department that the Joint Chiefs of Staff believed Israel "already had arms in sufficient quantity, and that [Israeli] air power, in particular, was greater than that of all the Arab states put together" (Kagan, *Secret Battle*, p. 173). Figures that can be gleaned from the various sources cited in this chapter confirm the Joint Chiefs' judgment.

70. See, e.g., Kemp, *Arms and Security*, pp. 19–20; and Nadav Safran, *From War to War: The Arab-Israeli Confrontation, 1948–1967* (New York: Pegasus, 1969), p. 146.

taking into account circumstantial political and other variables external to the formal purposes of the rationing system itself.

Thus, when asked by Senator John Kennedy shortly after the Suez war whether Egypt had concluded the "Czech" arms deal "because the United States, the British, and the French under the tripartite agreement were enforcing equality between the Israelis and all the Arab countries together . . . , which meant that Egypt, in relation to Israel, was at a sharp military disadvantage," the Chairman of the Joint Chiefs of Staff, Admiral Radford, replied, "That is probably a good estimate of the situation."[71] Similarly, in February 1956, Secretary Dulles told Congress that "in the 1950 [Middle East] Declaration . . . we wanted to maintain a certain balance there, and we also did not want to start an arms race," but later added that, up until Egypt's purchase of Soviet-bloc weapons, "the State of Israel ha[d] procured more arms abroad than the neighboring Arab states have."[72]

Loy Henderson, who was Deputy Under-Secretary of State for Administration while the rationing system was in effect, recalls that "since Israel was one while the Arab states were many, the idea was to assure an Israeli defensive capacity sufficient to deter attack by any coalition of Arab states. Of course, Israel should be better armed than any one Arab state; however, there was no attempt to equate in quantitative terms arms going to Israel with arms going to all Arab states."[73] Raymond Hare, who negotiated the Tripartite Declaration in London and who later spent most of the 1950s as U.S. ambassador in Saudi Arabia, Lebanon, and Egypt, felt that the sought-for balance was perceived not in terms of units, but as a sort of "equilibrium," a notion Hare used at the time to convey what he felt the Western powers should seek to maintain between Arabs and Israelis.[74]

This view was shared by Parker Hart, who represented the United States on the NEACC. Hart maintained that the tendency to equate arms flowing to each side in the Middle East gun for gun was checked by the strong American desire to limit weapons transfers as an absolute objective in itself. It was the Israelis who constantly advocated the principle of parity between them and all the Arab states in their efforts to curtail Western supplies to their adversaries. Israel had the advantage, since she had managed to pick up a great deal

71. U.S. Congress, Senate, Committee on Foreign Relations and Committee on Armed Services, *The President's Proposal on the Middle East, Hearings,* 85th Congress, 1st session, Part I, January–February 1957, p. 429.

72. U.S. Congress, Senate, Committee on Foreign Relations, *Situation in the Middle East,* pp. 17 and 49.

73. Loy Henderson interview.   74. Raymond Hare interview.

of surplus and other arms from different sources in the years following the
1948 war; in fact, the British and the French on the NEACC attempted to
rationalize their desire to sell arms to the Arabs on that basis, with the French
adopting a pro-Israeli sales policy after the outbreak of conflict in Algeria.[75]

Among European decision-makers a similar set of attitudes was apparent.
Speaking in Parliament on November 22, 1955, about arms supply policy,
Prime Minister Anthony Eden observed that "[t]here is nothing about a
balance in the Tripartite Agreement," which, to the contrary, obligated its
signatories to "deliver to the Middle Eastern countries certain supplies of
arms." There was, however, a Western desire for fairness in arms distribution:

> Mr. H. MORRISON: Is there not a moral or other obligation on the part of
> Her Majesty's Government to maintain some sort of equity and fairness in the
> supply of arms between these unfortunately competing nations? Is it not the
> case that Israel should have a supply of arms which is roughly equitable in re-
> lation to the supply of arms to the Arab States together?
>
> The PRIME MINISTER: The right hon. Gentleman is perfectly right in
> saying that we should try to maintain a balance of arms. Indeed, I myself gave
> that assurance to the House, and that is what we have done, without doubt,
> ourselves and to the best of our ability, with our French and American allies. . . .[76]

And on December 12, 1955, Eden stated on the same subject:

> [Arms] are coming from all parts of the world to Israel and to the Arab States
> on a very large scale. We have done what we could ourselves during this period,
> and when it was my responsibility at the Foreign Office we spent a great many
> hours trying as far as we could to see that the balance of deliveries was kept as
> fairly as we could contrive, not only by ourselves, but together with the United
> States and France, our principal Allies. . . .
>
> Perhaps it is unwise, but I think I should say it. Israel is not, in my belief, at
> a military disadvantage today in relation to any Arab State, or, indeed, to any
> combination of Arab States who are on her frontier. I think that that is about a
> true estimate of the situation.[77]

Some of the qualitative elements that London took into account in its
conception of arms balance were outlined by Selwyn Lloyd in February 1953
to justify the sale of jet planes to Egypt. "There are many considerations

75. Parker Hart interview.

76. *Parliamentary Debates* (Commons), November 22, 1955, col. 1263. The question
is as significant as the answer. Herbert Morrison was Britain's Foreign Secretary in
1951, when arms deliveries to Egypt had been suspended.

77. Ibid., December 12, 1955, cols. 961–970. It should be noted that Eden's
statement was made two and a half months *after* the announcement of the Soviet-
Egyptian arms deal.

other than those of actual numbers," he explained to the Commons. "There are, for example, considerations of serviceability, technical skill, the capacity to keep the aircraft in the air, geography, and so on. . . . So far as the question of parity is concerned, that is not a matter of a mathematical formula, but the relative strength of the air forces is certainly one of the features to be taken into consideration." [78]

In the French capital, similar evaluations of the regional balance of military strength prevailed. Israeli Ambassador Jacob Tsur noted in March 1954, after a meeting with the Secretary-General of the Foreign Ministry, Alexandre Parodi: "I gathered the impression that there is a conviction in governmental circles that our army is much stronger than all the Arab armies put together and that, consequently, any additional arms for Israel would endanger the balance in the region. This problem of a balance undoubtedly is a factor that militates against us each time that the arms question is raised." [79]

In May 1955, the Minister of National Defense and one of the main architects of the Franco-Israeli connection, General Pierre Koenig, also declared himself "against any notion of a mechanical balance between Israel and the Arab States." By this he did not imply that Israeli qualitative superiority should be taken into account, however, but rather that arms transfers to Israel need not be restricted by the amount of arms the Arabs were receiving. While assuring the Israelis that they held the military upper hand and should not fear "Arab supremacy," Koenig promised his immediate attention to and support for the "long list of armaments" that the Director General of Israel's Defense Ministry, Shimon Peres, had just come to Paris to purchase.[80]

THE REGIONAL IMPACT OF THE TRIPARTITE POLICY

When the Declaration was issued in May 1950, the Israeli government welcomed it with no reservations, since it guaranteed Israel's borders, including the territorial gains of 1948, and explicitly acknowledged Israel's need for armaments on a par with the Arab countries. As a Foreign Ministry statement indicated, Israel considered the Declaration as putting an "end to

78. Ibid., February 17, 1953, cols. 1080 and 1086.
79. Tsur, *Prèlude à Suez*, pp. 61–62, entry for March 10, 1954.
80. Included in this list were twelve additional Mystère-IIs, twelve Mystère-IVs, heavy artillery, antiaircraft guns, SS-10 antitank missiles, radar equipment, and ammunition; Bar-Zohar, *Suez: Ultra Secret*, pp. 81 and 107. At about the same time, Koenig offered Israel the newly developed Vautour jet fighter-bomber; ibid., p. 107. The Vautour would first enter service with the Israeli air force in 1958.

the discrimination hitherto practiced in the supply of arms and war materials to countries of the Middle East." [81]

The official Arab response was cautious and mildly critical, particularly of the Western guarantees of the status quo, while the press was more outspoken in its opposition to what was seen as a new form of political tutelage by the imperialist powers. [82] The Declaration's implications from an arms supply perspective seem to have left the Arab governments relatively untroubled, however. In a lengthy statement issued by the Arab League on June 21 in response to the Declaration, the only direct reference to the arms balance that the Tripartite Powers would seek to implement was a rather mild remonstrance to the effect that sovereign states have a right to determine the size and strength of their own armed forces, which are "subject to various factors, chiefly the size of the population, the area of the country and the length and diversity of its frontiers." The Arab governments also pledged that all arms they would procure would be used for defensive ends, and they reiterated their peaceful intentions toward Israel. [83]

Their mild reaction may be ascribed to the fact that the Arab states were then being favored over Israel in terms of arms supplies, and the Declaration's reference to the need for armed forces for regional defense seemed to fore-shadow more of the same. Indeed, *Al-Misri*, the organ of the Egyptian ruling Wafdist Party of Premier Mustapha An-Nahas, was able to maintain that the statement was "not made in the interests of the Arabs, but at the same time it is not entirely to their detriment." [84] *Al-Ahram*, on the other hand, sounded a note of caution, warning that unless the tripartite regime was evenhandedly administered, Israel might acquire offensive weapons that would be withheld from the Arabs, thereby tipping the arms balance. If this were to happen, the editorial queried, "before what court could we bring our complaint? . . . What guarantee of fairness do we have?" [85]

In the end, the new approach to arms supplies vindicated Israel's optimism and the Arabs' fears. The net short-run impact of the Declaration was to enable the West to begin selling arms to the Jewish state without facing major

81. *Jerusalem Post*, May 26, 1950. See also the statement by Prime Minister Ben-Gurion to the Knesset; text in J. C. Hurewitz, *Diplomacy in the Near and Middle East, A Documentary Record: 1914–1956*, reprint edition (New York: Octagon, 1972), pp. 309–310.

82. See e.g., the lead editorial in *Al-Ahram*, May 30, 1950.

83. The text is in Hurewitz, *Diplomacy*, pp. 311–312.

84. Quoted in the *New York Times*, May 29, 1950.

85. "The Declaration of the Three on Arming the Jews and the Arabs," *Al-Ahram*, May 27, 1950.

political difficulties or other negative repercussions from the Arab camp, and without qualms about fuelling an arms race, since these weapons were being provided subject to commitments against their use for aggressive purposes and within the framework of a military balance. Also, by putting all arms transactions under the supervision of the NEACC, the arrangement placed an effective ceiling on the quantities and types of military equipment that Britain could sell to her major clients, Iraq, Jordan, and especially Egypt, which made up the bulk of the arms flow to the Arab world. It is not clear exactly how much the British supplies to Egypt were affected by the new policy, for the dispute over the Suez base intervened in 1951. Since it was pressure stemming from such British sales that motivated the United States to seek a coordinated rationing of arms in the first place, it may be assumed that Cairo's weapons acquisition efforts would have been adversely affected—at least temporarily— even if there had been no deterioration in Anglo-Egyptian relations.[86]

The changes wrought by the arms rationing in the pattern of arms pro-curement by Middle Eastern countries are reflected in the figures for military expenditures by these countries in the years immediately before and after the announcement of the 1950 Declaration.

Table 8 shows that, although there was a slight decrease in Israeli expendi-tures in 1950 compared with 1949—which saw the largest proportion of the GNP devoted to defense in the country's history, because of the all-out effort made in the 1948 war—these expenditures picked up in the following year, surpassing the amounts spent in 1949 and increasing thereafter at the very high average rate of 21 percent. The drastic decreases in 1954 and 1955 were due to the devaluation of the Israeli pound. While in 1949–1953 the army was allocated foreign exchange at the minimal rate of U.S. \$1 = I £0.357, in January 1954 this rate became U.S. \$1 = I £1, and in June 1955 it was U.S. \$1 = I £1.80; i.e., there was a fivefold devaluation within a period of eighteen months.[87] However, the actual effect on Israel's defense establishment was not so drastic as the figures would suggest. Only that portion of overall expenditure devoted to the purchase of military equipment abroad suffered, while domestic expenditures on defense felt the impact of inflationary pressures gradually over the years and to a lesser extent as well, as can be seen from a comparison of columns 1 and 2.[88] Furthermore, these figures do not reflect

86. The London correspondent of *Al-Ahram* wrote in the May 27, 1950, issue that official British sources anticipated some limitation of arms sales to Arab countries under the new tripartite policy.

87. See asterisked note in Table 8.

88. The year 1952 was chosen as the base year because then the assigned value of the

Table 8. Israeli Military Expenditures, 1949–1955

Year	I £ (*millions*) Current Prices (1)	I £ (*millions*) Constant (1952) Prices (2)	U.S. $ (*millions*) Official Exchange Rate★ (3)
1949	46.6	77.7	132.9
1950	41.8	79.3	117.1
1951	52.8	84.1	147.9
1952	63.9	63.9	180.0
1953	74.1	60.3	207.6
1954	118.2	87.5	118.2
1955	160.0	104.5	124.4

SOURCES: Don Patinkin, "The Israel Economy: The First Decade," The Falk Project for Economic Research in Israel, *Fourth Report 1957 and 1958* (Jerusalem, November 1959), Tables 12, 18, 43; the figure in column (1) for 1949 was extrapolated from fiscal year figures in Table 6 of the Falk Project's *Third Annual Report, 1956*.

NOTE: Figures include the defense budget and the special budgets, which are lumped together by Patinkin as military expenditures. See also Nadav Safran, *From War to War: The Arab-Israeli Confrontation, 1948–1967* (New York: Pegasus, 1969), pp. 423–424.

★ During this period, Israel maintained several official exchange rates. The one used here is the lowest, which was the one applied to the foreign exchange allocated to the Ministry of Defense for purchases abroad; Alex Rubner (former advisor to the Israeli Ministries of Finance and Trade and Industry), *The Economy of Israel* (London: Frank Cass, 1960), pp. 226–227. This rate was five times higher in 1955 than in 1949 in respect to the dollar; details appear in Patinkin, "The Israel Economy," Table 43.

total Israeli military outlays, because additional classified expenditures and other security-related disbursements, such as the subsidization of high-cost defense industries, are included in the civil sector.[89]

From Table 8 it would appear that Israel had less resources available for arms purchases in 1954–1955, when the French supply source opened up, than in previous years. On the other hand, the years 1952–1954 witnessed relative calm on the Arab-Israeli borders, which meant that a larger share of the pie could be spared for purchases of equipment abroad, and a foreign exchange reserve could be built up for later procurement efforts. Also, the Franco-Israeli political relationship was one that allowed for more extensive credit arrangements than had been the case in previous Israeli experience, when cash purchasing had been the rule.

Turning to Table 9, we see that Egypt, by contrast, could not reach a level of expenditures similar to that which she had attained in 1949—when her

Israeli pound was closest to its "true" value; Don Patinkin, "The Israel Economy: The First Decade," in The Falk Project for Economic Research in Israel, *Fourth Report 1957 and 1958* (Jerusalem, 1959), p. 46.

89. Ibid., p. 58. Patinkin says that "[n]o estimate is available of the costs involved in these additional defense activities, but there are grounds for believing that they are substantial."

Table 9. Egyptian Military Expenditures, 1949–1955

Year	E £ (*millions*) Current Prices	U.S. $ (*millions*) Official Exchange Rate*
1949	34	126.2
1950	31	89.0
1951	33	94.8
1952	35	100.5
1953	37	106.3
1954	47	135.0
1955	71	203.9

SOURCE: Stockholm International Peace Research Institute (SIPRI), *Yearbook of World Armaments and Disarmament, 1969–1970, 1973* (New York: Humanities Press, 1970 and 1975).
* The exchange rate was as follows: up to September 1949, E £ 1 = U.S. $ 4.133; September 1949–June 1962, E £ 1 = U.S. $ 2.872.

arms purchase agreements with Britain had been concluded—until 1954, registering in 1950–1953 an average yearly increase of only about 5 percent. Overall expenditures were at all times lower than Israel's. From the data in Tables 6 and 9, it appears that Britain was able to use the NEACC effectively so as to supplement her own shutoff of arms to Cairo with a virtual embargo by all suppliers while the Suez problem remained unresolved. The 35 percent increase registered in 1955 came after the collapse of the tripartite regime as Soviet arms began to arrive in Egypt.[90]

Finally, Table 10 shows how the Israeli military effort compared with defense expenditures in the Arab countries adjacent to Israel (Egypt, Jordan,

Table 10. Military Expenditures of Selected Middle Eastern Countries, 1950–1955 (*in U.S. $ millions, at current official exchange rates*)

Year	Israel	Egypt	Syria	Iraq	Jordan	Lebanon
1950	117.1	89.0	31.1	19.6	14.0	6.7
1951	147.9	94.8	31.3	21.6	24.1	8.2
1952	180.0	100.5	31.5	33.0	25.5	8.2
1953	207.6	106.3	39.7	42.6	27.7	9.7
1954	118.2	135.0	34.7	46.8	28.6	9.8
1955	124.4	203.9	37.4	48.2	29.4	12.2

SOURCE: For Israel, Table 8 above; for Egypt, Table 9 above; for other Arab countries, Stockholm International Peace Research Institute (SIPRI), *Yearbook of World Armaments and Disarmament, 1972* (New York: Humanities Press, 1972), p. 88.

90. For an account of the successful British pressure on Washington against supplying arms to Egypt in 1953, see Chapter 6, below.

Syria, and Lebanon) or directly involved in the Palestine conflict (Iraq, which participated in the 1948 war and later refused to conclude an armistice agreement). Computed in U.S. dollars at the official rates of exchange, these figures should not be considered as indicative of the extent of resources these countries could devote to defense, but rather as expressing in comparable terms their relative ability to procure arms abroad. This is so because figures for Israel are computed at the lowest exchange rate, which was more favorable than the actual *domestic* cost of the defense burden was, given the high rate of inflation then current in the country. Thus, Table 10 tends to overestimate somewhat the whole Israeli military budget in comparative terms, particularly in 1953. It does not overestimate the Israeli ability to purchase arms from *foreign* suppliers, however, which is what we primarily want to measure.[91] With this caveat in mind, the figures show that in 1950–1953 Israel exerted in dollar terms a military effort which was (1) equal to that of the five Arab countries put together—due allowance being made for the wasteful duplication in ancillary services inherent in maintaining five separate military establishments; (2) larger than the combined efforts of the three most likely opponents in war, Egypt, Syria, and Iraq; and (3) much larger than that of her principal adversary, Egypt.

Thus, budgetary figures lead to the same evaluation of the effect that the arms rationing system had on the regional military balance as was reached from the analysis of Israeli and Egyptian weapons procurement above, and also to the same evaluation of the stated objectives and/or perceptions of the decision-makers. Israel was able to maintain effective military superiority over any likely coalition of Arab opponents throughout the operant tenure of the system. Insofar as the three Western controlling governments did regulate the flow of arms from their countries to the Palestine conflict area with reference to a preferred power correlation between Israel and the Arab states, one may

91. By allocating a large amount of finite foreign exchange to the military at the lowest possible rate, the Israeli leadership deprived other sectors of such scarce resources and increased the military share of the GNP much beyond the proportions suggested by published figures in local currency. The real extent of the defense burden was shielded from the public's eye by secrecy and a number of fiscal devices, including the reporting of foreign exchange allocations by using the average rate of exchange rather than an actual breakdown according to the multiple rates in operation. The Israeli economist Alex Rubner comments on this: "The leaders of the State rightly ask themselves what the attitude of the population would be if, by proper accounting, the real burdens of investment, defence and colonization were exposed to view in plain figures. Would they vote, voluntarily, for a lowered standard of living in order to provide more steel plants, more tanks and more settlements on hilly land?" (*The Economy of Israel* [London: Frank Cass, 1960], p. 229).

conclude that such an outcome was desired or, at the very least, willingly tolerated by them. As has been observed of the large increases in Israeli defense outlays in the early 1950s, they "betray the looseness of the rationing under the Declaration or the degree to which it could be circumvented." [92] By April 1953, one year before the large secret French arms deals, Prime Minister Ben-Gurion could assert that "since the end of the War of Independence, [Israel's] military strength in terms of manpower and equipment alone has been tripled." [93]

The status of the Arab-Israeli military balance was not the only major concern of the tripartite arms suppliers, however. Aside from economic and other incentives discussed earlier, there was one other factor that drastically affected their arms supply policy, particularly in the case of the United States. An outstanding American objective in the general area of the Middle East at the time, especially in the Dulles era, was the formation of a regional defense organization under Western sponsorship. The coordination of arms transfer practices among the major suppliers that the 1950 arrangement instituted permitted Washington to use military aid or sales as a potent lever with which to pursue its Cold War interests locally. By so doing, the United States (and Britain too, though for rather different reasons) risked turning an agency of conflict control that derived its legitimacy from the nominal impartiality of its averred purpose—the avoidance of a destabilizing regional arms imbalance— into an instrument of pressure at the service of extraneous unilateral political objectives.

In 1953, and again in 1955, these two roles of military balancer and pressure lever came most clearly and forcefully into conflict in Egypt. Nasser's arms requests from the United States thus became the litmus test of Western intentions and of the continued viability of the 1950 policy when subjected to the stresses of immediate political expedience. This is a test that all international arms control systems sooner or later must face. The U.S.-Egyptian encounter is the subject of the following chapter.

92. Safran, *From War to War*, p. 161.
93. Quoted in the *New York Times*, April 21, 1953.

CHAPTER 6   ARMS FOR EGYPT: THE LITMUS TEST

> I have been impressed with the difficulty of determining what
> our policy was in the Middle East during these last three or
> four years. I am unable to find any consistent theme or principle
> involved in our attitude toward Egypt. At one moment we
> seemed to encourage Nasser and at another to thwart him
> without any compelling reason for such shifts being evident, at
> least to me. Such rapid changes of attitude were, I am sure,
> confusing to our allies and friends as well as to our enemies.
>
> > Senator J. William Fulbright, 1957
> > Kennett Love, *Suez: The Twice-Fought War*

One of the hottest arms races in the world today," wrote Harold Hovey in 1965 in a standard work on American arms aid policies, "that of the Middle East, is clearly not related to United States military assistance."[1] At best, this statement was only partially true. At worst, it betrayed a grave and all too common misconception of the role that arms transfer policies of the major powers play in the international system.

Granted, in the period 1950–1956 (and subsequently until 1962), the United States did not provide weapons in substantial amounts to any of the principal actors in the Arab-Israeli conflict. To that extent, the U.S. may have been innocent of directly contributing to the regional arms buildup. Nonetheless, Washington was greatly influential in determining the nature of the military balance of forces in the area. This was by virtue of (1) its participation in the tripartite arms rationing system; (2) its influence on the weapons supply practices of the main exporters of military hardware to the region—Britain and France—which influence it exercised as a major financial underwriter of their weapons industries and through NATO; and, most importantly, (3) its own arms supply policies toward individual Middle Eastern countries. Thus,

---

1. Harold H. Hovey, *United States Military Assistance: A Study of Policies and Practices* (New York: Praeger, 1965), p. 223.

in paradoxical contrast to Hovey's conclusion, by repeatedly refraining from selling arms to Egypt in 1953–1955, the United States precipitated a quantum jump in the Israel-Egypt arms race in 1955–1956, starting an upward-spiral effect that has continued unabated to the present time.

As shown in Chapter 5, the concerted Western arms transfer policy implemented in 1950–1954 did in effect impede the establishment of a true balance of military power between Israel and the Arab states, and helped to maintain the superiority that accrued to Israel in the aftermath of the 1948 war. One prevalent argument has it that this deliberate policy, aimed at balancing the military capability of Israel against that of all the Arab countries conjointly, was based on the premise that it was the latter who were actively bent on challenging the status-quo.[2] The validity of this adduced rationale is debatable, however. Repeated official and other Western evaluations of the situation in the Middle East throughout the entire 1950–1956 period denied the existence of a threat of aggression against Israel.[3]

The purposefulness with which a policy of "asymmetric balance" was pursued by the West must be explained in different terms. Strong domestic political support for the Jewish state in the supplier countries played a major role, as it did in bringing the Tripartite Declaration itself into existence in 1950. Once firmly in power, Nasser did not take long to realize that the tri-partite arms rationing was instrumental in preventing the establishment of Egyptian military parity with Israel. Whatever doubts remained on this score were finally erased in early 1955 by the disclosure of France's sale of sub-stantial quantities of modern arms to Israel—which, as far as the Egyptians were concerned, were being made with British and U.S. approval—as well as by the surfacing of more information on Israeli military strength, and the accentuation of a sense of military inferiority in the wake of the Gaza raid. These developments were sufficient to put the continued existence of the arms

2. Nadav Safran, *From War to War: The Arab-Israeli Confrontation, 1948–1967* (New York: Pegasus, 1969), p. 146; Geoffrey Kemp, *Arms and Security*, Adelphi Paper, No. 52 (London: The international Institute for Strategic Studies, October 1968), pp. 19–20.

3. See, e.g., the statement by Secretary Acheson in January 1950, *New York Times*, January 16, 1950; a similar statement by the Acting Assistant Secretary for the Near East in 1953, in U.S. Congress, Senate, Committee on Foreign Relations, *Mutual Security Act of 1953, Hearings*, 83d Congress, 2d Session, p. 274; the letter from the Assistant Secretary of State for Congressional Affairs to Representative Emanuel Celler on August 11, 1954, stating that "we fail to find evidence that any Arab state is desirous or capable of sustaining an aggressive move against Israel" *New York Times*, September 8, 1954); and the British and U.S. intelligence reports mentioned in ibid., October 6, 1956.

control system in jeopardy—a jeopardy arising from the fact that a major arms producer in the shape of the Soviet bloc was available to Egypt—unless the Tripartite Powers took remedial action by satisfying to some extent Cairo's demand for military equipment.

More important, however, were the Western—particularly the American—determination to use arms supplies as a prize to be granted only in exchange for Arab acceptance of anti-Soviet regional defense plans, and the refusal of Arab nationalists to accept these political strings. Launched in 1951 with the Middle East Command proposal, the policy of regional security never knew smooth sailing, and eventually, in 1955, ran aground for good on Egyptian sands. By the time Nasser came to know of the surreptitious French transfers, the arms control regime was already seriously endangered by another set of negative attitudes in Cairo fostered by the growing conviction that the arms monopoly was being exploited to exact political and defense commitments from the local governments that would perpetuate Western domination of the area. This was a conviction that Nasser would find easy to sustain in light of the American response to his various attempts to purchase U.S. weapons, which spanned practically the entire period from the revolutionary coup of July 1952 to the Soviet arms deal of September 1955.

NASSER'S FIRST BID FOR U.S. ARMS: THE SABRI MISSION

The Egyptian army emerged from the Palestine war of 1948 extremely weakened, both in its equipment and its morale. In the officer corps, to the onus of defeat was added a spreading resentment at the corruption and political irresponsibility of the Faruq regime, particularly in the field of national security.[4] The munitions scandals of war profiteers that were soon to erupt into the public light and help set the stage for the Free Officers' revolt were well known to the military, for they implicated its own top leadership.[5]

4. A few days before the entry of Egypt into the war against Israel, the top army officers advised the Palace not to engage in the conflict, for which the army was ill-prepared. See the text of the judgment issued by the Criminal Court in June 1952 in the case of the munitions scandal, in *Al-Ahram*, July 7, 1953; the judgment accused the "politicians" of having brought Egypt into the war "despite the scarcity of arms, supplies, and ammunition, and despite the opposition of Egypt's military men, who unanimously" recommended against it. See also Jon Kimche, *Seven Fallen Pillars: The Middle East, 1945–1952* (New York: Praeger, 1953), pp. 369–370.

5. Inquiries into the affair led to the dismissal of the Commander in Chief of the armed forces, General Mohamed Haydar, and the Chief of the General Staff, General Osman Al-Mahdi. After the 1952 coup, General Hussein Sirri Amer and about a thousand officers and civil servants were convicted of complicity in this and other similar incidents of venality.

The situation was rendered even more critical by the emergence of Israel as a strong, victorious enemy that the Egyptians—and other Arabs—regarded as inherently expansionist. In July 1949, Premier Abdul-Hadi announced an ambitious three-year rearmament program, calculated to cost about $300 million, which envisaged the construction of a small and medium-sized armaments industry, a strengthening of the air force, and the addition of a full armored division to the land forces.[6] Military outlays for 1949–1950 amounted to $100 million, a sixfold increase over expenditures prior to the Palestine war. Arms procurement efforts abroad, particularly in Western Europe, were accelerated and were particularly successful in Britain, where they resulted in agreements for the purchase of Vampire and Gloster-Meteor jet fighters, Centurion tanks, and frigates. The actual strengthening of the army proceeded extremely slowly, however, since the Anglo-Egyptian disputes eventually delayed the transfer of most of this equipment until 1955.

The Egyptian government also approached Washington with requests for military hardware. In February 1949, Abdul-Hadi had called for Marshall Plan-type aid such as that then being granted to Turkey and Greece.[7] This was the period of intensive Zionist pressure that preceded the formulation of the Tripartite Declaration, and Cairo's approaches did not find receptive ears. Moreover, the United States continued to consider Egypt as pretty much within Britain's preserve. As was mentioned earlier, a further unsuccessful bid was made by the Egyptian Foreign Minister while he was in Washington in the fall of 1950, after Britain had suspended the delivery of tanks and air-craft on September 12. Sounding a note that would be often repeated to Egyptians and other Middle Easterners in the future, Assistant Secretary of State McGhee told Salaheddin that the question of arms would be determined in the light of two crucial issues to which Cairo had not yet given an acceptable response: a pro-Western orientation in the Cold War, and progress in regional defense.[8]

The need to obtain U.S. arms did not assume an urgent character for Cairo until Britain froze all outstanding arms purchase agreements in October 1951, marking the beginning of a three-year span during which Egypt was to acquire no heavy weapons from the West aside from four aircraft in 1953. In February 1952, Egypt again approached the United States, this time pri-marily in search of arms suitable for riot control and other internal security purposes. Bloody clashes between the British army and Egyptian police in the

6. *New York Times*, June 27 and July 4, 1949; and *Akhbar El-Yom* (Cairo), April 14, 1951.

7. *New York Times*, February 20, 1949.   8. *Al-Ahram*, October 22, 1950.

Canal zone had led to ugly demonstrations in Cairo that culminated in the burning and looting of most of the downtown district by gangs of political extremists and common criminals on Saturday, January 26th. "Black Saturday," the fruit of a combination of pent-up frustrations and grievances engendered by the continued British occupation, the ineffectual, corrupt, and irresponsible national leadership, and a host of unattended social ills, marked the beginning of the end for the monarchy and the existing political system.[9] It also disquieted the U.S. government, which feared that rampant instability might lead to a Communist-inspired revolution and a recrudescence of Anglo-Egyptian problems, both highly unwelcome prospects.[10] A cash-reimbursable military sales agreement was concluded between the two countries, under which Egypt undertook to honor the conditions imposed by the Mutual Security Act on all recipients of U.S. arms aid.[11] Contracts were drawn up for the purchase of $5 million worth of armored cars, two-pound guns, bazookas, armor-piercing ammunition, sidearms, gas masks, and other equipment useful for internal security enforcement.[12] But these arms were also suitable for paramilitary warfare against the British soldiers and installations in the Canal zone. Whether due to British pressure or to the lack of sufficient time, this equipment was still undelivered when Lt. Colonel Gamal Abdel Nasser's Free Officers, under the nominal leadership of General Mohamed Nagib, took over power on July 23, 1952.

The Americans welcomed the new developments in Cairo. The coup came as no surprise to Washington, which had been aware of the existence of an underground anti-Faruq conspiracy in the army.[13] Contact had been made

9. For good descriptions of the domestic situation in the last few months of Faruq's regime, see Jacques Berque, *Egypt: Imperialism and Revolution* (London: Faber & Faber, 1972); and Anouar Abdul Malek, *Egypt: Military Society* (New York: Random House, 1968).

10. For an overdrawn but essentially accurate description of State Department thinking during this period, see Miles Copeland, *The Game of Nations* (New York: Simon and Schuster, 1969), chap. 3.

11. *New York Times*, February 29, 1952; testimony by former U.S. Assistant Secretary of State for the Near East, Henry Byroade, in U.S. Congress, Senate, Committee on Foreign Relations and Committee on Armed Services, *The President's Proposal on the Middle East, Hearings*, 85th Congress, 1st Session, 1957, p. 757.

12. Mohamed Hassanein Heikal, *The Cairo Documents* (Garden City, N.Y.: Doubleday, 1973), pp. 36 and 40; Parker Hart interview; and August 30, 1973, interview with General Abdelhamid Ghaleb, who was then military attaché at the Egyptian Embassy in Washington and who became deputy foreign minister in the Nasserist era.

13. Except where otherwise noted, the factual material in the remainder of this chapter is based on extensive conversations with American and Egyptian individuals

with the Free Officers in the spring of 1952, and the State Department had ascertained to its own satisfaction that the movement was not leftist in its ideological orientation or programs but solidly nationalist, was aware of the need for social change but determined to maintain law and order, and was inclined to the West internationally but bent on preserving its freedom of action. In sum, the new regime would be one of strong, no-nonsense military rule rather than of socialist revolutionaries as earlier feared, a regime that would become an important stabilizing factor in the region by virtue of its expected ability to take unpopular decisions in reaching an accommodation with Britain and a permanent peace settlement with Israel. As the experienced U.S. Ambassador in Cairo, Jefferson Caffery, put it shortly after the coup, this was a government that Washington "could do business with."[14]

Within days of its coming to power, the junta apprised Caffery of its desire to purchase modern arms and equipment for both the army and the police force.[15] The request was accompanied by public assurances given by Nagib that the arms would not be used against Israel,[16] and by a secret approach to the U.S. Embassy in September which offered broad cooperation and participation in a regional defense pact in return for military and economic aid.[17] Washington was responsive, and on November 5, William Foster, then Deputy Secretary of Defense, visited Cairo to acquaint himself with the military needs of the Egyptians. He was accompanied by the Assistant Secretary of Defense for International Security Affairs, who handled the political aspects of military aid for the Pentagon, and he met with Nagib and later with Nasser for several hours, promising the latter some $100 million in military equipment. It later transpired that Foster had exceeded his authority

---

who were participants in or had direct contact with events discussed herein. A selected list of persons interviewed appears following the Bibliography.

14. Useful sources on Egyptian-U.S. relations in the early years of the Nasser regime are: Copeland, *Game of Nations*; Harry B. Ellis, *Challenge in the Middle East* (New York: Ronald Press, 1960), chap. 3, an account by the longtime Middle East correspondent of the *Christian Science Monitor* that anteceded by a decade Copeland's "revelations"; and Heikal, *Cairo Documents*, chap. 2. These relations were underpinned by informal and unofficial but extremely important continuing contacts between key members of the military junta, including Nasser himself, and a number of Americans in Cairo, such as Copeland, Kermit Roosevelt, James Eichelberger, William Lakeland, Colonel Wilbur Eveland, and Charles Cremeans, whose affiliations and associations ran the gamut from the U.S. Embassy to the State Department, the CIA, and the Pentagon.

15. *New York Times*, August 8, 1952.   16. Ibid., August 7 and 10, 1952.

17. Dean Acheson, *Present at the Creation: My Years in the State Department* (New York: Norton, 1969), pp. 566–567.

in making this pledge, that the U.S. had a much smaller figure in mind, and that aid would be closely linked to a solution of the problem surrounding the British base at Suez. Nasser did not know this, however, and later that same month he dispatched Ali Sabri—a wing commander in the air force and the Free Officer who had first established contact with the Americans at the time of the July coup—to Washington with a detailed arms shopping list and high expectations.

Sabri's list included tanks, artillery, antitank guns, and transportation equipment sufficient to equip an armored division, as well as three squadrons of jet fighters. Together with the military attaché in Washington, Abdelhamid Ghaleb, Sabri spent the next several weeks negotiating the transaction, in the course of which several meetings were held with representatives of the Departments of State, Defense, and the Treasury, as well as with the Chairman of the Joint Chiefs of Staff, General Omar Bradley. Now the Egyptians learned that they would have to settle for considerably less than they had been led to expect. Early in January, tentative agreement was finally reached on a detailed arms deal valued at some $10 million, which, in Ghaleb's words, fulfilled the "absolute minimal requirements" of the Egyptian armed forces. Sabri cabled his success to Cairo, elated at what could only be described as a major breakthrough, as in those years the total value of weapons sold annually to all Middle Eastern countries—including Israel—averaged less than $25 million.

The Egyptians' joy was premature, however. The transaction broke down at the eleventh hour, with the United States withdrawing on the same day that the final agreement was to be signed.[18]

No one single factor was responsible for the rebuff dealt to the Sabri mission, a rebuff that left Cairo bitterly disappointed and mistrustful of American arms-aid objectives.[19] Even after extensive investigation, only a

18. Abdelhamid Ghaleb interview. For a brief published account by Ghaleb of the abrupt manner in which the arms sale was brought to a halt, see *The Scribe* (Cairo), May 1964, pp. 8–9. Heikal, in *Cairo Documents*, pp. 38–40, also describes some of the difficulties encountered by the Sabri mission in Washington. The account in Copeland, *Game of Nations*, pp. 171–173, confuses Dulles's promises of aid during his visit in May 1953 with William Foster's in November 1952 and errs chronologically in placing the Sabri mission after the Dulles visit.

19. "You will regret this decision beyond your imagination," Ghaleb says he told Wells Stabler, the official in charge of the Egyptian desk at the State Department, when Ghaleb was informed of the indefinite postponement of the arms sale. "We shall consider this a change of policy. It will be a terrible shock for our Government, to whom we have already reported that we had reached a final agreement" (Ghaleb interview).

mixed and rather confused picture emerges of the reasons for the failure of the negotiations. Some difficulties that were also encountered in subsequent American-Egyptian talks on arms arose from restrictive U.S. legislation. By Nasser's own account, the United States insisted on (1) sending a Military Assistance Advisory Group (MAAG) to Egypt as part of an arms grant package, and (2) Egyptian acceptance of conditions for the use of weapons as outlined in the Mutual Security Act. Egypt's refusal of these terms precluded the granting of aid, and an outright purchase deal was substituted. Even a straight commercial sale agreement required undertakings that the equipment supplied would not be used for aggressive purposes or be transferred to third parties. Egypt had already agreed to the required undertaking under Faruq in February 1952, and the new regime confirmed this in late 1952 as well.

Political strings, equally unacceptable to Egypt, were another significant factor. They included, in addition to reaching a compromise with the British over Suez (which will be treated below), the related issue of defense co-operation arrangements with the West. Egyptian participation in a regional defense pact in exchange for withdrawal from Suez was to be an important British objective in the Canal base negotiations, and Washington was supportive of this with its arms supply leverage. Eventually, such a quid pro quo was dropped, following Secretary Dulles's visit to the region in May 1953, but only temporarily. In the Secretary's estimation, "obtaining political advantage" was a major justification for the granting of military equipment or its sale, as he confided in a memorandum written upon his return from the Middle East.[20]

Finally, but no less importantly, there were problems arising from the impact that the new influx of arms would have on the local military balance and Egypt's own armed potential. Israel and her American sympathizers began exerting the usual pressures as soon as the possibility of an arms sale being concluded became publicly known. These protests were coordinated with appeals to influence London not to supply jet fighters to the Arabs as was then being proposed,[21] in a manner reminiscent of the identical campaign waged in 1950.[22] Ironically, while they themselves were willing to give Cairo

---

20. Quoted in Kennett Love, *Suez: The Twice-Fought War* (New York: McGraw-Hill, 1969), p. 275.

21. See Chapter 5.

22. The Israeli government was reported on January 1, 1953 to have demanded from Washington that no arms be sold to the Arab states. Israeli ambassador Abba Eban conferred with Secretary Acheson on January 5 and February 13 on this subject. The American Zionist Council also wrote to the State Department. See *New York Times*, January 1, 6, February 14, 1953.

a few Gloster-Meteors, the British were dead set against the U.S. transaction. Any strengthening of the Egyptians, particularly if small arms were involved, would decrease British leverage in the negotiations with the Revolutionary Command Council (RCC) over the future status of Suez.[23] Even more than the military aspect, the British feared the political effect that the sale of U.S. arms on the scale proposed would have, for it would signal to Nasser that the Western powers were not united on the need to maintain direct control of the strategic Suez position.

In fact, the British attitude was probably the weightiest factor that tipped the scales against arms aid to Egypt in early 1953. The Suez negotiations about to begin opened up vital questions regarding the future of Britain's presence in Egypt and hence her position in the whole Middle East, regional defense in the face of the "Communist menace" from the north, and the Anglo-American division of responsibilities in the area, much in the same fashion that the British withdrawal from Greece and Turkey in 1947 had done with respect to Southeast Europe and the Mediterranean.

This political context, which operationally coalesced largely around the issue of regional security arrangements deserves further analysis, for the question of arms supplies to Nasser's Egypt—both at the time of the Sabri mission and later on—was to become unavoidably entangled in its web.

Middle Eastern Defense

Under the faltering but tenacious leadership of Winston Churchill in the twilight years of his political life, the British government in 1952–1953 remained determined to keep some form of direct control over Suez, preferably through continued unilateral military occupation, or if that proved unfeasible, by association with Egypt in a regional defense arrangement. This posture was dictated more by a semiautomatic impulse to retain long-held imperial strongpoints than by any thoughtful reappraisal of the actual strategic importance and costs of continued occupation of the Canal base. For Churchill, Suez had become a symbol, "the test of Britain's survival as a Great Power," as he told the Commonwealth Prime Ministers in June 1953.[24]

In the end, the harsh facts of life prevailed over outdated imperial ambitions.

23. In a Commons debate over the issue, Minister of State Selwyn Lloyd assured the House that the sale of the jet fighters to Egypt was "quite different from the sale of something like a machine gun which can be conveniently used behind a hedge or from a window in a house. In my submission this weapon does not involve any real threat to our Forces" (*Parliamentary Debates*, February 17, 1953, col. 1082).

24. Jon Kimche, *The Second Arab Awakening* (London: Thames and Hudson, 1970), p. 85.

The Empire had been almost completely liquidated; Britain's financial resources were severely strained; Egypt and the oil-rich Arabian peninsula were no longer in danger of falling to conquest by other European powers (the traditional fear that had motivated British occupation); and the atom had changed the very nature of large-scale war. Henceforth, regional economic and other interests could be better protected by a policy of adjustment to local nationalist aspirations than by one that exacerbated already strong anti-British feelings. Had a reassessment along these lines taken place in 1952 rather than two years later, when the realities of strategy in the nuclear age belatedly dawned on Prime Minister Churchill—an inspiration undoubtedly induced in large measure by Egypt's aggressive resistance to continued British occupation—convincing him of the strategic obsolescence of the Suez base and opening the way to the Agreement of July 1954, the future course of events in the entire region could have been substantially different. [25]

As it was, beginning in the summer of 1951, beset by economic problems and hoping that a strong show of Western solidarity and cooperation would strengthen her hand against Egyptian demands, Britain sought an American ratification of her Suez policy. The first attempt to solve the issue on other than a bilateral basis with Cairo came shortly thereafter, while the Laborites were still in office. At London's initiative, Anglo-American talks were held in Washington during the first week of September to plan a joint Western–Middle Eastern military structure for the defense of the Middle East against Soviet aggression, to be headquartered in the Suez Canal zone. This Middle East Command proposal would be sponsored by the United Kingdom, the United States, France, and Turkey; Egypt would be offered membership on an equal basis with its founders, on condition that she place the Canal base under the authority of the Command and contribute military forces to it. In return, she would be granted military aid, and the Anglo-Egyptian alliance of 1936 would be terminated. Whatever the merits of the proposal from the standpoint of regional security, for Foreign Secretary Morrison—who had replaced the ailing Ernest Bevin in March—the main attraction of the project, as he frankly put it, was that "Britain would remain in Egypt without incurring any charge of British 'occupation.'" [26]

---

25. The change in British thinking is reflected in Royal Institute of International Affairs, *British Interests in the Mediterranean and Middle East*, a Report by a Chatham House Study Group (London: Oxford University Press, 1958) especially pp. 12–13.

26. For the text of the proposal, see the *Department of State Bulletin*, October 22, 1951, p. 647; also see ibid., November 19, 1951, pp. 817–818, for an explanatory statement of principles by the four sponsoring powers. The Middle East Command

The Command proposal was presented to Egypt on October 13, without any prior consultation with Cairo on its contents. Practically any Egyptian government would have found extreme difficulty in accepting the Western proposal as presented. The Wafdist cabinet of Prime Minister Mustapha An-Nahas, characterized by irresponsibility and widespread corruption in the management of domestic affairs, had fallen back on a stridently nationalist foreign policy committed to securing unconditional British withdrawal as its only claim to popular support. The project was rejected outright, on the justifiable grounds that it was a transparent attempt to maintain foreign occupation under a different flag. Two days later, Nahas carried out his threatened abrogation of the 1936 Treaty, which formed the legal basis for the British presence. London responded immediately by clamping down a total embargo on arms supplies, in anticipation of armed clashes between the Canal garrison and Egyptian forces.[27]

With the Command idea stillborn, the new British Prime Minister, Churchill, soon hit on another idea for propping up Britain's position in Suez. While visiting the United States in January 1952, he suggested to the Americans that some U.S. forces be stationed in the Canal zone. The idea met with a frigid reception in all quarters. More than a year later, in March 1953, still seeking American backing, the British asked for formal U.S. participation in the Anglo-Egyptian negotiations with the RCC. Throughout, London was insistent that no arms aid or sales be provided to Cairo.

Yet, American officials were not uninterested in helping out their British allies. To the contrary, United States policy in the early 1950s called for maintenance of British military preeminence in the Middle East, together with work toward some regional grouping for defense against the perceived threat of Soviet expansion or internal Communist subversion. Cold War considerations were uppermost in the minds of American policymakers, however, and support for London's position would be predicated on its concordance with the requirements of regional security as perceived by Washington. As Secretary Acheson explained to Defense Secretary Marshall

---

idea and British policy toward Egypt in general are amply discussed in many published works. Particularly useful are: Acheson, *Present at the Creation*, chap. 58; John C. Campbell, *Defense of the Middle East* (New York: Praeger, 1960), chap. 4; M. A. Fitzsimons, *Empire by Treaty* (Notre Dame, Indiana: University of Notre Dame Press, 1964), pp. 98–116; and Anthony Eden, *Memoirs: Full Circle* (London: Cassell, 1960), chap. 10.

27. On this aspect, see Chapter 5.

in January 1951 in a letter requesting a Pentagon review of Middle East policy:

Our idea was that the primary responsibility of the British and the Commonwealth to supply armed forces for the defense of the area and the considerable assistance that we were furnishing to individual countries there could be made more effective if all this could be coordinated under a plan for the defense of the area as a whole. The general plan upon which we wanted the Pentagon's help was, after making our purpose clear to all the countries involved, to make available to the Arab states and Israel small military training missions, an increased number of places for their officers in U.S. military schools, and token amounts of arms and ammunition for training purposes.[28]

In essence, this was the thinking that produced the Middle East Command project, which fitted both American specifications and British needs. It soon became apparent, however, that the two American objectives were mutually exclusive. Protection of Britain's hegemony entailed support for London's efforts to maintain military control of Suez, but this would inevitably forfeit Egyptian cooperation, for Cairo had repeatedly made clear that its demand for complete evacuation of Egyptian territory was non-negotiable.

By the end of 1951, the State Department had become aware of these inconsistencies. The quick failure of the Command idea surely was enlightening in this respect. Moreover, reluctance to appear ranged on the side of an already waning colonialism and disappointment with the British postwar diplomatic record in the Middle East, plus the alternative provided by the increasing projection of U.S. local military power in the form of the Sixth Fleet, inspired a gradual disengagement from active support for British policies. With particular reference to Suez, Acheson now frankly confided to Churchill that sending U.S. troops to the Canal would not do, for "Anglo-American solidarity on a policy of sitting tight offered no solution, but was like a couple locked in warm embrace in a rowboat about to go over Niagara Falls. It was high time to break the embrace and take to the oars."[29] While Washington would continue to work in support of the Middle East Command concept, the British were told that their troops and facilities at Suez could not come within its compass "until Egypt accepts the MEC proposals," and that a "reasonable amount of Egyptian cooperation [was] necessary to gain that objective."[30]

28. Acheson, *Present at the Creation*, p. 562.   29. Ibid., p. 600.

30. Steering Group on Preparations for Talks Between the President and P.M. Churchill, Negotiating Papers on "Middle East Command" and "Egypt," January 3 and 4, 1952. PSF, Subject File, Truman Papers, Truman Library.

Thus, when Nagib and Nasser sounded out the United States on military and economic aid in the fall of 1952, they encountered a positive response, after which William Foster visited Cairo. In January 1953, with the Sabri mission already in Washington with its shopping list, the State Department recommended to President-elect Eisenhower that economic aid to Egypt be started immediately, and military assistance was also urged. The Joint Chiefs were asked to prepare a specific program of military aid.[31]

The new Republican administration came in strongly committed to regional defense as a means of warding off the Soviet threat. President Eisenhower observed that "[y]ears of frustration in their attempts to reason with the increasingly powerful and ruthless Soviet government had led free nations to begin looking anxiously to their own capacity for self-defense. Obviously, free nations . . . would each, standing alone, be in mortal danger. . . . The answer to Communist ambitions had to be in some form of collective defense."[32] Secretary of State Dulles was no less enthusiastic about this general strategy; he too, "from the first days of assuming office . . . was certain the Soviet Union had begun a covert effort to turn that vast area [of the Middle East] into a Communist sphere of influence, and that the United States was the only nation capable of preventing it."[33] Within weeks of assuming office, Dulles told a news conference that the administration was considering the formation of a Middle East Defense Organization along principles similar to those proposed to Egypt in 1951.[34] Accordingly, aid was made contingent on a Suez settlement—to oblige the British—and on Egyptian participation in the proposed MEDO. The Cairo junta had privately offered to seriously consider the latter in return for U.S. aid, although with the proviso that such consideration would only follow British withdrawal.

By tying aid for Egypt to a Suez settlement, however, Washington temporarily reversed the trend of disengagement for British policies set in the second half of 1952 by the outgoing Truman Administration. The movement toward a more neutral posture was only resumed after Dulles's subsequent visit to Cairo in May convinced him of the depth of anti-British emotions there and of the need to dissociate the United States from "British colonial and

31. Acheson, *Present at the Creation*, p. 567.
32. Dwight D. Eisenhower, *The White House Years: Mandate for Change, 1953–1956* (New York: Doubleday, 1963), pp. 137–138; see also Copeland, *Game of Nations*, p. 133.
33. Louis L. Gerson, *John Foster Dulles*, The American Secretaries of State and their Diplomacy series (New York: Cooper Square, 1967), p. 241.
34. *Department of State Bulletin*, March 16, 1953, p. 403.

imperalistic policies." [35] In March 1953, a "package deal" was worked out by Dulles and Foreign Secretary Eden, in close consultation with President Eisenhower. It included (1) withdrawal of British troops from Egypt on the understanding that the Canal base would be kept in readiness under British supervision for reactivation in case of war, (2) Egyptian participation in a MEDO, and (3) a program of military and economic assistance to Egypt. [36] The deal was to be offered jointly by Britain and the United States, and the latter was to join the Anglo-Egyptian negotiations as a full-fledged participant.

While lining up the Americans on their side was the main desideratum for the British, Eisenhower was moved by the desire "that the discussion of the canal would include the broader problem of the defense of the entire Middle East," as he told Nagib in correspondence. [37] But American participation in the discussions was made contingent on Egypt's acquiescence, as in Eisenhower's view there was no other basis for it. Eden candidly argued that "there was a direct relationship between the arming of the Egyptians and defense arrangements in the Middle East." [38] Since Egypt was shopping for arms in Washington, the United States was entitled to something in return. At the urgent behest of the State Department, the President maintained his position both to protect the "special relationship" that had developed between the U.S. and the new military regime in Cairo, and to preserve the credibility of the American mediating position, on which Ambassador Caffery was heavily relying as the only means to bring about a Suez settlement without provoking a catastrophic Anglo-Egyptian showdown. When Egypt predictably refused to invite the United States in, the projected tripartite talks fell through. And so did the laboriously constructed "package deal."

A third victim was the arms deal that the Egyptians were seeking in Washington. Frustrated in her attempt to draw the United States into the Suez talks on her side, Britain endeavored to prevent the further strengthening of the RCC. During his March visit, Eden had already "made strong representations to Mr. Dulles," which he later repeated to the American ambassador in London, against the imminent conclusion of the arms agreement, [39] on whose progress the British were presumably keeping tab through the NEACC. A Foreign Office memorandum with a similar request was transmitted to the State Department, and Churchill communicated directly with

---

35. Dulles's private memorandum on his trip, quoted by Louis L. Gerson, *John Foster Dulles* (New York: Cooper Square, 1967), p. 253.
36. Eden, *Memoirs*, p. 251.   37. Eisenhower, *Mandate for Change*, p. 150.
38. Eden, *Memoirs*, p. 250.   39. Ibid., pp. 253–254.

Eisenhower, urging him to withhold all forms of support from Cairo.[40] As we have seen, the deal was eventually stopped at the last minute, and in a manner highly injurious to Egyptian sensibilities. During his talks in Cairo, Dulles warned Nasser that no arms would be sent before the Suez problem was solved.[41] On June 10, Eisenhower wrote to Churchill that "the United States would continue to defer arms aid to Egypt pending a final settlement between Nagib and the British."[42] But a solid promise was extended to Egypt. In mid-July, President Eisenhower assured Premier Nagib in an exchange of letters that "firm commitments" of economic assistance and of military aid for "strengthening your armed forces to discharge their increased responsibilities" would be extended to Egypt "simultaneously" with the conclusion of an amicable settlement over Suez.[43]

Assessment

In dealing with this first attempt by Nasser to obtain arms from the United States, there appears to have been on the American side a discontinuity of policy, as well as a disregard for Egyptian feelings, that frustrated the objective of improving American-Egyptian relations which had prompted the arms negotiations in the first place. Perhaps more importantly in the long run, this failure considerably dampened Egyptian confidence in the United States as a reliable source of military hardware by conveying to the new regime a very negative impression of the political conditions under which U.S. arms would become available.[44] For Western policymakers, deriving what Dulles called "political advantage" from all arms aid was a pursuit whose legitimacy was practically taken for granted. To a revolutionary nationalist regime whose

40. Eisenhower, *Mandate for Change*, p. 153; and Heikal, *Cairo Documents*, pp. 39–40. Heikal singles out British objections as the main reason for the U.S. refusal to grant the Egyptian request. He says, however, that, according to Dulles, President Eisenhower was mistakenly shown the shopping list submitted in February 1952 under Faruq, which consisted mainly of light weapons, and this accounted for the refusal. While bureaucratic bungling provided a handy excuse for the Secretary to mollify his Egyptian hosts, it is far from persuasive. On British pressures, see also Anthony Nutting, *Nasser* (New York: Dutton, 1972), p. 49. Nutting at the time was Parliamentary Undersecretary of State for Foreign Affairs in Churchill's government.

41. Eisenhower, *Mandate for Change*, p. 158.   42. Ibid., p. 157.

43. *New York Times*, July 31, 1954.

44. "We asked for arms [from the West], but what was the result?" asked Nasser in the speech announcing the arms deal with Czechoslovakia in September 1955. "The result . . . makes a long and bitter story. . . . We humiliated ourselves when we asked for arms, when we begged for arms. . . ." The full text is in Muhammad Khalil, *The Arab States and the Arab League: A Documentary Record*, Vol. 2: *International Affairs* (Beirut: Khayats, 1962), pp. 903–907.

main appeal was its promise of securing full independence from external intrusion, however, Washington's attitude appeared designed to abort these purposes by maintaining a tight Western hold on Egypt's foreign policy. Furthermore, Washington's attitude suggested that in the arms transfer field, the United States would maintain the common front established under the Tripartite Declaration with the British and French colonial powers. To that extent, the experience of the Sabri mission predisposed Nasser to consider alternative sources of armaments in the Soviet bloc, a predisposition that was reinforced by the strikingly similar manner in which his second bid for U.S. military aid, in 1955, was treated by Washington.

The inconstancy of U.S. policy toward Egypt at this early stage may be partly laid to the inevitable disruptions contingent upon any changeover of administrations, magnified in 1953 by the vigor with which the incoming Republicans had denounced the foreign policies of the Truman era across the board, and their determination to introduce a "new look" into all aspects of the country's foreign affairs. On the other hand, the inconstancy exemplified an erratic or, at best, ambiguous pattern of behavior that would characterize Dulles's dealings with the Middle East in general, and Nasser in particular, throughout his tenure.[45] Eisenhower's willingness to accommodate the British —always greater than Truman's—also played a role. Prime Minister Churchill had visited the President-elect at the end of December 1952 and impressed upon him the need to "coordinate our views and decisions . . . and act jointly in the affairs of the family of nations."[46] Both Eisenhower and Dulles were receptive in their first months in office to London's appeals for the withholding of arms and to the view that an agreement on regional security prior to Britain's withdrawal from Egypt was essential to the Western position in the Middle East.[47]

This was in contradistinction to the view shared by U.S. officials in the field and area specialists in the State Department and other Washington agencies that priority be given to gaining the confidence and future cooperation of the new Egyptian regime by supplying the arms that the United States had already agreed to provide.[48] If the overall American purpose toward Cairo at

45. Senator Fulbright attested to this in 1957; see Love, *Twice-Fought War*, p. 279. For Dean Acheson's comments on what he called "the ambivalence of American policy in regard to Egypt" during this period, see his testimony in U.S. Congress, House of Representatives, Committee on Foreign Affairs, *Economic and Military Cooperation with Nations in the General Area of the Middle East, Hearings*, 85th Congress, 1st session, January 1957, pp. 166–167.

46. Eisenhower, *Mandate for Change*, p. 157.   47. Eden, *Memoirs*, p. 249.

48. For Ambassador Caffery, "the job which he considered to be the important one

this stage was indeed "to hasten the day when Egypt would be prepared to cooperate voluntarily in Western defense,"[49] the renewed emphasis on MEDO while the British were still at the Canal and postponement of the arms transaction were singularly self-defeating measures. Dulles would realize this during his May sojourn in Cairo. The RCC had been willing to give serious consideration to the idea of a Middle East defense pact during its first months in power; and as late as December 1952, Premier Nagib could say that Egypt would be ready to join in area defense arrangements with the West, "provided our aspirations are met first."[50] Even in October 1954, after the final Suez agreement had been concluded, an RCC communiqué offered a "closer association with the Western Powers" following a "period of complete independence during which mutual confidence would be established."[51] With the passage of time, Nasser's growing perception that active leadership of an independent Arab bloc was the optimal role Egypt could play in the area, as well as the constraints imposed on American flexibility by the domestic and international imperatives of the Arab-Israeli conflict, rendered Egyptian participation in Western-sponsored pacts less and less of a realistic possibility. There is little doubt, however, that the withholding of arms from Cairo in 1953 did much to determine the new regime's attitude toward these issues as well as its general political orientation.

PROMISES TO KEEP: NASSER'S SECOND BID

The visit by the Secretary of State to Cairo in May 1953 had as one tangible result the realization by Dulles that the menace of Communism was far down on the list of Egyptian concerns, while getting rid of the British was uppermost; and that, consequently, a western-Arab defense organization was not feasible for the time being. Addressing the nation upon his return, he called MEDO "a future rather than an immediate possibility."[52] Dulles

[was] getting a military agreement between the Egyptians and the Americans that would provide our Government with the basis for giving Nasser the arms he needed . . ." (Copeland, *Game of Nations*, p. 137).

49. Campbell, *Defense of the Middle East*, p. 66.

50. Interview with C. L. Sulzberger, *New York Times*, December 11, 1952. Nagib went on to declare: "There are only three possible courses for a free Egypt: to remain neutral—and this is at the very least extremely difficult, if not impossible; to join the Eastern bloc, which is out of the question as we are not Communist; or to join the West. It is our natural inclination to work with the West whose people we know."

51. Quoted in a useful article by G[eorge] E. K[irk], "The Turco-Egyptian Flirtation of Autumn 1954," *The World Today* (London), November 1956, pp. 447–457.

52. The full text of Dulles's report on his trip is in *Department of State Bulletin*, June 15, 1953, pp. 831–835.

found a better disposition to cooperate in regional defense among the "northern tier" of Middle Eastern countries—including one Arab state, Iraq —that were closest to the Soviet Union geographically, and to these he directed his principal attention.

Nonetheless, he did not give up on Egypt, except temporarily. His conversations with Nasser led him to believe that active support for Egypt over Suez would bring the junta around to support for the MEDO concept.[53] Also, for the first time, Dulles had a firsthand look at the extensive damage to U.S. prestige and influence that American postwar policies of support for Britain and for the Zionist cause in Palestine had wrought in the Arab world. "The United States position . . . is not good," he privately concluded, "and the loss of respect for the United States varies almost directly with the nearness of the respective Arab states to Israel. The Israeli factor, and the association of the United States in the minds of the people of the area with French and British colonial and imperialist policies, are millstones around our neck."[54]

Following Dulles's return to Washington, solutions were sought in a more evenhanded position on the Arab-Israeli conflict, postponement of joint defense schemes, and extension of economic as well as military assistance to revive American influence. At least the *intention* to do these things existed by the end of the Dulles journey. The matter of aid had been discussed by Nasser and the Secretary in Cairo, and the latter had further fuelled Egyptian hopes of large-scale assistance from the United States. The positive attitude shown by the previous administration in its last few months seemed now to be reinforced by the commitment of the new American government. Shortly thereafter came President Eisenhower's pledge to enter into "firm commitments" of economic and military aid upon conclusion of a Suez agreement. The magnitude of the assistance became a matter of contention at a certain stage, with the Egyptians protesting that they had been promised amounts several times larger than the economic or military assistance that Washington was willing actually to provide. But that a solid understanding on the principle of U.S. aid as a quid pro quo for an evacuation agreement existed was not doubted by those officials in the State Department and the CIA who were directly engaged in the conduct of U.S.-Egyptian relations.[55]

One year later, in July 1954, Britain and Egypt initialled an agreement on

53. Heikal, *Cairo Documents*, p. 41; and Richard P. Stebbins et al., *The United States in World Affairs, 1954* (New York: Harper, 1956), p. 341.

54. Dulles's memorandum, quoted by Love, *Twice-Fought War*, p. 275.

55. Interviews with Kermit Roosevelt and with Peter Chase, who was the political officer of the U.S. Embassy in Cairo at the time.

the Canal base, and the final settlement was concluded in October. All British forces would be withdrawn within twenty months, but Britain maintained the right to return in case of armed attack by an "outside Power" on any Arab state or on Turkey. The compromise inclusion of Turkey established a tenuous link between Egypt and NATO. American behind-the-scenes participation in the negotiations had been of crucial importance. In the judgment of many observers, it is likely that no agreement at all would have been obtained without Ambassador Caffery's repeated interventions.

But the U.S. role, and the "special relationship" between Cairo and Washington on which it rested, had been made possible primarily by promises of aid. The solution of the Suez problem thus set the stage for another test of American intentions.

The evacuation agreement presented the RCC with urgent problems of military preparedness that made the quest for arms abroad a matter that henceforth could brook no deferring. The long-standing British buffer in the Canal zone was being quickly dismantled, and Egypt now faced Israel alone. The military inferiority of the Egyptian army became a source of intense concern, particularly after a series of incidents that began in mid-1954 and culminated in February 1955 with the major Israeli raid on the Gaza Strip. In July and August 1954 came the capture and trial of an Israeli intelligence ring that had engaged in a series of sabotage attempts directed at British and American installations in Cairo and Alexandria with the purpose of disrupting the impending Suez agreement and what Tel Aviv saw as an ominous rapprochement between Egypt and the West.[56] At about the same time, the Israeli government publicly acknowledged its policy of border reprisals carried out by its regular armed forces. The previous October, the Israelis had launched a border raid on the Jordanian village of Qibya, initiating a policy of large-scale and disproportionate across-the-border retaliation for frontier incidents that greatly increased the tension on all armistice lines.[57] In

56. This adventure triggered the well-known and recurrent "Lavon" affair in Israel. Pinhas Lavon was Defense Minister at the time, and was held accountable for the miscarriage of the sabotage operation in Egypt. This had been arranged behind his back, however, by David Ben-Gurion's "activist" protégés in the Ministry, notably the Director-General, Shimon Peres, and the Chief of Staff of the Army, General Moshe Dayan. Ben-Gurion replaced Lavon in February 1955.

57. For an authoritative, officially inspired description of this policy, see Moshe Brilliant, "Israel's Policy of Reprisals," Harper's, March 1955, pp. 68–72. Useful analyses are in Love, Twice-Fought War, pp. 53–63; in Edward Luttwak and Dan Horowitz, The Israeli Army (New York: Harper & Row, 1975), pp. 105–112; and in a book by the commander of the U.N. truce supervision organization at the time, Lt.-General E. L. M. Burns, Between Arab and Israeli (London: Harrap, 1962), chap. 5.

late September, on the eve of the final signing of the Suez agreement, Israel sent the *Bat Galim*, a ship of Israeli registry, up the Gulf of Suez to test Cairo's determination to uphold the blockage of Israeli shipping through the Canal after Britain's withdrawal. The ship and its cargo were confiscated by the Egyptians and the crew imprisoned.

This multifaceted outburst of Israeli militancy was prompted mainly by the increasing feeling of political isolation that had been engendered by the Dulles policy of "evenhandedness" on the Palestine problem and his courting of the Arabs for purposes of securing their support for Western defense plans. The American decision in April 1954 to give military assistance to Iraq complemented the noticeably close relations with Cairo since the Free Officers' coup. Now, the Suez agreement removed the major remaining irritant in Egyptian-Western relations. U.S. arms and economic aid would become available to the RCC, which might eventually endanger Israel's military superiority. The situation, in Abba Eban's words, "gave the Israeli public the impression that American friendship for Israel had been a fleeting and accidental circumstance of history, linked organically with the Truman administration. . . . Therefore a greater policy of militance should develop in Israel for two reasons: both as a compensation for American friendship and, perhaps, as a way of forcing the U.S. to recoil from any change adverse to Israel. . . . The response in Israel was one toward greater self-reliance, a very active policy of retaliation on the frontiers."[58]

The most fateful border raid to develop from this policy came on the night of February 28, 1955, when Israeli paratroopers attacked an Egyptian army camp in Gaza, in an operation that left thirty-six Egyptian soldiers killed and twenty-nine wounded, and shattered the relative calm on the Israeli-Egyptian border that had lasted since the 1949 armistice.[59] The raid destroyed Nasser's consistent attempt since the revolution to isolate Egypt from the Arab-Israeli dispute as much as domestic opinion allowed him to, and exposed for all to see the comparative weakness of his army.

Military impotence in the face of external challenges was bad enough, but it also posed domestic dangers. Internally, the critical relationship of dependence between the Cairo regime and the armed forces made the need for

58. Interviewed by Love, *Twice-Fought War*, p. 63.
59. The Israelis lost eight men, and nine were wounded. For descriptions of the raid, its political context, and its impact on Nasser's attitude toward Israel, see Love, *Twice-Fought War*, pp. 5–20; Burns, *Between Arab and Israeli*, pp. 17–21; and Avi Shlaim, "The Gaza Raid, 1955," *Middle East International*, No. 82 (April 1978), pp. 25–28.

military modernization and strengthening no less compelling. As Nasser himself repeatedly pointed out, the lack of equipment and the low morale in the army had been at the roots of the Free Officers' coup. Moreover, after two years of rule and consolidation, the regime had not yet been able to develop an alternative power base, and remained totally dependent on the support of the armed forces for its political survival. To make things worse, the Nasser-Nagib struggle for power in the first half of 1954 had produced serious rifts in some sectors of the military.[60] The British arms embargo had resulted in a steady deterioration of the Egyptian arsenal through obsolescence and attrition.[61] General Hassan Al-Badri, a military advisor to Nasser in later years, disagrees with the commonly held notion that until February 1955 the junta concentrated on internal reform and only decided after the Gaza raid that they had no recourse but to strengthen the army. The intention to develop a strong army was there from the first day, but the problem was the lack of suppliers. Nasser had been able to keep the officers in check with promises, but, after Gaza, promises would no longer do. "What Gaza did was to convert the question of armaments into a life-or-death issue for Nasser and his team as the leadership of the government."[62]

On the inter-Arab plane as well, Egyptian policy came to require increased military strength. Iraq, the longtime rival for Arab leadership, was to receive substantial military aid from the United States under the April 1954 agreement, and, in the second half of that year, she was clearly moving toward joint defense arrangements with the West. This not only threatened Cairo's inter-Arab primacy established since the mid-1940s through the medium of the Arab League; it would also break Arab solidarity in the face of Western blandishments. Nasser, who relied on a common Arab front under Egyptian stewardship as his main bargaining counter with Britain and the United

60. See Robert Stephens, *Nasser: A Political Biography* (New York: Simon and Schuster, 1971), chap. 5.

61. According to Major Salah Salem, a leading member of the RCC and the Minister of National Guidance in 1954–1955, at the time of the Gaza raid "Egypt had six serviceable planes; about thirty others were grounded for lack of spare parts; Britain had stopped deliveries. We estimated that our tank ammunition would last for a one-hour battle. Nearly sixty percent of our tanks were in need of major repairs. Our artillery was in the same deplorable state. We were even short of small arms" (Interview with Patrick Seale, in *The Struggle for Syria* [London: Oxford University Press, 1965], p. 235).

62. Al-Badri interview, August 7, 1973. Khalid Muhhieddin, one of the dozen RCC members who formed the core of the 1952 revolutionary junta, similarly asserted to this author that military strength was "a major concern of the new leadership from the moment it came to power . . . and a key issue in the Revolution's dealings with the West" (Interview, August 10, 1973).

States on the crucial issue of regional defense, was constrained to launch a new foreign policy of stronger identification with pan-Arab causes, necessary for legitimizing Egypt's claims to bloc leadership. This entailed a more militant rhetorical stance in regard to the retrieval of Palestinian rights, a more rigid and uncooperative public attitude toward Western defense initiatives, and an increased emphasis on the Arab nature of Egypt and the need for united action.[63] The instrument for the implementation of these pan-Arab policies, Nasser insisted, should be purely indigenous, along the lines of the Arab collective security pact that had been adopted by the Arab League at Egypt's behest in 1950 but had remained a paper arrangement. For such a pact to become a credible reality vis-á-vis other powers, including Israel, as well as within the Arab World, military rearmament was a crucial prerequisite.

The envisioned sources of arms for Egypt were to be in the West.[64] Following the Suez settlement, Britain had offered to restart arms shipments; and in August 1954, the British Quartermaster-General, General Roberts, visited Cairo to negotiate the resumption of arms supplies with Foreign Minister Mahmud Fawzi and to arrange for the British withdrawal.[65] France also agreed to sell Egypt some arms during this period, including AMX-13 tanks and heavy guns. The primary source that the Egyptians looked to was the United States, however, as the time had come for Eisenhower to fulfill his part of the Suez bargain.

For a brief time, it seemed as if an arms deal would be worked out smoothly and speedily. One week after the initialling of the Canal base agreement, Ambassador Caffery met with Foreign Minister Fawzi on the matter of U.S. economic and military aid,[66] while his Egyptian counterpart, Ahmad Hussein, met with Assistant Secretary Henry Byroade in Washington for the same purpose.[67] In early September, an Egyptian military mission left on a visit to

63. A good analysis of this aspect of inter-Arab relations and the birth of Nasser's Arab policy is in Seale, *Struggle for Syria*, chaps. 16 and 17.

64. Echoing this line on a bloc-wide level, a meeting of the Arab Foreign Ministers held at the Cairo headquarters of the Arab League in December 1954 unanimously resolved: "(a) That no alliance should be concluded outside the fold of the Arab collective security pact; (b) That co-operation with the West was possible, provided a just solution was found for Arab problems and provided the Arabs were allowed to build up their strength with gifts of arms" (quoted by Seale, *Struggle for Syria*, p. 211).

65. *Al-Ahram*, August 16 and 19, 1954. The British embargo was lifted at the end of August; ibid., August 30, 1954. In September, the Egyptian Foreign Ministry announced that Spain, Belgium, and Sweden had also offered to sell arms to Egypt; ibid., September 19, 1954.

66. Ibid., August 3, 1954.

67. Ibid., August 4, 1954. Byroade supplanted Caffery as ambassador to Cairo in February 1955.

the United States; it included the Chief of Staff of the army, the Director of military training, and the Military Attaché in Washington.[68] The U.S. offer of arms amounted to some $20 million. But several problems were soon encountered, and though for a time each appeared singly capable of a compromise resolution, in combination they proved eventually insurmountable and wrecked the entire edifice of American-Egyptian friendship and cooperation.

The first obstacle arose from Military Assistance Program (MAP) legislation requiring the recipient of grant aid to accept a Military Assistance Advisory Group (MAAG), which would provide training, coordinate arms procurement, and see to it that the arms provided were not used for aggressive ends or transferred to third parties. Nasser categorically refused to go along with this requirement, telling the Americans that "he might be accused of selling his country to another big power before the British even got out of the place."[69] Nasser at the time was encountering heavy domestic opposition to the evacuation agreement, mainly from the strong Muslim Brethren organization, on the grounds that it did not get rid of the British quickly and thoroughly enough. Strong feelings against foreign military missions arose from experience under Britain's occupation, when British advisors had weakened and partly dismantled the Egyptian army.[70]

American efforts to persuade Nasser to accept a more restricted type of mission did not succeed either. Toward the end of October, two high Pentagon officials, Colonels Harrison Allan Gerhardt and Wilbur Eveland— the latter with considerable Middle East experience—were dispatched on a highly confidential assignment to Cairo. The two men met with Nasser and several other key members of the RCC secretly at night several times during the week they spent in the Egyptian capital. Part of their task was to "sell" to the RCC a "diluted" version of the standard MAAG. Not only did they offer a much smaller mission, but "they offered to Nasser even to send the mission in civilian clothes; it would accompany the arms shipments, transfer the equipment to Egyptian hands, and shortly return home permanently. Nasser refused even this diluted formula."[71]

68. Ibid., September 7, 1954. The mission met with Nasser before its departure.

69. Byroade testimony, in *President's Proposal on the Middle East, Hearings*, p. 730; and *Al-Ahram*, November 5, 1954.

70. Mahmud Y. Zayid, *Egypt's Struggle for Independence* (Beirut: Khayats, 1965), pp. 125–126. See also Nasser's Suez nationalization speech of July 26, 1956, in Khalil, *Documentary Record*, p. 750.

71. Parker Hart interview. According to Samir Souki, who was press counsellor to the Egyptian Embassy in Washington in 1953–1954 and was close to Nasser during this

The Baghdad Pact: Collision Course

The Defense Department envoys had another message to convey to the Egyptian leadership that was of far greater import. From Miles Copeland, who was present at the crucial meeting, we learn that Nasser was told in no uncertain terms that "whether it made sense [to Nasser] or not, [U.S.] military planners wanted to see a workable area defense plan, and that all military and economic aid to Middle Eastern countries would be proportionate to their respective degrees of enthusiasm for the idea." The envisaged arrangements would be restricted to the direct participation of local powers, but "the planning assumption" was that it would be directed against the Soviet Union, and it would thus be in close coordination with NATO.[72] What the Americans were talking about was what would soon become known as the Baghdad Pact.

In other words, Nasser now learned that to the aid promised him as an incentive to a Suez settlement were attached new conditions, and conditions that both sides well knew were unacceptable to Egypt.[73]

Following the Suez evacuation agreement, American policy in the Middle East was directed full-steam toward the formation of a regional defense grouping. Secretary Dulles had succeeded during the summer of 1954 in promoting SEATO in Southeast Asia, and the Manila Pact was signed in September. The Middle Eastern underbelly of the Soviet bloc remained as the only gap in the chain of containment, and Dulles now moved to fill it. "What we had in mind," NEA Assistant Secretary Byroade testified in 1957, "was a defense organization of the Middle East which would be worked out with Egypt and the other states of the area. . . . I am not talking about MEDO or MEC; but we hoped to be able, as soon as this base dispute sore with the West was healed, to be able to organize with the Arabs some kind of a defensive arrangement."[74] The planned setup was different in conception from SEATO or the 1951 Middle East Command idea in that it envisaged an exclusively local pact, at least in its early stages, without direct U.S. or

---

period, the talk on the U.S. side initially was of some 500 instructors and technicians; when this was refused, the number was de-escalated to 200, and eventually to no more than 40, who would be quartered at the U.S. Embassy as "assistant military attachés" and would not be conspicuous; Souki interview, June 27, 1973.

72. Copeland, *Game of Nations*, pp. 145–148; and Copeland and Roosevelt interviews.

73. Of course, demands that Cairo join a regional defense pact under Western tutelage had been pressed as far back as 1951, as we have seen. They were "new" only in the sense that they were now being revived by Washington, while they had not figured in the understandings that preceded the Suez settlement.

74. *President's Proposal on the Middle East, Hearings*, p. 712.

British participation.[75] Dulles thereby hoped to blunt Egypt's vociferous hostility to Western pacts, and neutralize Israel's bitter opposition to any formal defense agreements that would encompass the United States and Arab governments but inevitably exclude her.[76]

This Middle Eastern grouping would not be purely Arab, however; it would be linked to both NATO and SEATO through the joint memberships of Turkey and Pakistan, respectively. The governing conception actually was that of the "northern tier," formulated by Dulles after his 1953 Middle Eastern trip. Those countries whose proximity to the Soviet Union would make them much more aware of the Communist threat could be expected to take the initiative in combining their defensive efforts against Communism. In exchange, they would receive generous Western economic and military assistance.

The American effort began to take shape in April 1954 with the conclusion of a Turko-Pakistani agreement for friendly cooperation, which would be open to adherence by other countries whose participation was considered "useful" by the signatories. This was followed by the signing of a U.S.-Pakistani mutual defense agreement on May 19, which permitted Washington to grant aid to Karachi under the Mutual Security Program. Turkey was a long-standing recipient of Western aid, first under the Truman Doctrine and later as a member of the NATO alliance, and was already considered a formidable military power by regional standards. In facts, the United States saw Turkey as both the military mainstay of the projected link between NATO and SEATO, and the principal diplomatic "recruiter" for the new defensive system. The latter was a role that the active and strongly pro-Western Turkish Prime Minister, Adnan Menderes, played with great vigor in the following months.

In Baghdad, Nuri As-Said appeared as the most eager of Middle Eastern leaders to accept Washington's initiative, and this suited Dulles's northern-tier concept perfectly. The inclusion of Iraq in the projected alliance appears

75. Gerson, *Dulles*, pp. 258–259; and Campbell, *Defense of the Middle East*, pp. 60–61. On August 27, 1954, *Al-Ahram* reported statements to this effect by "official American sources." See also the useful article by James W. Spain, "Middle East Defense: A New Approach," *Middle East Journal* 8 (Summer 1954), 251–266, especially p. 261.

76. Two articles that describe very well Israel's position on regional defense and Western military aid to the Arabs in 1954–1955 from a Zionist viewpoint are Hal Lehrman, "American Policy and Arab-Israeli Peace," *Commentary* 17 (June 1954), 546–556; and Hal Lehrman, "Arms for Arabs—and What for Israel?" *Commentary* 18 (July 1954), 423–433.

to have been a cause of some contention in Washington at the time. For those who favored an understanding with Nasser and realized that the state of public opinion in the Arab area would not tolerate too close an association with the West, it would mean alienating Cairo and thrusting the whole project into the messy thicket of inter-Arab politics, in addition to antagonizing the Israelis. For the majority of those who had an input into the matter, however—including Secretary Dulles and, at this stage, NEA Assistant Secretary Byroade—Iraq's involvement opened up the possibility of winning over other Arab countries such as Lebanon and Jordan, and perhaps even Syria. This would provide the defensive organization with the territorial depth required for an adequate military function, and would counteract the trend toward neutralism fostered by Egypt. In mid-May 1954, a meeting of U.S. ambassadors in Istanbul discussed Moscow's growing popularity in the Arab world as a result of its increasingly anti-Israel stand at the United Nations. Byroade was reported as telling the assembled envoys that the United States was basing her entire Middle Eastern policy on the premise that the new Turko-Pakistani alliance could be broadened to include other states in the area.[77]

As a preliminary, the U.S. government approved on April 21, 1954, an Iraqi request for military assistance that had been submitted by Baghdad in March 1953. In October, Secretary Dulles sent a new ambassador to the Iraqi capital, Waldemar J. Gallman, with instructions that he do his utmost to bring Iraq into an alliance with Turkey and Pakistan. Gallman's brief was practically identical to that of the Gerhardt-Eveland mission:

> Dulles called on me in mid-1954, while I was ambassador in South Africa, because he wanted someone with broader, non-Middle Eastern experience to bring the leaders of the northern-tier countries into a defense arrangement. Dulles asked me to make it crystal-clear to Nuri that the degree of economic and military aid he could expect from the United States would be dependent on his readiness to bring Iraq into such a pact. . . .
> Iraq did get considerable amounts of military material in the 1950's. Nuri did not want to build a large, efficient military machine. What he wanted were showy pieces of equipment, of political value domestically and in inter-Arab terms. "Big guns" was the ever-present plea on Nuri's lips, repeated practically every time he and I met.[78]

77. *New York Times*, May 16 and 21, 1954.

78. Waldemar Gallman interview. See also his book, *Iraq under General Nuri* (Baltimore: Johns Hopkins University Press, 1964), especially pp. 31, 48, 51, and 63. Gerhardt and Eveland visited several other Arab capitals besides Cairo in connection with the projected regional defense system. John Robinson Beal's statement in his biographical work, *John Foster Dulles* (New York: Harper, 1957), that the Baghdad

Nuri As-Said needed no convincing. By tying Iraq to the West, he expected to reap sufficient benefits in arms aid and political support to wrest the mantle of Arab leadership from Cairo. Moreover, if he could persuade other Arab governments to follow suit—and he fully believed that he would— he then would be in a better position to further his old aims of Fertile Crescent unity. A third objective that had become particularly pressing once Britain and Egypt reached agreement on ending the British occupation of Suez in July was the renegotiation of the Anglo-Iraqi treaty of alliance of 1930; with Iraq joining a Western defense organization, Nuri expected to be able to end British control of the Habbaniyyah and Shuaibah air bases, a focus of troublesome nationalist agitation. Following a series of visits to Ankara, London, and Cairo, and despite intense Egyptian pressure, Iraq and Turkey announced on January 12, 1955, their intention to conclude a military alliance between them; and on February 24, the Turko-Iraqi Pact was signed in Baghdad. In April, the United Kingdom acceded to the Pact and simultaneously transferred the two air bases to Iraqi hands. Pakistan joined in September, and Iran in October.

The United States government elected to stay out of the alliance, however. By so doing, it remained faithful to its initial conception of a purely indigenous organization. Of course, London's accession in April changed the rules of the game. By this time, two major elements in the situation had also changed, however. First, the British, with Nuri As-Said's collaboration, had taken over the initiative in the last quarter of 1954. Having lost the Suez base, they were faced with the need to consolidate their presence in Iraq and Jordan or lose their major remaining footholds in the Arab Middle East. Given the nationalist ferment, only a revamping of their treaty relationships within the framework of a new and multinational defense organization could guarantee continued tenure. Britain therefore identified her primary interest as membership in any prospective defense system, not mere sponsorship and assistance from without, as the Dulles concept envisaged. Furthermore, British regional interests were mostly located in Arab countries, London argued, and the U.S. focus on the northern tier failed to take this into account. While Britain's

---

Pact came as a surprise to Dulles, who "had taken no step to urge the pact" from 1953 to 1956 (p. 249), is erroneous. See Gallman, *Iraq under General Nuri*, pp. 29–32, on the repeated Gallman-Said conversations in December 1954 in preparation for the Menderes visit of early January 1955, in the course of which the gestation of the Pact was announced. Also erroneous is Love's assertion (in *Suez*, p. 273) that Dulles did not wish to see Iraq or any other Arab country in the northern-tier alliance, and that the Pact was "concocted by the British and Iraqis "behind Dulles' back." On the British role, see below.

diplomatic role in the period that saw the establishment of the Baghdad Pact is yet to be revealed,[79] it is clear that this role was a very active one, and that the U.S. State Department regarded it and the subsequent British accession with mixed feelings.

The second, and probably the principal, factor accounting for the U.S. attitude toward the Pact was the intensity of the anti-Iraqi reaction in Cairo and Nasser's ability in the weeks and months that followed the announcement of the Pact to deter any other Arab government from following in Iraq's footsteps. The Egyptian campaign was waged both diplomatically, through the Arab League and other governmental contacts, and by direct propaganda appeals to the Arab populations over the heads of their governments, carried mainly through the powerful Cairo press and radio. The pivotal country was Syria, ringed by pro-Western Turkey, Iraq, Jordan, and Lebanon, ard ruled in late 1954 and early 1955 by political coalitions dominated by pro-Iraqi parties.[80] In February 1955, Syria opted against joining the Baghdad Pact, a decision that was to a degree induced by France's staunch opposition to the "Anglo-Saxon" alliance, in addition to intense Egyptian pressure.[81] In the end, far from bringing Nuri As-Said ascendancy over the Arab world, the Baghdad Pact brought about Iraq's isolation from the mainstream of Arab politics and the final forfeiture of bloc leadership to Egypt. Nasser's efforts in fact were so effective that they succeeded in completely discrediting on nationalist grounds the notion of Arab defense cooperation with the West, and put a prohibitive price on Washington's own adherence to the Pact. Byroade himself, within days of his arrival as ambassador in Cairo at the end of February 1955, changed his mind about the wisdom of having encouraged Iraqi participation and became a strong proponent of U.S. cooperation with Egypt.

79. Eden's memoirs are singularly obscure on this aspect of his Middle Eastern policy (*Memoirs*, pp. 243–244).

80. The best account of the inter-Arab struggle over regional defense is by Seale, *Struggle for Syria*, chaps. 16 and 17.

81. On Syrian President Hashim Al-Atasi's fears regarding a French-engineered coup in Damascus and Turko-Iraqi appeals to the United States for intercession with Paris, see Gallman, *Iraq under General Nuri*, p. 53. For the French attitude toward the Baghdad Pact, see Metellus, "Politique de la France au Proche-Orient," *Politique Etrangère* 20 (December 1955), 677–688; General [Georges] Catroux, "Aspects actuels des problèmes du Proche-Orient," *Politique Etrangère* 21 (February 1956), 5–20; and Edouard Sablier, "La tension en Proche-Orient et la politique des grandes puissances," *Politique Entrangère* 20 (January–February 1955), 21–26. For a French government note to the British and U.S. governments in this regard, see *The Times* (London), January 27, 1956.

But in the second half of 1954, Washington's misgivings about the course that Middle Eastern defense was taking under British guidance and its decision to stay out, at least for the time being, lay in the future. The United States was strongly supportive of the new alliance throughout the period of its inception (and would later join in some of its activities). The new conditions laid out for arms aid to Egypt soon after the Suez Canal base agreement thus fitted within an overall policy for the area that was being reactivated with increased resolve after the lull that followed the 1953 tour by the Secretary of State. But these conditions set Nasser and Dulles on a collision course, for they struck at the very roots of Nasser's evolving doctrine for the conduct of Egypt's foreign affairs. In the matter of regional defense and Arab-Western relations, this doctrine sought to capitalize on Egypt's primacy within the Arab League framework by insisting on the Collective Security Pact of 1950 as the only acceptable structure on which to build regional security while preserving Arab freedom of action.

Sensing the gravity of the evolving situation,[82] the Egyptian Premier sought to convey his position to the United States through every channel he could command, and in a manner that left no room for misunderstandings. A typical public "message" that he sent to Washington—one of many such signals in the second half of 1954—was the statement he gave to an Associated Press correspondent in August of that year. Without mincing any words, Nasser said that "(1) Egypt wishes to receive American assistance and is relying on the United States for her defense against an eventual aggression. (2) Egypt is openly at war against Communists, who follow orders from the U.S.S.R. . . . (3) Egypt knows that the West will not attack her. Only collective defense can be effective against aggression on the part of a Great Power. That is why the Arab States' collective security pact has been created."[83]

The same note was struck in several private contacts. One of these secret channels was Norman Paul, the Near East director for the Foreign Operations Administration, who happened to make an official visit to Cairo in mid-November to discuss matters related to economic aid. On the very first day of his visit, Paul was told by Ambassador Caffery that Nasser wanted to see him privately:

> I was driven the following evening to a house in the outskirts of Cairo . . . where I met Nasser. He was accompanied by several members of the Council of

82. Nuri As-Said visited Cairo on September 15 to convince Nasser of the advantages of a defense association with the West. The two leaders parted in strong, and lasting, disagreement. For details of their talks, see Seale, *Struggle for Syria*, pp. 206–208.

83. *Cahiers de l'Orient Contemporain* (Paris) 11 (1st semester, 1954), 124.

the Revolution, including [army commander-in-chief Abdelhakim] Amer, and probably Sabri. . . . To my great surprise, Nasser told me that he did not want to talk about economic aid but about military supplies. A long conversation ensued, in which Nasser did most of the talking, in a most impressive and convincing fashion. He was concerned with the amount and types of arms the U.S. was talking about supplying him with. He thought the amount too small and the types inadequate. He said he did not care much about economic aid, but now he heard of new strings being attached to the military supplies he had been led to expect. He eloquently told me why he could not accept the idea of joining a regional pact. He ended by quietly but firmly telling me that unless he received satisfactory arms supplies from the U.S. he would have to ask for Soviet aid. He had expected me to have some instructions on the subject of military aid. He was disappointed when he learnt that I had no idea the subject was to be discussed by us. Apparently, there had been a communications gap somewhere.

I felt at the time that Nasser was deeply concerned with the imbalance between his military capability and Israel's, which he thought was very substantial. Army morale was another factor he mentioned.

Immediately after the meeting ended, I went to the embassy and drafted a cable which Caffery initialled and was sent to Byroade, summarizing Nasser's message. . . . After I returned some two weeks later to Washington, Byroade agreed with my estimate that Nasser was dead serious about his felt need for arms and his determination to get them wherever he could.[84]

Despite the change in the U.S. posture, promised economic assistance was made available in the sum of $40 million on November 6.[85] But negotiations for arms grants-in-aid were stalemated by the linkage to regional defense and were soon shifted to an outright commercial purchase agreement. They continued on this basis until the Soviet arms deal was announced in September of the following year. Copeland says that these steps were contrary to the spirit of Dulles's policy toward Egypt at the time, which aimed at coercing Nasser into cooperation with the West by withholding all forms of aid, and were carried on by the "working levels" at the State Department.[86] This

84. Norman S. Paul interview, February 1, 1973. General Mohammed Naguib, who was deposed from the presidency on November 14, 1954, and placed in restraint at his home until his release by President Sadat in 1973, maintains in his memoirs that the Soviets were sounded out by him on military aid in December 1953; *My Testimony to History* [in Arabic] (Cairo: Dar al-Kitab al-Namuzagi, 1975). British War Secretary, Anthony Head, who signed the Suez Agreement with Nasser in July 1954, was told by the Egyptian Premier on that occasion that he would buy arms from Czechoslovakia if he could not get them from the West, a warning that Head says he transmitted to the British Cabinet upon his return to London; Love, *Twice-Fought War*, p. 186.

85. *Al-Ahram*, October 25 and November 7, 1954; and *New York Times*, November 7, 1954.

86. Copeland, *Game of Nations*, pp. 150–151.

seems hardly credible, although inconsistencies in policy toward Cairo were by no means rare, as we have already seen. A more plausible explanation is strongly suggested by the subsequent dilatory course taken by the arms negotiations, and the political context surrounding Middle Eastern defense arrangements that I have just described: A decision was made in the fall of 1954 not to supply military equipment to Nasser unless and until he cooperated on defense with the West, but not to cut off all negotiations either. Economic aid was permitted, however, in order to "keep the door open." Complete reneging on the Eisenhower pledge was not feasible if some influence and communication with Cairo were to be maintained. Moreover, as Nasser and other Egyptians had made abundantly clear, there was urgent need for arms, and Washington's bargaining leverage would therefore not be considerably diminished by granting the $40 million. Eventually, Washington expected, the Egyptians would relent and accept some form of defense association with the Free World, or at least acquiesce in other Arab countries' joining a Western-sponsored pact, in exchange for arms they could not do without for much longer.

Egypt Goes East

If this interpretation is correct, it would make comprehensible some of the more difficult to explain—and thus far unexplained—aspects of U.S. policy during the year that separated the initiation of the arms sales talks with Egypt and the announcement of the Soviet deal in September 1955.[87] By far the most curious of these aspects is the procrastination by the United States that bedevilled the negotiations, even when these were pushed by repeated interventions by Nasser himself, publicly and privately, particularly after the Israeli raid of February 28, 1955, underlined the urgency of rearmament. Furthermore, the U.S. Embassy in Cairo fully endorsed Nasser's urgings and became particularly insistent when reports of actual Egyptian approaches to Moscow began to surface.

A few days after the raid, in the first week of March, Nasser conferred with newly-arrived U.S. Ambassador Henry Byroade and told him that Egypt would need substantial amounts of heavy arms, including tanks and bomber aircraft, in view of the Israeli threat. While heretofore he had tolerated the slow pace of the negotiations with Washington, he could no longer safely do so.

87. A fully adequate explanation must await the future release of the relevant official records, although even these may not be of much help, judging from Senator Fulbright's comment (quoted above at the head of this chapter), which he made after an investigation by the Senate Foreign Relations Committee of the 1955 arms flap.

If the United States continued to insist on tying grant aid to conditions, then Egypt preferred to purchase the arms under the existing 1952 agreement. Byroade said he would transmit the Egyptian views to Washington and promised to support the arms request, which he believed would not upset the existing regional military balance.[88] No breakdown of the details of Egypt's March request is available, but its potential impact on the Arab-Israeli military equilibrium apparently was not such as to disquiet U.S. officials. Upon seeing a list of the weapons sought by Cairo, President Eisenhower is reported to have exclaimed, "Why, this is peanuts!"[89]

Nevertheless, Washington stalled. Dulles continued to hope that the arms carrot might yet change Nasser's mind on the merits of regional defense, if only to the extent of toning down the violent Egyptian campaign under way against Iraq and the emerging Baghdad Pact.[90] The Gaza clash with Israel had heightened Western anxiety over the military situation on the armistice lines. Cairo had taken another step on the road to neutralism by accepting an invitation to the Bandung conference of nonaligned nations being prepared under active Chinese sponsorship, much to Dulles's displeasure. On March 31, in a widely publicized speech on foreign policy, Nasser spoke to sixteen hundred army officers in pessimistic terms about the likelihood of receiving U.S. arms and recalled the earlier experiences of the Sabri mission:

[The West] talked with us about military aid and about economic aid, and said they would give us all this. We said we accept military aid, but without imposed conditions. We are not ready to sign on conditions with which you tie other countries' hands. You help us militarily and we naturally shall not use [the arms] except for legitimate defense. . . .

[The U.S.] said we shall give you $20 million worth of arms in 1954–55. So far, the whole big deal has yielded nothing but sweet words.

We told them—we are willing to buy. But we have not reached any conclusion with them, except that arms will come. I told you this two years ago, and a mission with An-Naklawi and Ali Sabri went there, and long negotiations ensued, but nothing came of it. Jewish influence and Zionist influence has very great impact there, and I believed it would be a miracle of miracles if we ever obtained anything.[91]

88. Nasser said this to Love, *Twice-Fought War*, p. 281. See also Heikal, *Cairo Documents*, p. 47; and Copeland, *Game of Nations*, pp. 151–154. Both Copeland and Ellis (*Challenge in the Middle East*, pp. 37–42) describe the good working relationship established between Byroade and Nasser.

89. Love, *Twice-Fought War*, p. 88, quoting a U.S. ambassador.

90. During this time, the U.S. was urging all the remaining Arab countries to join the Turkish-Iraqi alliance, according to a report by Lebanese ambassador to Washington, Charles Malik, to his government; *Al-Ahram*, February 14, 1955.

91. Ibid., April 1, 1955.

The public appeal to Washington implied in these words was made even more urgent by the news of the surreptitious French arms supplies to Israel that began to reach Cairo in early 1955. In January, the shipment of British surplus Sherman tanks and tank guns through private French dealers brought an angry protest from Nasser to the British Ambassador, Sir Ralph Stevenson, and a request that the latter transmit to Eden a personal message that unless British or U.S. arms became available to Egypt, "he would have to get them where he could. Stevenson was certain that Nasser would do as he said."[92] In March, the Syrian and Lebanese press published accounts of the French shipment of jet warplanes and tanks to Israel, and reported the actual delivery of fifty tanks.[93] On the 29th, the day before Nasser's important address at the Officers' Club, it became known that Israel had purchased fifteen Mystère-II fighters from France.[94] Details of further purchases, including one hundred AMX-13 tanks, 75-mm. guns, and 155-mm. guns, were to surface in May. Not announced at the time was the acquisition of twelve Ouragan jet fighters, which were contracted for in 1954 along with the other weapons.

These sales, particularly of the Mystère aircraft, represented a qualitative jump in the until-then slackening arms race that left Nasser and his team no doubts about the nature of the "balance" that the three Western powers sought to maintain through the instrumentality of the NEACC regime. Arms were flowing to Israel while they were being denied to Egypt.[95] Yet, as the American President himself later admitted, "in early 1955 there was no question that, should war break out between Israel and Egypt, the latter would be decisively defeated." Even if all "surrounding governments" were to concert their efforts, he observed, the Israelis had about the same quantitative military power, while Israel's army "was certainly better motivated, better trained, and more effective as a fighting force."[96] Eisenhower's

92. Sir Ralph Stevenson said this to Robert Stephens, *Nasser: A Political Biography*, pp. 157–158.

93. *Al-Ahram*, March 18, 1955. The same report said that the Syrian government planned to submit a formal protest in Paris.

94. *New York Times*, March 30, 1955.

95. According to Anthony Nutting, by March 1955 Britain had not even responded to the Egyptian arms request that he had been handed by Nasser himself after the signature of the final Suez accord in October 1954 and which he had carried back to London; Nutting, *Nasser*, p. 97. Sir Humphrey Trevelyan, who became U.K. ambassador to Cairo in August 1955, reports that whatever British arms were sold to Egypt that year were sent without ammunition or after great delays; Humphrey Trevelyan, *The Middle East in Revolution* (London: Macmillan, 1970), p. 27.

96. Eisenhower, *Waging Peace*, p. 24.

assessment of the military balance was concurred in by the other U.S. officials as well as by other Western governments, as we have seen.[97]

Thus, Nasser's pessimism regarding the availability of U.S. arms, a pessimism considerably justified by previous experience, was compounded in the crucial months of March–May 1955 by large-scale supplies to Israel of offensive weapons of the latest design by one of the tripartite powers— despite Israel's decisive arms superiority and the fact that she had shortly before carried out against territory under Egyptian control the largest military operation the area had witnessed since the Palestine war. Simultaneously, an alternative source of arms was opening up in the Soviet bloc, and Nasser had given the Western capitals repeated warnings that he would resort to it if left with no other acceptable choice. In these circumstances, the treatment to be accorded by the United States to the post-Gaza approach by Nasser for military supplies was destined to be viewed in Cairo as the final test of Washington's willingness to provide Egypt with the arms she had been promised and her security clearly required. As it turned out, the request was met with dilatory tactics aimed at preventing Nasser from acquiring the armaments he wanted until he compromised on the issue of regional defense, while dissuading him from turning to non-Western sources by keeping alive his hopes of a favorable outcome by means of protracted negotiations. As Eisenhower candidly explained the U.S. response in his memoirs, "Nasser requested arms—$27 million worth. Our State Department, confident that he was short of money, informed him that payment would be expected in cash rather than barter."[98]

The following account of the developments surrounding these negotiations and the stages undergone by the Egyptian request between March and September 1955 can be assembled from available information:

The arms request communicated by Nasser to Byroade in early March included items that the United States did not wish to see in Egyptian hands— offensive weapons that the Sabri mission had sought to acquire in 1953.[99] Nasser left Cairo on April 9 for Bandung without having received any response from Washington. While on his Asiatic trip, he both gained considerable exposure while attaining new stature as an important figure in the Third

97. See Chapter 5, above. Byroade testified at congressional hearings in 1957 that, militarily, Egypt in 1955 "was not half as strong as Israel" (*President's Proposal on the Middle East, Hearings*, p. 755).

98. *Waging Peace*, p. 24.

99. JCS Chairman Admiral Radford's testimony, in *President's Proposal on the Middle East, Hearings*, p. 438.

World, and opened new options for arms procurement by seriously approaching the Soviet bloc for major arms supplies. The Kremlin's attitude toward the military junta originally had been characterized by suspicion if not outright hostility, which Nasser's ruthless suppression of local Communists and other leftists had done nothing to discourage. This began to change in late 1954 and early 1955. Cairo's determined stand against a continued British presence at Suez, and particularly its stout opposition to the Baghdad Pact, broke the ice, created a community of interest between the two countries against continued Western entrenchment in the area, and coincided with an ideological re-evaluation in Moscow of the role of Third-World petty bourgeois nationalist regimes in the struggle against Western capitalism. In conversations with Chinese Premier Chou En-lai during his journey to Indonesia, Nasser was encouraged to expect a favorable response from the Soviet Union on arms supplies, which Chou promised he would personally promote.

The details of the Soviet-Egyptian arms negotiations—later conducted and consummated under a Czech cover in order to minimize negative Western reaction—fall outside the scope of this study.[100] It is sufficient to note here

100. For material on the antecedents and progress of the Soviet arms deal, see below. Also see Heikal, *Cairo Documents*, pp. 47–51; Heikal, *The Sphinx and the Commissar* (New York: Harper & Row, 1978), pp. 57–63; Heikal broadcast, "Political Enquiry: The Search for an End," Part I, Cairo Home Service, December 25, 1958; Love, *Twice-Fought War*, chap. 8; David J. Dallin, *Soviet Foreign Policy after Stalin* (Philadelphia: Lippincott, 1961), pp. 389–395; and Walter Z. Laqueur, *Communism and Nationalism in the Middle East* (New York: Praeger, 1956), chap. 19. Surprisingly, Nikita Krushchev, who was the Soviet leader most responsible for this signal Soviet achievement, devotes only one short, particularly vague paragraph to the transaction in his memoirs, *Khrushchev Remembers* (Boston: Little, Brown, 1970), p. 433.

One published work on the arms deal deserves special mention, for it has gained some currency as an authoritative source. This is an extensive analysis by Uri Ra'anan in his book *The U.S.S.R. Arms the Third World: Case Studies in Soviet Foreign Policy* (Cambridge, Mass.: M.I.T. Press, 1969). Ra'anan sets out to prove that the Soviet-Egyptian arms agreement was firmly concluded, in principle if not in its details, in January–February 1955, and that, from that point on, Nasser's repeated requests to the United States were nothing but a charade designed to throw dust in the eyes of the West while the deal with Moscow was being completed. Ra'anan's otherwise valuable study of the evolving Soviet strategy toward the Middle East and relations with Egypt is marred by a series of faulty interlocking assumptions, based on flimsy and circumstantial evidence, and by a rather abusive application of content-analysis techniques to a number of Soviet and Egyptian documents and statements. Ra'anan bends over backwards, in 150 pages of text, to establish a thesis that apparently is primarily designed to "absolve" Israel of some putative "responsibility" for precipitating Nasser's "loss" to the Soviets by her attack on Gaza on February 28, 1955, and for the leaks on arms purchases from France. In any case, his version is not borne out by any of the several accounts subsequently published by individuals who were direct

that upon his return to Cairo at the end of April, Nasser informed the RCC about the Soviet option and obtained their agreement to pursue it. Only a very small number of officials were let in on the secret. A committee was set up to study the issue of arms procurement from the Soviet bloc from the standpoint of its technical military implications, such as changes in doctrines, training, etc. The committee was chaired by General Mohammed Hafez Ismail, who was then Director of the Office of the Commander in Chief of the armed forces, and who would play a leading part in the ensuing negotiations. On May 18, Nasser asked the Russian ambassador, Daniel Solod, about the possibility of purchasing large quantities of weapons from the U.S.S.R.; and on May 21, Solod communicated Moscow's positive response.

Now armed with the Russian alternative, the Egyptian Premier formally informed Byroade on June 9 that he would obtain arms from the Eastern bloc unless the United States proved more forthcoming on the pending requests.[101] Cairo at this stage still preferred to obtain its armaments from traditional Western sources. Not only was this politically safer (the example of U.S. intervention in Guatemala in 1954 after the Arbenz government had purchased arms from Czechoslovakia was still fresh in the minds of RCC members); it was also economically cheaper for equivalent increments of fighting power, and much less disruptive of the existing military establishment, which was exclusively Western in equipment and training. In the words of Lt. General Mohsen Idriss, who was on Hafez Ismail's staff in 1955 and intimately involved in the preparation of arms requests:

On the one hand, we were glad a source of arms had opened up that, according to Nasser, was ready to give Egypt all the armaments she wanted without restrictions or conditions. On the other hand, the fact that such a radical shift would entail practically scrapping all the equipment already in Egypt's possession, nullify all efforts made and under way to get arms and ammunition from the West, and need a complete change in doctrines, tactics, strategy, training, etc., boggled our minds. . . . Our feeling simply was one of worry about the

---

participants in or close observers of the Egyptian diplomatic scene in 1955, nor by the extensive field research and interviewing this author has conducted in Britain, the United States, and the Middle East on the subject of Egypt's search for arms, all of which support the standard version that places the origins of the arms deal in the Nasser-Chou talks of April 1955 at the earliest. While much remains to be revealed about this celebrated episode—including any official documentation—one may say with reasonable confidence that the Ra'anan thesis has no basis in fact.

101. Statement by official Egyptian government spokesman reviewing U.S.-Egyptian arms negotiations, *Al-Ahram*, November 9, 1955; and Nasser interview, *Daily Herald* (London), November 8, 1955.

unknown future. With the Czech deal, Egypt would burn her bridges to the West. What if Russia changed her attitude six months later?[102]

The State Department chose to regard Nasser's threat as pure bluff;[103] and as late as the end of August, both Secretary Dulles and the new Assistant Secretary for Near Eastern Affairs, George V. Allen, considered arms to Egypt from the Soviet bloc as "out of the question."[104] Dulles personally regarded it as empty blackmail, and he would not be blackmailed.

The British Foreign Office reacted differently when Byroade informed Ambassador Stevenson of Nasser's declared intentions. Whitehall instructed Stevenson to warn the Egyptians that no further British arms would be supplied to them if they took any from Russia. Nasser considered this warning as intolerable, for London was already withholding arms from him because of his opposition to the Baghdad Pact. From that day on, he would have no more conversations with the British over arms. As Sir Humphrey Trevelyan, who succeeded Stevenson in August 1955, acidly commented, "the Foreign Office were acting as if the Egyptians could still only look to the West for arms and they could use their position as a monopoly supplier to put on political pressure."[105]

Despite its skepticism, the State Department decided in mid-June to reply to Nasser's approach, most probably at Byroade's urgent insistence.[106] On June 22, the U.S. Ambassador informed the Egyptian government that Washington would make arms available for purchase, and invited them to make a specific formal request, which Egypt did make on June 30.[107] Although there was no intention to provide all the offensive weaponry demanded by Cairo, basic objections regarding the type of armaments to be supplied were not raised with Nasser. Nor could they be if negotiations were to be maintained, since Nasser's first priority now was precisely to obtain those weapons

102. Interview with the author, August 12, 1973.

103. Eisenhower, *Waging Peace*, p. 24; Love, *Twice-Fought War*, p. 282; and Kermit Roosevelt interview.

104. Copeland, *Game of Nations*, p. 156. Kermit Roosevelt says that Allen maintained, even as late as September, that the Soviets did not dispose of sufficient arms to sell abroad in large quantities; interview with the author.

105. Trevelyan, *Middle East in Revolution*, pp. 28–29.

106. Ambassador Byroade strongly felt throughout this period that the maintenance of cooperative relations between Cairo and Washington would not be possible without fulfillment of Nasser's arms needs, and he pressed the State Department on this issue constantly. See his testimony before the Foreign Relations Committee, in *President's Proposal on the Middle East, Hearings*, especially pp. 714–715 and 728–731.

107. U.S. Statement on Egyptian-American arms negotiations released by the U.S. Embassy in Cairo; *Al-Ahram*, October 16, 1955.

that could provide a deterrent to the Israeli threat, and if necessary, the means for retaliation against further large-scale incursions. Furthermore, it had become public knowledge that Israel was being supplied with late-model heavy arms precisely at this time by a tripartite power (France). This is why Byroade's reply to the June 30 request was that some of the desired items had been authorized by Washington and could be supplied, but that others had to be negotiated.[108] While objections to the qualitative aspects of the weapons sought by Cairo were thus downgraded, recourse was made to imposing financial conditions for the sale that it was assumed Egypt could not meet.[109] Nasser was told that the arms he desired would cost $27 million, and that immediate payment was expected in cash.[110]

The pricing policy that was in effect in the United States during most of the 1950s in regard to arms destined for export *sales* was a peculiar one, given the overly liberal American practices when arms were granted free. The policy had the overall effect of rendering U.S. products noncompetitive on the world arms market because of their high cost. This policy required that the purchaser of a certain item pay the cost of replacing that item in the American inventory, even if the equipment had been used for years, was obsolescent, or was on the point of being scrapped by U.S. military forces. Since the replacement value was computed on the basis of prevailing procurement costs of comparable but modern equipment in production at the time of purchase, this resulted in price tags for American arms much higher than those of other suppliers for similar weapons. Hence, most U.S. arms exports during this period were on a grant rather than sales basis, for political expedience often dictated the provision of arms to foreign governments that could not afford them.[111]

This same pricing yardstick was applied to the arms requested by Nasser. As Peter Chase, who was political officer at the U.S. Embassy under Byroade, has noted, "the fact that payment in cash at non-reduced off-the-shelf prices was demanded was an indicator that Washington did not want to give arms to Egypt and was therefore imposing conditions expected to lead the Egyptians to withdraw or freeze their request. Cairo told us at the time that such a condition would tie up all their dollar exchange, and complained that this was

108. Byroade testimony, in *President's Proposal on the Middle East, Hearings,* p. 279.

109. Eisenhower, *Waging Peace,* p. 24.

110. Egyptian spokesman, *Al-Ahram,* November 9, 1955; and U.S. Embassy statement, *Al-Ahram,* October 16, 1955.

111. Hovey, *United States Military Assistance,* pp. 182–183; and Dulles testimony, in *Situation in the Middle East, Hearings,* p. 17.

no way for the U.S. to treat a friendly government."[112]The stratagem worked. When Nasser proclaimed his inability to pay in cash dollars[113] and offered part payment in Egyptian currency, Washington demurred. Although the American Embassy in Cairo prepared a detailed credit program that would have permitted Egypt to pay for the arms over a number of years, no authorization to proceed on this basis came from Dulles throughout the summer, and there the matter rested.[114]

Egyptian contacts with the Soviet bloc, which had been officially halted in mid-June in response to the new American initiative, were now resumed. The Russians were aware of Nasser's preference for Western aid and became suspicious that he was playing them off against the United States; they reportedly pressed for serious consideration of their offer.[115] As for Nasser, if anything was needed to convince him that no large-scale supply of U.S. arms could be expected on terms that he could live with, Washington's continued silence on his appeal for relaxation of the stiff financial conditions laid out for the sale spoke louder than words. On July 21, Dimitri Shepilov, who was the editor of *Pravda* and a member of the Central Committee of the CPSU, arrived in Cairo at Egyptian invitation to discuss with Nasser the possible terms of an arms deal, including quantities, timetables, and terms of payment. According to Mohamed Awad Al-Quni, who became Egyptian ambassador to Moscow in August 1955, the purpose of Shepilov's visit "was mainly to take a final, good look at the Egyptian scene and the regime before giving the green light to the deal, and to assure the Egyptians of Moscow's good will and good intentions."[116] The Soviet visitor concluded his stay on July 29, and the venue of Soviet-Egyptian negotiations was moved to Prague.

Two days later, Nasser queried Washington about his arms request through Ambassador Hussein.[117] Similar inquiries were made throughout the month of August and the first half of September, both directly through formal channels and by means of "unofficial" Americans close to the Cairo regime.

112. Peter Chase interview.

113. According to a statement by the Egyptian Minister of Finance and Economy, Abdel Mun'im Al-Qaisouni, the foreign exchange available to the Egyptian government as of February 26, 1955, amounted to 51.6 million pounds sterling, 41.5 million U.S. dollars, and about 10 million Egyptian pounds in other currencies. If sterling accounts from British war debts that were blocked in London are included, the total amounted to 274 million Egyptian pounds; *Al-Ahram*, March 31, 1955.

114. Parker Hart interview. Hart became the deputy chief of mission at the U.S. Embassy in Cairo in August 1955.

115. Nutting, *Nasser*, p. 103.

116. Interview with the author, August 12, 1973.

117. *New York Times*, September 26, 1955.

No definite reply was forthcoming from Washington, however, despite warnings by the CIA and the U.S. Embassy that an Egyptian arms deal with the Soviets was imminent. In late August, at the request of the acting CIA Director, General Cabell, Kermit Roosevelt—the Agency's "specialist" on Egypt and one of the Americans closest to Nasser—prepared a two-page memorandum on why Intelligence was convinced that such a deal was in the making. Roosevelt took it to Secretary Dulles, and they went over it together. Roosevelt has said since then that he thought he had made a convincing case but that Dulles did not agree with his conclusions. Unbelievably, the Secretary said that such a step by the Russians would be "contrary to the spirit of Geneva."[118] Consequently, he did nothing.

Dulles's strangely misplaced idealism; his belief that Nasser would not dare make such a drastic and perilous shift in basic foreign orientation towards the Communist orbit; his pugnacious and stubborn determination to bend the Egyptian leader to his own will and policy before he would grant the much-desired aid; his reluctance to disturb the Middle Eastern military equation established by the tripartite arms transfer regime at a time of increasing Egyptian-Israeli border tensions and pay the domestic political price of arming the Arabs: all these were factors that were present and combined to produce the American immobility in the face of the impending Soviet deal.

What the precise combination was and which of these elements weighed most heavily in the Secretary's calculations must remain largely subject to conjecture, however. It was part of the Dulles working style that he kept his own counsel. Although he sought information and advice from experts and associates, there was little give-and-take in the actual making of decisions, a process which, as a rule, he shared with no one and in which he followed rationales that remained locked in his own head.[119] The upshot often was perplexed ignorance in the minds of even his closest collaborators as to where he stood on matters that required immediate decision until he announced it, as well as confused ambiguity regarding the longer-term direction of policy or the ultimate ends towards which the Secretary was working. The subject of U.S.-Egyptian relations was no exception to this pattern.[120] This of course

118. Kermit Roosevelt interview. The first Great Power summit meeting since wartime years was held in Geneva in July 1955, and was touted as heralding an era of relaxation of tensions between East and West.

119. For more on this, see, among others, Townsend Hoopes, *The Devil and John Foster Dulles* (Boston: Little, Brown, 1973), pp. 141–142.

120. Dulles's immediate predecessor—whose decision-making practices had been much more methodical and institutionalized, and who had made better use of the professional talent and experience available at the State Department and other agencies

had its disjunctive effects on American actions as such—best exemplified by the incongruous position in which Ambassador Byroade found himself: sent to Cairo just a few months earlier in order to cement the growing relationship of friendship and cooperation with the Officers' regime, he was now helplessly witnessing the unraveling of this relationship by Washington's silence and its potential supplanting by close ties with the Soviet arch-rival. And Dulles's behavior also makes it extremely difficult for the analyst to precisely determine the motives that impelled the Secretary to sit tight while events unfolded. As Kermit Roosevelt has remarked, probably no one besides the Secretary knew what the latter's strategy towards Nasser actually was in the summer of 1955. "It was all in Dulles' head. The working levels did not even have a clue as to whether arms would be given, or what were the conditions under which they would be given."[121]

The interplay of these factors was also affected to a degree by personal idiosyncrasies and the vagaries of circumstance, which have often been so crucial at historical turning points. The apparent breakdown in communication between the Cairo Embassy and the higher levels at the State Department is probably the most curious aspect of this misadventure. The sense of urgency that Byroade sought to convey in his repeated warnings does not seem to have made its mark on Dulles's thinking until the penultimate hour. Why this was so is, again, difficult to determine. A likely explanation may be provided by the enigmatic role played by the Assistant Secretary for Near Eastern Affairs, George Allen. As already mentioned, Allen did not believe the Soviets could or would give Egypt arms on a substantial scale. Whether for this reason, or because he concurred in Dulles's belief that Nasser was simply bluffing and would not venture to embark on such a radical course, or because he did not wish to upset the Secretary, he appears to have withheld from Dulles the full import of the judgments made by the men in the field. Allen was a kind but rather weak man, who showed no particular leadership at the head of the NEA bureau as a successor to the dynamic Byroade, and who was determined not to "make any waves." He felt that Byroade's constant requests for a positive decision on arms to Nasser were a thorn in his neck. He told Dulles what he thought Dulles wanted to hear. On the other hand, he was not alone in this. The Secretary's relationship with his Department subordinates was never one that encouraged dissent, strong advocacy, or bold initiative.

---

of government—was highly critical of the Secretary on this score; Gaddis Smith, *Dean Acheson* (New York: Cooper Square, 1972), pp. 395–396.

121. Kermit Roosevelt interview.

In a more fundamental sense, the obstacles in the way of an arms agreement with Egypt were a direct expression of the inescapable contradiction between a policy of arms balance on the one hand, and the formation of a militarily significant regional defense organization on the other, to which we have referred in a previous analysis of U.S. arms transfer practices.[122] Given the political realities in the region, Israel would have necessarily been excluded from any regional organization that included Arab states. The injection of sufficient arms into the area to turn the proposed defense pact into a useful military bulwark against Soviet attack would have done away with the 1950 tripartite intent to keep arms levels down. Moreover, if shipments to pact members were not counterbalanced with supplies to Israel, the long-term security of the Jewish state would have been put in jeopardy, a situation that for domestic political and other reasons the Western powers would not be likely to allow. If, on the other hand, such counterbalancing arms transfers were to be made, a regional arms race would be certain to develop, and the probability of renewed general Arab-Israeli warfare would be greatly increased.

The only way out of this dilemma, and one that U.S. and British policy-makers most likely had in mind in 1954–1955, was to create a regional alliance with the Middle East that would in fact rest, not on indigenous military strength invigorated by large-scale arms aid, but on a significant Western military presence in pact bases scattered strategically through the region (Iraq, Cyprus, Libya, Saudi Arabia), buttressed by the true political signifi-cance of the pact: the signalling to the Communist bloc that the Middle East was now a staked-out area within the Free World perimeter, and no longer a part of the so-called "grey areas."[123] Regardless of the rhetoric, arms aid would therefore need to be given only in token quantities, sufficient to build up internal security forces and provide the prestige trappings of a modern army (Nuri As-Said's "big guns"), but not to create a major threat to Israel or require casting aside the 1950 tripartite arms policy.

This line of thinking, however, failed to take account of the new type of leadership that had lately come to power in some countries of the area, particularly in Egypt (and in Syria as well), the drives that motivated it, and

122. See Chapter 5, above.
123. Thomas K. Finletter, *Power and Policy* (New York: Harcourt, 1954). As Coral Bell has aptly put it in her excellent book *Negotiation from Strength* (London: Chatto & Windus, 1962), p. 88: "Seato and Cento and the mutual defence treaties with countries like Iran and Pakistan were not, except in a minor and subsidiary way, attempts to create military organizations or military strength on the ground in the manner of Nato: they were so many devices for defining a perimeter, 'Thin Ice' signs erected for the benefit of observers in Moscow."

the prevailing popular mood in the Arab world, to which this new leadership proved much better attuned than the traditional regimes could ever be. For Nasser, how much military aid the Western powers would provide to the Middle Eastern members of the proposed defense pact, and to what ends and on what conditions the aid would be provided, were fundamental issues. His insistence on the Arab League's Collective Security Pact as the only possible basis for a regional defense setup emanated not only from a desire to protect and reinforce Egypt's leading position in the area, but also from a need to secure autonomy and flexibility in the use of Arab military forces in roles other than anti-Communist ones, if necessary against Israel herself. In the words of the RCC spokesman, Major Salah Salem, "unless the Palestinians are repatriated in accordance with the U.N. resolutions . . . , no leader in Egypt or any other Arab country will be prepared to agree to any alliance with the West. . . . The Russian threat may or may not become a reality. How then can the Arabs disregard a danger at the very center of their existence, in order to contemplate another danger . . . which . . . has not yet made itself felt ?" [124]

Thus, willy-nilly, the Israeli factor stood firmly in the way of Egyptian adherence to Western defense plans. By the same token, it precluded large-scale military aid or sales by the United States to Egypt—or, for that matter, to any other country.

Washington clearly understood this. It was in this context that, parallel to the American campaign to induce the Cairo junta to change its mind on Middle Eastern defense by diplomatic pressure and offers of economic and military assistance, Dulles deployed in the last few months of 1954 a strong effort within the U.S. government to appraise the possibilities open to it of bringing about an Arab-Israeli peace settlement. In October, he appointed Ambassador Francis H. Russell as his special assistant in charge of co-ordinating Administration activities related to the Palestine question. According to one of Dulles's biographers, from "October 1954, to August 1955, the Arab-Israeli problem got the most exhaustive examination from all agencies of the U.S. government involved in foreign policy, including the National Security Council, that it was possible to give." [125] Early in 1955, this same source adds, the conclusion had been reached that the conflict was indeed capable of a negotiated solution, but that this required energetic Great-Power

124. This was said to a group of Turkish journalists visiting Egypt in December 1954; it is quoted here from George Kirk, "The Turco-Egyptian Flirtation of Autumn 1954," *The World Today* 12 (November 1956), 454.

125. Beal, *John Foster Dulles*, 252. Also on this project, see Gerson, *Dulles*, pp. 261–263; and Trevelyan, *Middle East in Revolution*, pp. 40–42.

initiative and participation. The principal results of the review were embodied in a major address delivered by the Secretary of State on August 26, 1955.[126] The United States, the Secretary announced, was ready to promote a political settlement of the Arab-Israeli dispute with economic aid in the repatriation or resettlement of refugees, formal treaty engagements with the parties to deter future wars, and active diplomacy in behalf of drawing permanent boundaries.

Needless to say, the American initiative soon foundered amid the mounting succession of crises that engulfed the area shortly thereafter, starting with the announcement of the Soviet arms deal and its reverberations, soon to be followed by the Aswan High Dam loan episode, the nationalization of the Suez Canal Company, and the Suez War.[127] Probably the most significant aspect of this demarche from the perspective of the present study is the rather leisurely pace at which it seems to have moved. Considering the swift increase in tensions and border clashes especially between Israel and Egypt after the Suez base settlement in mid-1954, including the serious Gaza raid in February, and considering the fact that the main outlines of the U.S. proposals apparently were already set in early 1955, the delay of the Dulles speech until late August can be explained in terms of a feeling among the top American decision-makers that time was on their side. This same feeling must largely account for U.S. behavior as regards Nasser's arms request; the strategy of stringing the Egyptians along on military supplies until they accepted American conditions was feasible only on the assumption that overall control of the regional situation would remain in Western hands for the foreseeable future.

How seriously Dulles and his collaborators had miscalculated began to dawn on them only a few days after the Secretary's address. By the first week of September, indicators of an impending Soviet-Egyptian arms transaction from diplomatic and intelligence sources had become too numerous and too plausible to be dismissed. Finally, when no doubts remained that such an agreement was indeed about to be signed, it was disclosed on September 25 that the United States would agree to sell arms to Egypt on credit. This was a futile gesture. Byroade had been notified of the formalization of the

126. The text is in the U.S. Department of State *Bulletin*, September 5, 1955, pp. 378–380.

127. That Egyptians were keenly sensitive to the relationship between regional defense alliances and the Arab-Israeli conflict as a key to U.S. conduct toward Cairo in 1954–1955 is shown in a short but perceptive monograph by Mohamed H. Heikal, *The Psychological Complexes that Control the Middle East* [in Arabic] (Cairo: Arab Printing and Publishing Co., 1958), especially pp. 57–60.

Czech-Egyptian agreement on the 21st.[128] The CIA was convinced that the point of no return had been crossed weeks before this date, to the extent that Kermit Roosevelt, who was dispatched by Dulles to Cairo on the 23rd in a last-ditch effort to salvage the situation, made only a halfhearted effort to talk Nasser out of the agreement, and tried instead to use the opportunity to elicit from the Egyptians a softening of their attitude toward Israel.[129]

On September 27, Nasser announced to the world that a major weapons agreement had been signed with the East.

128. Byroade testimony, in *President's Proposal on the Middle East, Hearing*, p. 731.

129. For details of the American maneuvers to cope with the political repercussions of the arms deal, including the notorious visit by Assistant Secretary Allen to Cairo, see Copeland, *Game of Nations*, pp. 156–169; and Love, *Twice-Fought War*, pp. 283–290. Both accounts are substantially accurate, and supporting evidence can be found in Ambassador Trevelyan's memoirs, *Middle East in Revolution*, pp. 29–33. Heikal's account in *Cairo Documents*, pp. 51–52, is purposely misleading on the timing of Kermit Roosevelt's mission.

PART III

CONCLUSIONS

CHAPTER 7   THE USE AND
MISUSE OF ARMS CONTROL

> Any attempt to achieve a unilateral advantage must doom arms
> control, [for] the purpose of arms control is to enhance the
> security of all parties.
>
> Henry Kissinger
> *The Necessity for Choice*

I argued in the initial chapters of this study that the problems created by the large-scale international transfer of armaments from the standpoint of its impact on international tensions and the incidence of wars could be tackled best on a regional basis. The global approach exemplified by proposed multilateral treaty undertakings of restraint and worldwide registration of arms transfers is fraught with daunting obstacles. It is too ambitious in scope, presenting enormous problems of implementation and supervision of compliance; it is of dubious legitimacy on grounds of its inherent inequity toward nonproducers of arms; and it can ill contend with the political strains and stresses that come with universal membership. Besides, the regional focus demands priority because the urgent threats to international stability deriving from conventional arms are localized in a small number of regional arms races that account for a major absolute share of the arms flow. Practical considerations that should make arms control for crisis areas more easily attainable have also been discussed.

From a regional perspective, much of the available literature on the arms trade and arms control is of very limited relevance. Most contemporary analyses apply a macroscopic focus to the global transfer process. As a rule, they are heavily skeptical of the chances of achieving meaningful restraints in this field. This is a proper conclusion, which they base on the strength of the multifarious incentives and motivations driving arms producers to sell their products abroad, and nonproducers to shop for their military needs in a free market. But for specific conflict situations involving a limited number of countries, additional, more immediate and particular considerations intrude that render such generalizations partially meaningless and make separate appraisals of each particular conflict situation necessary.

To the maximum extent feasible, such appraisals should be based on investigation into the political and historical circumstances prevailing in the subject conflict-region within a relevant time-frame, for such circumstances are likely to be as determinative of the outcome of any arms control attempt as the more general and abiding incentives and motivations of weapons suppliers and their clients. Despite the fact that considerable analytical and descriptive attention has been paid to a number of important individual arms transactions—particularly the 1955 Soviet-Egyptian arms deal—only prefatory and scattered efforts have been made thus far to discover and assess the relationships between the supply of military equipment, arms control, and the diverse factors that affect governmental policy and inter-state relations in specific conflict areas.

For this neglect I have sought partial remedy in the Middle Eastern case study that forms the body of this work. Special significance attaches to this region, not only because it has witnessed for three decades the most virulent and unstable arms race, but also because it was uniquely subjected to an arms control system. Furthermore, the tripartite regime might serve, with modifications, as a protype of future arms control attempts in the Arab-Israeli area, and perhaps elsewhere. What lessons can be derived from the 1950–1955 experiment that such future endeavors should not ignore?

A systematic, detailed evaluation of the *mechanics* of the tripartite system has been precluded until now by the lack of public information on the workings of the Near East Arms Coordinating Committee, which administered the actual rationing. Such definitive assessment must await the release of the relevant records. Hence, the conclusions that can be derived from the preceding analysis—in addition to the many already made in passing—must perforce be of a general character. On the other hand, the Middle Eastern experience strongly suggests that it is the political environment in which the arms control scheme is implemented that is crucial to its success, rather than any single specific feature of its machinery or its guidelines. It is to defining this environment that the larger part of what follows is devoted.

BASIC SHORTCOMINGS OF THE TRIPARTITE REGIME

From an arms control and conflict management perspective, the particular arms-rationing regime applied by the tripartite Western powers was not successful. The system came to an ignominious end with the single largest arms transaction concluded by a Third World country up to that time, a development that, as the case study shows, was provoked by the tripartite rationing policy itself. Within one year, a full-scale war broke out between the two principal regional adversaries, with the active participation in the hostilities of two of the three rationing powers.

Given the obstacles that even this limited arms control device had to face, however, it is highly unlikely that the alternative control option—that is, a total supply cutoff—would have been any more effective, assuming that it would have been feasible in the first place. The embargo imposed on the combatants during the 1948 Palestine war was ineffective. While it may be justifiable to consider "arms trade" and "arms control" as basically antithetical, a combination of both may still be the only practical means of checking regional weapons buildups and curtailing their disruptive effects.

The failure of the tripartite attempt may be largely attributed to:

- the absence of serious concurrent efforts to settle the underlying dispute between Israel and her Arab neighbors that fuelled the race;
- the exclusion of other potential major arms suppliers;
- the informality and limited authority of the administrating body (the NEACC);
- the disparities in the regional political aims of the participating supplier governments; and
- the failure to maintain a regional military balance minimally acceptable to all the local parties.

Significantly, the circumstances in which the rationing was begun were as nearly optimal as can be reasonably expected in any region characterized by a high level of inter-state conflict. There were negligible domestic arms manufacturing capabilities in the local countries; existing military establishments were small, and economic resources were very limited; the political context all but denied to any Middle Eastern government the option of resorting to the only other major source of heavy arms existing at the time—the Soviet bloc; and the rationing powers exercised strong political and military influence in the region. The failure of the system despite these favorable conditions underlines the vulnerability of this particular conflict-limiting device to the encroachment of independent political variables. Such a device will serve its purpose effectively only so long as its overseers choose to abide by it, and one desertion can be fatal. It will last only so long as its target governments feel that it does not place an intolerable political or security burden on them. This vulnerability is further compounded if the arms rationing is to be applied to a large number of countries, for an indefinite period of time in conditions of relative peace, or to a region of great strategic, political, or economic value to several major powers, as in our Middle Eastern case.

The tripartite experience also demonstrates the weakness of any control system that does not involve all the major weapons exporters. The exclusion of the Soviet Union eventually resulted in the system's breakdown, for, apart from all additional political considerations that were inherent in the 1955 arms deal, such exclusion in and of itself provided Moscow with a strong motivation to undermine the entire arrangement by supplying arms to Egypt on such a scale as to render untenable the arms balance sought by the West.

Even universality is no guarantee of effectiveness, however. One or more of the participating suppliers may at one point find it politically advantageous to commence or increase arms sales to one of the "rationed" countries, secretly if necessary, on a scale that would disrupt the equilibrium on which the control regime is based, as France did in 1954. Such "scabbing" could be made much more costly in political terms—and therefore less likely—if the control system is implemented through a more formal, public, and institutionalized instrument than the NEACC was designed to be. The system would thereby acquire an international visibility and legitimacy that would strengthen it considerably.

Furthermore, defections are much less likely to occur if the control system is of limited duration. An open-ended undertaking, such as the tripartite one was assumed to be, becomes unavoidably subject to the stresses of changing political and other circumstances that prompt participating arms suppliers to challenge or evade it. Hence, it may be hypothesized that, if any arms rationing system or arms embargo is to succeed, it must be of short duration and must therefore be seconded by substantial efforts to solve the political dispute that underlies the military confrontation at issue. Long-term regional stability in conflict areas cannot be secured through a perpetual adjusting of military inventories by external powers according to some abstract conception of a "military balance," which is partly based on a number of qualitative and therefore subjective and necessarily arbitrary elements. Sooner or later, it must be sought in a negotiated solution to the basic political quarrel. At best, arms control can only be a useful adjunct to peaceful means of conflict resolution, not a substitute for them. The NEACC was relatively successful in restraining and balancing the flow of arms for approximately four years, but the stability of the political environment was due to the strong local military presence of the rationing powers, particularly Britain, which greatly limited opportunities for maneuver by Middle Eastern regimes.

A major source of difficulties that will face any arms-transfer regulation scheme is well illustrated by the history of Egypt's quest for arms during the 1950–1955 period and since. That is the crucial role played by weapons acquisition in determining overall relations between the major powers and Third World countries—particularly if the latter are ruled by the military or are involved in an international quarrel. The importance assigned by recipient countries of crisis areas to the strengthening of their military forces is such that this factor is likely to critically influence *all* other aspects of their relations with supplier governments, if not their entire foreign policy. As Washington learned to its chagrin in 1955, the costs to the suppliers of imposing restrictions on the procurement efforts of the recipients may in the long run adversely affect the whole range of interests that these suppliers have in the recipient countries. This in turn does not necessarily imply that a generous supply of arms is a reliable political lever.

Such negative consequences may be averted—and the control system safeguarded—only if all the recipient governments perceive the regional military equilibrium established by the suppliers as politically tolerable and not a hazard to their security. Seen from this perspective, it becomes clear how detrimental to the tripartite regime was the attitude adopted by the United States towards Egypt's arms requests. Although the arms balance that the West maintained in the first four years strongly favored Israel on an individual-country basis, this did not seem to unduly concern the Egyptian leadership so long as the overall Arab-Israeli equation remained stable and the confrontation continued in a state of relative quiescence. But, starting in late 1954, France's violation of the control arrangements and the concurrent assumption by Israel of an aggressive posture toward Egypt made the Nasser government acutely aware of its comparative military weakness. These developments—in addition to the creation of the Baghdad Pact around rival Iraq in return for U.S. arms aid to the Iraqis—rendered remedial action necessary. The American refusal to redress the balance except in exchange for political concessions by Cairo that were unrelated to the stated purpose of the arms rationing system destroyed the credibility of the Western guarantees under the 1950 Declaration that underlay the system, and left Nasser with no alternative but to seek arms wherever he could obtain them.

Perhaps the single most important conclusion to be drawn from the Middle Eastern experience of 1950–1955 is that the success of any arrangement by arms suppliers to limit the flow of weapons to conflict areas requires that all other goals of arms transfer be subordinated to the aim of maintaining a military balance acceptable to the conflicting parties.

This raises fundamental issues of political purpose.

THE POLITICS OF ARMS CONTROL

In any specific conflict situation, it is not enough to identify the objective material conditions that make arms control relevant—such as levels of military competition, quantity and quality of available weapons systems, likelihood of war, etc.—and to determine the optimal operational specifications for the machinery of its implementation. It is also imperative to come to grips with the political variables, which will be fundamental determinants of measurable success or ultimate futility. The hard political questions are the ones that have most often gone unanswered—or been gingerly sidestepped with no more than perfunctory reference—in the arms control literature, particularly that which has dealt with the Middle East and other regional crisis areas. In any particular conflict relationship, who will benefit from which arms control steps? To the advantage of which side would increased stability work? Does the restriction of military tools for challenging the status quo amount to its indefinite prolongation?

Judging from the results of the tripartite system, at least three political preconditions appear to be essential to the workability of any future endeavor to control the Arab-Israeli arms race and, by extension, other similar regional contests.

1. Provision of Effective Nonmilitary Avenues for Conflict Resolution. The restriction of armed violence is not always an absolute good or a supreme goal for states in conflict. The attractiveness of arms control is strongest in situations, such as the strategic arms race between the superpowers, where war as a policy option is almost unthinkable and the ever-present threat and costs of unplanned Armageddon are such that arms limitation is a matter of the first priority regardless of political differences. For small states involved in territorial conflicts with their neighbors, the issue is not so clear-cut. It may be true that their mutual security may be enhanced rather than reduced by a mutual relaxing of armed competition. Additionally, the possibility of effecting much needed economic savings should in and of itself be sufficient to interest them in arms control.

In certain conflict situations, however, neither security nor economy but the alteration of an intolerable status quo may be the paramount objective—as it has been for the front-line Arab states in the Middle East dispute since the

1967 war, for instance. The benefits of arms control are much less persuasive to decision-makers when the perceived stakes are so critical that military action becomes a feasible choice (assuming that the expected outcome is not a catastrophe). Under such circumstances, nothing will undermine the support of arms recipients for the principle of arms limitation faster than suspicion that what is being offered is in fact a devious means of weakening their position or jeopardizing their vital interests.

On the other hand, military action is never an end in itself. "Sir, do you want war?" Bismarck was once asked. "Certainly not," he replied, "I want victory." For the parties to any international quarrel, the impact of arms control on their chances of securing a favorable outcome—or at least a face-saving draw—will be their primary concern. If arms control is to win their acceptance, it must be supplemented by the provision of nonviolent means for challenging the status quo—such as diplomatic negotiations, arbitration, or legal adjudication. In other words, a resolution of the dispute must be actively and concurrently sought through peaceful means.

2. Dissociation of Regional Arms-Transfer and Control Arrangements from Unilateral Benefits. Whatever its putative advantages, the willing acquiescence of Arabs and Israelis in arms control will be difficult to secure. Aside from issues of national sovereignty, prestige, and equality, there is no evading the fact that arms control does affect the core of a nation's strength and limits policy options. If only for these reasons, recipients are likely to be intensely suspicious of any supplier initiatives designed to limit the flow of arms to them. For Middle Eastern countries in particular, history provides further solid grounds for apprehension. Past arms limitation proposals or arrangements promoted by the major weapons suppliers have been geared principally to serving their own immediate political objectives in that strategic region. The tripartite system was imposed during a period of Western monopoly over arms supplies, and was designed to protect a political and territorial situation seen as favorable to Western interests and explicitly guaranteed in the Tripartite Declaration of May 1950. At the height of the Cold War, Khrushchev's proposals of 1956–1958 for an embargo on arms transfers to the region sought to capitalize on the foothold the Russians had recently gained by virtue of the "Czech" arms deal and subsequent military assistance to Syria so as to graduate the Soviet Union into a position of equal partnership with the West and frustrate the latter's strategy of containment. Finally, the renewal of U.S. interest in limiting the transfer of weaponry to the Middle East in 1967 came at a time when Israel had just achieved a position of clear regional military supremacy. In fact, in his address of June 19, 1967, President Johnson's call for "limits on the wasteful and destructive arms race" was made while the Syrian, Egyptian, and Jordanian military machines lay practically in ruins.

It does no violence to the record to maintain that regional arms control as a genuine tension-reducing and conflict-limiting instrument remains to be tried. In the few instances when the major powers have turned to conventional-arms control, they have done so for its utility as one additional instrument of policy at the service of immediate interests—though conflict attenuation may have been a welcome incidental benefit. Designed for unilateral advantage, arms limitation schemes aroused the immediate opposition of those they were designed to victimize.

In the final analysis, the practicability of genuine regional arms control admittedly cannot be decided by intellectual fiat, nor can it be determined on the basis of the very limited experience yet accumulated. Its true potentialities can be exposed solely by application to situations where armed conflict is a lively possibility, with reduction of the likelihood of war as *the* overriding objective. Dissociating regional arms control arrangements from objectives that translate into unilateral political, military, or strategic benefits, however difficult, is essential for their success. The Middle East rationing system of 1950–1955 failed to observe this cardinal requirement, both in conception and execution.

3. Participation of Regional Parties Subject to Control in the Framing of the Arms-Limitation System. Since 1948, the need to secure friendly, reliable, and adequate sources of armaments has conditioned the foreign relations of the major participants in the Arab-Israeli conflict more than any other single factor. For Egypt, Israel, and Syria, obtaining the weaponry their security was perceived to require has been their first priority, determining foreign policy orientations and alliances, as well as taking up the lion's share of the national effort. Any initiatives purporting to restrict their access to military hardware, from whatever source, will be highly suspect to these governments, if not downright unacceptable. That they have waged five wars in three decades can only sharpen their resistance.

The last round in 1973 may have had additional important repercussions for arms control prospects in at least three negative respects. To the Israelis it demonstrated a new Arab ability to take the military initiative, to act in coordination, and to fight effectively, all novel elements that call for an increased state of military readiness and a stronger military posture. The front-line Arab states have found in war a seemingly useful instrument of policy, which may increase their opposition to any curtailment of their future ability to engage in it. Finally, the successful use of the "oil weapon" to extract political concessions from the industrialized countries has provided the Arab bloc with a potent lever that, together with the immense funds yielded by oil revenues, will frustrate any efforts by arms suppliers to unilaterally impose arms rationing or embargo schemes along the lines of the earlier tripartite experience.

Not that weapons suppliers generally have been or will be overly eager to curtail their business with Middle Eastern clients. To see the light of day, any limitation on the flow of military materiél must overcome, not only the reluctance of recipient governments, but also strong economic inducements for producers to sell their wares. The range of incentives for arms sales, whether strategic, economic, or political, needs no belaboring here. The reluctance of traditional suppliers to forego the lucrative Middle East market is further reinforced by the growth in the number of weapons-producing countries that are eager to claim a share of the export market and are unencumbered by the regional political or strategic interests that may predispose the major powers to favor arms control. Given this set of attitudes on the part of recipients and producers, it is clear that any substantial control measures, if they are to be effective, cannot follow the previous precedent of outright imposition by the suppliers witnessed under the 1950–1955 regime, or the similar conception of a Soviet-American agreement advanced by Washington after 1967. Of course, the supply of certain types of very advanced weapons systems and other sophisticated military hardware—such as electronic countermeasures (ECM)— not currently available from other sources could be curtailed by such a superpower concert. These limited cuts, however, would neither affect the basic capability of the adversaries to wage major wars nor improve the stability of the Arab-Israeli balance. On the contrary, an increase in instability might well result, for instance, from the diversion of funds to the purchase of larger numbers of less costly and less advanced but not less effective weapons from other, willing suppliers.

Hence, a third political prerequisite of successful arms control in the Middle East must be the securing of the cooperation of parties at both ends of the transfer process in the envisaged limitations. The specific arms controls must be negotiated with the participation or approval of the conflicting parties, and must be consensually arrived at. Then, and only then, is their enforcement not likely to be perceived by any one of these parties as a threat to its relative power position.

This does not mean that the *initiative* must be left to the recipients. In fact, the major suppliers are in a better position to advance proposals for arms restrictions in regional situations characterized by acute conflict than local principals who will be concerned lest any such overture be interpreted by the adversary as signalling a loss of nerve. For such proposals to reach fruition, however, a strategic dialogue—which may be encouraged and facilitated in a variety of ways—between Israel and her neighbors will be required to produce a matrix of mutual conceptual and situational understandings essential to the joint approval of specific arms control measures.

IN SEARCH OF STRATEGIC STABILITY

The Arab-Israeli dispute is an active, ongoing conflict that has produced five wars in a quarter-century; thus, arms supplies are perceived by the participants as vital to their national security. In the international politico-economic contest of the 1980s, it is clear that planning for potential arms control measures for the Arab-Israeli area must come to grips with a fundamental axiom: to be feasible and effective, any such arms control measures must have the *acquiescence* (which could be tacit) of the Middle Eastern countries involved. Such measures can no longer be imposed from without, by the major conventional-arms suppliers, on the model of the 1950 Tripartite regime. The structural shortcomings of coercive arms control, seriously debilitating even in optimal circumstances, have already been addressed. In addition, the dynamics of the Arab-Israeli arms race, no less than the political matrix in which it is embedded, have undergone significant change since the 1950s. The following are only some of the salient factors shaping the contemporary situation.

- The number of major weapons suppliers has multiplied in recent years; the advent of new weapons technologies—e.g., precision-guided munitions (PGM)—is a further spur to the proliferation of arms sources.
- The two key suppliers to date—the United States and the U.S.S.R.— remain locked in a competitive ideological/influential struggle in the region; their arms supply policies follow a "hegemonic" pattern that is least conducive to cooperative arms control endeavors.
- For all Western arms suppliers, higher costs of imported oil have created balance-of-payment and broader economic crises, and arms sales to the Middle East do much to help alleviate these problems.
- Most Middle East arms recipients are oil-rich or have access to petrodollars; in addition to enormous purchasing power, control over oil production provides a highly effective bargaining chip and countercoercive tool.
- There are increasing, though asymmetrical, domestic arms production

capabilities in several Middle Eastern countries, some of which are able to produce major weapons systems.

• Last but not least, given the possibility—and a growing record—of intra-regional weapons transfer, an externally imposed arms limitation regime would need to include not just the front-line protagonists but the entire twenty-state membership of the Arab League in addition to Israel, and Iran as well. The added difficulties and complications inherent in such a scheme would be staggering.

If one admits the basic proposition that arms controls must be acceptable to the local powers, indeed negotiated with their participation, then two important corollaries follow:

First, the types of feasible arms control arrangements will be largely dependent on the local parties' perceptions of the status of the political dispute at the time when these arrangements are to become operative. No progress toward arms limitation is likely under current volatile conditions. This volatility stems mainly from the fact that one side to the conflict finds the present status quo intolerable, is bent on altering it, and to this end is seeking to maintain and enhance a credible military option. To obtain Arab support for arms control measures, the political settlement process must reach a stage whereat not only Egypt but also Syria, Jordan, and the PLO become willing to work toward a relationship of long-term military stability with Israel, keyed to maintenance and defense of the new territorial and political arrangement rather than its revision. As long as some principal to the conflict continues to have unrequited grievances, so that, as a result, destabilizing revisionist claims remain active, the quest for military superiority—or simply for maximal freedom of military action—will not abate, ruling out any but the most perfunctory arms control measures. At present, deterrence is central to Israel's strategic posture; except in a narrow, tactical sense, it is only of secondary importance to the Arabs.

Second, descending one step to the level of operational defense planning, workable arms control must also take into account the major strategic doctrines and perceptions of both sides and accommodate them in some complementary fashion to elicit compliance. In the Arab-Israeli context, strategic doctrines have been historically determined principally by the geographic/territorial dimension. This is not fortuitous. The contiguity of the warring states and the narrow compass of the theater have dictated this constraint and will continue to do so in the future. Hence, to be meaningful, any detailed discussion of arms control measures must be anchored in some specific conception of the final territorial settlement that will emerge from a political negotiation. For example, the Israeli and Egyptian military postures and preferred weapons-system choices in the 1980s will be significantly affected by the ultimate disposition of Sinai—the degree of demilitarization, dimension of buffer zones, and collateral security measures such as warning stations and international peacekeeping forces. On the eastern front with Syria and Jordan, where territorial flexibility is of necessity far more limited, it is probable that the determination of these issues will in turn be heavily affected by expectations regarding the likelihood and nature of supporting weapons limitation agreements.

Thus, to put it starkly, barring a comprehensive settlement of the Arab-Israeli dispute, it would appear futile to seek in arms control a means to help minimize the risk of another Middle Eastern war. An exception to this might be a discreet Soviet-American negotiation of understandings designed to regulate superpower behavior in the event of war with a view to limiting the duration and scope of hostilities through their arms resupply policies and the exercise of influence. The superpowers might agree to:

- limit clients' weapon stockpiles/prepositioning;
- limit provision of spare parts;
- refrain from major resupply efforts during war;
- negotiate rapid cease-fires; and
- share information pointing to impending outbreaks of war.

Again, the overruling objective would be to shorten the duration and scope of war. The chances of movement toward a political settlement in the aftermath of the next war will naturally be affected drastically by the scale of that war. A major clear-cut defeat for either side—whether measured in territorial losses or destruction of its armed forces—could make a peaceful solution unattainable for years or decades to come. On the other hand, an outcome that does not substantially alter the status quo ante despite the high material costs and human losses likely in any full-fledged future hostilities would without a doubt enhance the prospects of a quick settlement. An important additional benefit of a Soviet-American accord along these lines would be the reduction of opportunities for superpower confrontation in the event of war in the Middle East.

No overwhelming disincentives for either superpower are readily discernible that would preclude an agreement of this nature. Admittedly, the U.S.S.R. does rely on its arms-supplier role as the mainstay of its presence in the Arab world, and would be loath to have it circumscribed. On the other hand, over the medium term at least, Israeli superiority makes a significant defeat more likely for the Soviet clients rather than the American one in a prolonged sixth war. On the American side, the United States is Israel's almost exclusive weapons source and is bound to the latter in a relationship conditioned by salient domestic political factors. It has became generally recognized, however, particularly since 1973, that the only "winning" solution to the agonizing dilemmas of U.S. Middle East policy lies in the speedy achievement of a comprehensive Arab-Israeli settlement.

Were an overall settlement involving all principal parties to emerge from a resumed negotiating process, a number of substantial arms control measures would appear feasible. What the particular package might look like—such measures would need to complement one another in some integrated fashion— would depend, as already noted, on the set of territorial arrangements that are agreed upon. Although these arrangements are likely to be partly influenced by the envisaged supporting arms control measures, weightier agents such as domestic opinion and politics within Israel, Jordan, Syria, and Egypt, and inter-Arab factors where the latter three countries are concerned, will be determinative. For the purpose of focusing the remainder of this analysis, the following assumptions are made regarding relevant elements of a posited inclusive settlement:

1. Israel withdraws from the territories occupied in 1967, following "minor border rectifications." Demilitarized areas are established in a ratio proportional to territorial size astride the new international borders between Israel and Syria (20 km.-wide; 1:3 ratio) and Israel and Egypt (110 km.-wide; 1:10 ratio). The West Bank is subjected to severe limitations on weaponry and forces beyond the requirements of internal security.

2. Agreements regarding the status of Jerusalem, disposition of refugee claims, and the nature of autonomous Palestinian rule in the West Bank are reached that settle the major components of the "Palestinian" issue.

3. Israel and its Arab neighbors sign peace treaties that recognize the legitimacy, territorial integrity, and sovereignty of the parties within their new international borders and terminate all acts of belligerency.

Despite the comprehensiveness of a settlement of this nature, a significantly high level of tension, military readiness, and cautious expectancy will remain in being for a number of years, given the historical record of animosity and mistrust among the parties. Nonetheless, a basically stable situation will have been created, enabling the parties for the first time to favor policies that would render arms control attractive to them: (1) defensive military postures; (2) stability of mutual deterrence; and (3) reduction of defense burdens.

Within the framework of an emerging political settlement broadly supported by all major protagonists, a variety of arms control measures could be designed with the central purpose of enhancing strategic stability. This would be achieved by *concurrently*:

1. Strengthening deterrence.
2. Minimizing the likelihood of surprise attack.
3. Discouraging countervalue doctrines.

The Strengthening of Deterrence

Since it is assumed that the protagonists will have become status quo powers, the structuring of armed forces for the purpose of war prevention should be such as to (1) avoid provocative postures and capabilities that may cause misperceptions; and (2) deny quick and cheap military conquests that may tempt some future political leadership. This can best be achieved through a strengthening of defensive capabilities relative to the offensive power of both sides.

Qualitative measures tending in this direction would be: (a) reducing the number of tanks and the number of aircraft of the fighter, bomber, and multi-role variety; (b) augmenting tactical PGM, armored personnel carriers, and helicopter platforms; and (c) reducing or banning long-range PGM and some area weapons.

Quantitatively, inventory ratios that have applied since the early 1960s and that take into account both Israeli superiority in manpower quality and Arab superiority in manpower size have proved fairly stable and acceptable to the protagonists, to judge from the fact that none of the three wars that have occurred in the interim were caused by the arms race per se. Compare to this the Israeli decision to go to war against Egypt in the wake of the 1955 Soviet-Egyptian arms deal. Inventory ratios may therefore be maintained relatively unchanged without detriment to strategic stability.

As to combat unit limitations, the reduction of armored units in favor of more PGM-armed infantry would probably be the most effective way of bolstering the defense. The conversion of 25 to 40 percent of Israeli, Egyptian, and Syrian tank units would accomplish the desired effect and at the same time provide numerical guidelines for some of the qualitative controls envisaged above. On the Syrian and Jordanian fronts, the limited breadth of the demilitarized zones would make restrictions advisable on deployment of armored units and long-range artillery near border areas.

Minimizing the Likelihood of Surprise Attack

However favorable to stability may be the weakening of offensive options, clearly the major contribution will be the denial to either side of a disarming first strike (Israel, 1967) or, minimally, of a surprise opening strike capable of substantially affecting the entire course of the war (Egypt-Syria, 1973). The importance of surprise, demonstrated in 1956 as well as in 1967 and 1973, is further accentuated by the nature of the new military technologies. Surprise strategies can be discouraged in two complementary ways: by placing limits on weapons suited to this role, and by assuring the survival of retaliatory forces.

The first approach would involve restricting strike aircraft and long-range surface-to-surface missiles; the second can be effected through hardening of aircraft shelters, erection of dense, integrated missile defenses, and provision of advanced early-warning and reconnaissance systems. The existence of demilitarized zones would largely eliminate the surprise-offensive role for armor, or the related use of defensive weapons systems in a tactically offensive mode such as occurred on October 6, 1973. The weighting of the aircraft mix in the inventories of the parties in favor of interceptors and tactical ground-support aircraft would weaken their surprise-strike potential while reinforcing the impregnability of defenses against both air attack and armored thrusts. As for early warning, the 1975 Israel-Egypt disengagement agreement introduced a novel concept that could be extremely effective in providing notice of impending mass air attack, i.e., the placing of surveillance stations within the buffer zone, well in front of the sides' respective front lines rather than behind them. Similar facilities could be located in future demilitarized zones, as close as possible to the other side's demarcation line.

Discouraging Countervalue Doctrines

Although the principal contribution to Arab-Israeli stability will come from the establishment of territorial/political conditions that both sides can "live with," the post-settlement relationship will concomitantly become more sensitive to the evolving status of the arms balance. In the context of a formal peace, the primary threat to strategic stability will become the unbalanced acquisition by Egypt, Israel, and Syria of capabilities for posing significant threats of destruction to the parties' cities and key civilian/industrial complexes. Given the historical background of this conflict and resultant psychological and perceptual sets, the presence of such weaponry would set off powerful pressures for preemption in conditions where political crisis, ambiguous or misinterpreted signals, faulty intelligence, or catalytic behavior by other regional actors lowered the threshold of military action.

The limitation of long-range surface-to-surface and air-to-surface missiles, of strategic roles for advanced aircraft, and of nuclear weapons, or, alternatively, the balancing of such capabilities available to both sides, are principal arms control measures.

How achievable are controls such as these likely to prove? Their feasibility and potential effectiveness will be a function of (1) acceptability to the parties, (2) acceptability to outside powers/suppliers, and (3) susceptibility to verification.

Obviously, some major changes in current strategic doctrines will be required if controls limiting offensive options are introduced. Israel would face the more difficult choices, because of its traditional doctrinal reliance on preemption and strategic initiative, and because of the requirements imposed by its mobilization system. On the other hand, the postulated overall settlement would face Israel with a situation unlike any in its previous national history in at least two crucial respects. Israel would be at peace with its neighbors, who would have solemnly relinquished any further territorial claims and ceased hostile acts. And Israel would be separated from its major potential antagonist, Egypt, by a broad demilitarized band that, together with adequate collateral early-warning measures, would remove the need for preventive mobilization. An additional incentive for an Israeli doctrinal shift would lie in the enhancement of strategic stability allowed by a corresponding diminution of Arab incentives for preemption.

A similar dilemma for Israeli planners is entailed in the reduction of armored forces. Israel has traditionally relied on quick armored advances designed to move the battle to enemy territory, exploit surprise and the indirect approach, take advantage of demonstrated Arab weaknesses in highly mobile warfare, and bring about the rapid collapse of Arab forces through encirclement, disorganization, and logistic breakdown. This strategy also was seen as facilitating the achievement of set military objectives within the narrow time constraints imposed on Middle East wars by the international environment, and of keeping casualty figures down. Here too, however, Israel faces altered circumstances, with technology in this case dictating the need for change. As demonstrated in the October War, antitank PGM technologies have rendered quick armored thrusts self-defeating. Armor will henceforth require infantry support, which, while motorized, will force a slower pace dictated by the high attrition rates of PGM and the consequent need for constant and cumbersome logistic resupply. Furthermore, the mass availability of infantry-operated PGM will tend to produce extended, diffuse defensive front areas, thick with dispersed, small infantry units, both mobile and in hardened camouflaged positions, which will render mobile tank warfare extremely difficult to sustain.

Extraregional arms suppliers may be expected to support arms control steps that are acceptable to their weapons clients or sought by them. The Soviet Union might conceivably attempt to frustrate a peace settlement reached without its participation, or one that shuts it off from any subsequent major regional role—both unlikely contingencies—by engaging in destabilizing arms-supply behavior with other Middle Eastern states antagonistic to the settlement. A more prolific source of difficulties is likely to be the achievement of sufficient coordination of policy among the growing number of highly competitive arms suppliers that arms transfers to Middle Eastern states outside the settlement area will not prejudice Arab-Israeli strategic stability. To cope with Israeli anxieties regarding intra-Arab transfers, some form of regularized on-site inspection by Israel or, more likely, a superpower surrogate (the U.S.) may be required. A reciprocal mission within Israel by Arab observers or appropriate third-party substitutes would be demanded by the Arab side, primarily to monitor compliance with probable restrictions on the output of Israel's more advanced indigenous arms industries.

An additional role that major outside powers may have to assume is the potentially hazardous one of enforcement of the overall arms control system. This may entail not only a substantial presence on the ground but also the onerous burdens of arbitrating disputes and meting out sanctions for violations, ranging from compensatory arms transfers to direct military intervention. The acceptance in 1975 by both Israel and Egypt on the one hand, and the U.S. Congress on the other, of the stationing of American observers in Sinai is a precedent which suggests that more comprehensive arrangements of this nature are feasible in the context of a peaceful solution.

The requirement of enforcement raises a host of issues connected with the verification function, which cannot be dealt with in generalities but must be related to the specific weapons systems subject to control. Certainly, the degree of arms control that will prove feasible will be a function of the extent to which Israel and the Arab states concerned agree to lay their military establishments open to mutual inspection. Initially, their readiness to do so may be quite limited. Nonetheless, significant measures such as reduction of tank and strike-aircraft inventories, limitations on acquisition and deployment of long-range surface-to-surface missiles, a ban on production of nuclear weapons, and restrictions on deployment of combat units near border areas should be verifiable with minimal intrusions of a potentially provocative character, particularly if outside powers also participate in the process.

The obstacles that stand in the way of an effective curbing of the Arab-Israeli military competition are obviously great. The tripartite rationing experience of the 1950s illustrates those obstacles, and the violent course of the confrontation since then has not made them more manageable or less daunting. Nonetheless, the requirements listed above are not visionary or beyond reach. As these words are written, direct talks between the two major adversaries—Egypt and Israel—on the core issues underlying the Arab-Israeli dispute are in progress, for the first time in a generation, and a bilateral treaty of peace and normalization has been concluded. Furthermore, in the most pertinent arena of military affairs, a "strategic dialogue" of sorts has been under way between Arabs and Israelis for three decades. Their frequent armed encounters, at practically all levels of the escalation ladder, have given them multiple opportunities to learn about and test each other, and have created a reservoir of interactive experience rich in guidelines to their respective strategic and military postures.

What was missing until President Sadat's journey to Israel in November 1977, and what remains painfully absent as of this moment beyond the narrow scope of Egyptian-Israeli relations, is that minimal but indispensable commitment by both sides to deemphasizing military means in the conduct of their mutual relations in favor of political, diplomatic, and juridical instruments necessary for consensual arms control. Arab dissatisfaction with a status quo perceived as inequitable, coupled with despair of its alteration by peaceful means, is matched by Israeli distrust in the credibility of international compacts and Arab "paper" assurances, plus Israeli reliance on a forward-defense strategy of assertive military superiority, buffer territorial depth, and easily defensible borders. Only a qualitative change in this relational pattern embracing all the principal contestants can open up significant prospects for arms limitations that will enhance military stability, reduce current levels of weapons acquisition, and divert all-too-scarce economic resources to urgent developmental and other domestic social tasks.

Despite some partial setbacks, events such as the Israeli-Egyptian peace agreement provide solid grounds for hope that the process of change has begun. For those who put store in the utility of arms control for the mitigation of international conflict, it may be the greatest irony of all that it took four major wars to reach this turning point.

SELECTED BIBLIOGRAPHY

BOOKS AND ARTICLES

(This section contains only books and articles cited in the text.)

Abdul Malek, Anouar. *Egypt: Military Society*. New York: Random House, 1968.

Acheson, Dean. *Present at the Creation: My Years in the State Department*. New York: Norton, 1969.

Agha, Hassan. "Egypt, Israel and the Atom Bomb" [in Arabic]. *Al-Tali'ah* 11 (September 1975), 19–29.

Alcock, Norman S. "An Empirical Measure of International Threat: Some Preliminary Implications for the Middle East Conflict." In Peace Research Society (International), *Papers* 15 (1970), 51–72.

Amorai, Adiel. "The War Cost Will Lead to a Different Israel." *Jerusalem Post*, December 5, 1973.

Aronson, Shlomo. *Conflict and Bargaining in the Middle East*. Baltimore: Johns Hopkins University Press, 1978.

Azm, Sadiq Al-. *Self-Criticism after the Defeat* [in Arabic]. Beirut: Dar Al-Tali'ah, 1968.

Barnaby, C.F., ed. *Preventing the Spread of Nuclear Weapons*. London: Souvenir Press, 1969.

Bar-Zohar, Michael. *The Armed Prophet: A Biography of Ben-Gurion*. London: Arthur Barker, 1966.

———. *Suez: Ultra Secret*. Paris: Fayard, 1964.

Beal, John Robinson. *John Foster Dulles*. New York: Harper, 1957.

Beaton, Leonard. "Why Israel Does Not Need the Bomb." *New Middle East* (London), No. 7 (April 1969), pp. 7–11.

Bell, Coral. *Negotiation from Strength*. London: Chatto & Windus, 1962.

Bell, J. Bowyer. *The Long War: Israel and the Arabs since 1946*. Englewood Cliffs, N.J.: Prentice-Hall, 1969.

Berque, Jacques. *Egypt: Imperialism and Revolution.* London: Faber & Faber, 1972.

Black, Cyril E., and Richard A. Falk, eds. *The Future of the International Legal Order.* Vol. 3: *Conflict Management.* Princeton, N.J.: Princeton University Press, 1971.

Brecher, Michael. *Decisions in Israel's Foreign Policy.* New Haven, Conn.: Yale University Press, 1975.

Brilliant, Moshe. "Israel's Policy of Reprisals." *Harper's* (March 1955), pp. 68–72.

Burt, Richard. *Nuclear Proliferation and Conventional Arms Transfers: The Missing Link.* Santa Monica: California Seminar on Arms Control and Foreign Policy, December 1977.

Campbell, John C. *Defense of the Middle East.* New York: Praeger, 1960.

Catroux, General D. "Aspects actuels des problèmes du Proche-Orient." *Politique Etrangère* 21 (February 1956), 5–20.

Chaudhuri, General J.N. "The International Arms Trade: The Recipient's Problems." *Political Quarterly* 43 (July–September 1972), 261–269.

Childers, Erskine. *The Road to Suez.* London: MacGibbon and Kee, 1962.

Claude, Inis. *Swords into Plowshares.* New York: Random House, 1956.

Coleman, Herbert J. "Israel Aircraft Develops New Capabilities." *Aviation Week & Space Technology* (March 31, 1975), pp. 14–17.

Copeland, Miles. *The Game of Nations.* New York: Simon and Schuster, 1969.

Crosbie, Sylvia K. *A Tacit Alliance: France and Israel from Suez to the Six Day War.* Princeton, N.J.: Princeton University Press, 1974.

Dallin, David J. *Soviet Foreign Policy after Stalin.* Philadelphia: Lippincott, 1961.

Darin-Drabkin, Haim. "The Economic Aspects of Defense." *New Outlook* 18 (March–April 1975), 51–54.

Davenport, Elaine, Paul Eddy, and Peter Gillman. *The Plumbat Affair.* Philadelphia: Lippincott, 1978.

Digby, James. *Precision-Guided Weapons.* Adelphi Paper, No. 118. London: International Institute for Strategic Studies, Summer 1975.

Divine, Donna Robinson. "Why This War . . ." *International Journal of Middle East Studies* 7 (October 1976), 523–543.

Dougherty, James E. *Arms Control and Disarmament: The Critical Issues.* Washington, D.C.: Center for Strategic Studies, Georgetown University, 1966.

Dowty, Alan. "Israel and Nuclear Weapons." *Midstream* 22 (November 1976), 7–22.

Duchêne, François. "The Arms Trade and the Middle East." *Political Quarterly* 44 (October–December 1973), 453–446.

Dupuy, Trevor N. *Elusive Victory: The Arab-Israeli Wars, 1947–74.* New York: Bobbs-Merrill, 1977.

Eden, Anthony. *Memoirs: Full Circle.* London: Cassell, 1960.

Edwards, David V. *Arms Control in International Politics.* New York: Holt, Rinehart & Winston, 1969.

Egypt. Ministry of Foreign Affairs. *Records of Conversations, Notes and Papers Exchanged between the Royal Egyptian Government and the United Kingdom Government (March 1950–November 1951)*. Cairo: Ministry of Foreign Affairs, 1951.

Eisenhower, Dwight D. *The White House Years: Mandate for Change, 1953–1956*. New York: Doubleday, 1963.

———. *The White House Years: Waging Peace, 1956–1961*. New York: Doubleday, 1965.

Ellis, Harry B. *Challenge in the Middle East*. New York: Ronald Press, 1960.

Engelbrecht, H.C., and F.C. Hanighen. *Merchants of Death: A Study of the International Armament Industry*. New York: Dodd, Mead, 1934.

Evron, Yair. "Israel and the Atom: The Uses and Misuses of Ambiguity, 1957–1967." *Orbis* 17 (Winter 1974), 1326–1343.

———. *The Role of Arms Control in the Middle East*. Adelphi Paper, No. 138. London: International Institute for Strategic Studies, Autumn 1977.

Falk Project for Economic Research in Israel. *Third Annual Report, 1956*. Jerusalem, 1957.

Farley, Philip J., Stephen S. Kaplan, and William H. Lewis. *Arms Across the Sea*. Washington, D.C.: The Brookings Institution, 1978.

Fitzsimons, M.A. *Empire by Treaty*. Notre Dame, Indiana University of Notre Dame Press, 1964.

Fleming, Denna F. *The United States and World Organization, 1920–1933*. New York: Columbia University Press, 1938.

Foster, James L. "New Conventional Weapons Technologies: Implications for the Third World." In *Arms Transfers to the Third World: The Military Buildup in Less Industrial Countries*. Edited by Uri Ra'anan et al. Boulder, Colo.: Westview Press, 1978, pp. 65–84.

Frank, Lewis A. *The Arms Trade in International Relations*. New York: Praeger, 1969.

Franko, Lawrence G. "Restraining Arms Exports to the Third World: Will Europe Agree?" *Survival* 21 (January–February 1979), 14–25.

Friedlander, Saul. "Policy Choices before Israel." In *Political Dynamics in the Middle East*. Edited by Paul Y. Hammond and Sidney S. Alexander. New York: American Elsevier, 1972, pp. 115–154.

Gallman, Waldemar J. *Iraq under General Nuri*. Baltimore: Johns Hopkins University Press, 1964.

Gee, Jack. *Mirage—Warplane for the World*. London: McDonald, 1971.

Gerson, Louis L. *John Foster Dulles*. New York: Cooper Square, 1967.

Gray, Colin S. "Traffic Control for the Arms Trade?" *Foreign Policy*, No. 6 (Spring 1972), pp. 153–169.

Great Britain. Parliament. *Parliamentary Papers* (Commons), *1955–56*, Vol. 36: Accounts and Papers (Vol. 8). Cmnd. 9676, "Export of Surplus War Material."

Halevi, Nadav. "The Economy of Israel: Goals and Limitations." *Jerusalem Quarterly*, No. 1 (Fall 1976), pp. 83–92.

Harkabi, Yehoshafat. "Basic Factors of the Arab Collapse during the Six-Day War." *Orbis* 11 (1967), 677–691.

Harkavy, Robert E. *The Arms Trade and International Systems*. Cambridge, Mass.: Ballinger, 1975.

Heikal, Mohamed Hassanein. *The Cairo Documents*. Garden City, N.Y.: Doubleday, 1973.

———. *The Psychological Complexes that Control the Middle East* [in Arabic]. Cairo: Arab Printing and Publishing Company, 1958.

———. *The Road to Ramadan*. London: Collins, 1975.

———. *The Sphinx and the Commissar*. New York: Harper & Row, 1978.

Henriquez, Robert. *A Hundred Hours to Suez*. New York: Viking, 1957.

Hodes, Aubrey. "Implications of Israel's Nuclear Capability." *Wiener Library Bulletin* 22 (Autumn 1968), 2–8.

Hoopes, Townsend. *The Devil and John Foster Dulles*. Boston: Little, Brown, 1973.

Hoover Institution on War, Revolution, and Peace. *Arms Control Arrangements for the Far East: A Summary*. Stanford, Calif.: Hoover Institution on War, Revolution, and Peace, 1967.

Hourani, Cecil. "The Moment of Truth." *Encounter* 29 (November 1967), 3–14.

Hovey, Harold A. *United States Military Assistance: A Study of Policies and Practices*. New York: Praeger, 1965.

Huntington, Samuel P. "Arms Races: Prerequisites and Results." In *Public Policy*, 1958. Cambridge, Mass.: Harvard University, Graduate School of Public Administration, 1958, pp. 41–86.

Huntzinger, Jacques. "Regional Recipient Restraints." In *Controlling Future Arms Trade*. By Anne H. Cahn et al. New York: McGraw-Hill, 1977, pp. 163–197.

Hurewitz, J. C. *Diplomacy in the Near and Middle East, A Documentary Record: 1914–1956*. Reprint edition, New York: Octagon, 1972.

———. *Middle East Dilemmas*. New York: Harper, 1953.

———. *Middle East Politics: The Military Dimension*. New York: Praeger (for the Council on Foreign Relations), 1969.

———. "Weapons Acquisition: Israel and Egypt." In *Comparative Defense Policy*. Edited by Frank B. Horton III, Anthony C. Rogerson, and Edward L. Warner III. Baltimore: Johns Hopkins University Press, 1974.

International Encyclopedia of the Social Sciences, 2nd ed. New York: Macmillan, 1968. S. v. "Disarmament," by J. David Singer.

Isaac, Rael J. *Israel Divided: Ideological Politics in the Jewish State*. Baltimore: Johns Hopkins University Press, 1976.

Jabber, Paul. *Israel and Nuclear Weapons*. London: Chatto & Windus (for the International Institute for Strategic Studies), 1971.

———. "Israel's Nuclear Options." *Journal of Palestine Studies* 1 (Autumn 1971), 21–38.

———. "A Nuclear Middle East: Infrastructure, Likely Military Postures, and Prospects for Strategic Stability." In *Great Power Intervention in the*

Middle East. Edited by Milton Leitenberg and Gabriel Sheffer. Elmsford, N.Y.: Pergamon, 1979, pp. 72–97.

Jabber, Paul, and Roman Kolkowicz. "The Arab-Israeli Wars of 1967 and 1973." In *Mailed Fist, Velvet Glove: Soviet Armed Forces as a Political Instrument.* By Stephen S. Kaplan et al. Washington, D.C.: The Brookings Institution, for the U.S. Defense Advanced Research Projects Agency (September 1979), Chapter 10.

Jackson, Robert. *The Israeli Air Force Story.* London: Tom Stacey, 1970.

Jordan, Amos A. *Foreign Aid and the Defense of Southeast Asia.* New York: Praeger, 1962.

Kagan, Benjamin. *The Secret Battle for Israel.* Cleveland: World, 1966.

Kemp, Geoffrey. *Arms and Security: The Egypt-Israel Case.* Adelphi Paper, No. 52. London: The International Institute for Strategic Studies, October 1968.

———. "The International Arms Trade: Supplier, Recipient and Arms Control Perspectives." *Political Quarterly* 42 (October–December 1971), 376–389.

———. "U.S. Military Policy: Dilemmas of the Arms Traffic." *Foreign Affairs* 48 (January 1970), 274–284.

Khadduri, Majid. "The Scheme of Fertile Crescent Unity: A Study in Inter-Arab Relations." In *The Near East and the Great Powers.* Edited by Richard N. Frye. Cambridge, Mass.: Harvard University Press, 1951, pp. 137–177.

Khalidi, Ahmed S. "The War of Attrition." *Journal of Palestine Studies* 3 (Autumn 1973), 60–87.

Khalil, Muhammad. *The Arab States and the Arab League: A Documentary Record.* Vol. 2: *International Affairs.* Beirut: Khayats', 1962.

Khrushchev, Nikita S. *Khrushchev Remembers.* Boston: Little, Brown, 1970.

Kiernan, Thomas. *The Arabs.* Boston: Little, Brown, 1975.

Kimche, Jon. *The Second Arab Awakening.* London: Thames and Hudson, 1970.

———. *Seven Fallen Pillars: The Middle East, 1945–1952.* New York: Praeger, 1953.

Kirk, George. *The Middle East 1945–1950.* London: Oxford University Press (for the Royal Institute of International Affairs), 1954.

———. "The Turco-Egyptian Flirtation of Autumn 1954." *The World Today* 12 (November 1956), 447–457.

Kissinger, Henry A. *The Necessity for Choice.* New York: Harper, 1961.

Kochav, David. "The Economics of Defense—Israel." In *Military Aspects of the Israeli-Arab Conflict.* Edited by Louis Williams. Tel Aviv: University Publishing Projects, 1975, pp. 178–187.

Kuebler, Jeanne. "Traffic in Arms." *Editorial Research Reports.* Washington, D.C.: Congressional Quarterly Service, April 28, 1965, pp. 300–319.

Lambelet, John C. "A Dynamic Model of the Arms Race in the Middle East, 1953–1965." In *General Systems, Yearbook of the Society for General Systems Research* 16 (1971), 145–167.

Laqueur, Walter Z. *Communism and Nationalism in the Middle East.* New York: Praeger, 1956.

League of Nations. *Acts of the Conference on the Supervision of the International Trade in Arms and Ammunition and Implements of War.* A.13.1925.IX.

Lehrman, Hal. "American Policy and Arab-Israeli Peace." *Commentary* 17 (June 1954), 546–556.

——. "Arms for Arabs—and What for Israel?" *Commentary* 18 (November 1954), 423–433.

Leiss, Amelia C., with Geoffrey Kemp, John H. Hoagland, Jacob S. Refson, and Harold E. Fischer. *Arms Control and Local Conflict.* Vol. 3: *Arms Transfers to Less Developed Countries.* Cambridge, Mass.: Center for International Studies, Massachusetts Institute of Technology, February 1970.

Livneh, Eliezer. "Israel Must Come Out for Denuclearization." *New Outlook* 9 (June 1966), 44–47.

Love, Kennett. *Suez: The Twice-Fought War.* New York: McGraw-Hill, 1969.

Luttwak, Edward, and Dan Horowitz. *The Israeli Army.* New York: Harper & Row, 1975.

McDonald, James G. *My Mission in Israel, 1948–1951.* New York: Simon and Schuster, 1951.

Malik, Charles. *Charles Malik and the Palestinian Cause* [in Arabic]. Beirut: Badran, 1973.

Marlowe, John. *A History of Modern Egypt and Anglo-Egyptian Relations.* Hamden, Conn.: Archon, 1965.

Massachusetts Institute of Technology. Center for International Studies. *Regional Arms Control Arrangements for Developing Areas: Arms and Arms Control in Latin America, the Middle East and Africa.* Cambridge, Mass.: Center for International Studies, Massachusetts Institute of Technology, September 1964.

Mazrui, Ali A. "African Radicalism and Arms Policy." *African Scholar* 1 (1970).

Metellus. "Politique de la France au Proche-Orient." *Politique Etrangère* 20 (December 1955), 677–688.

Millis, Walter, ed. *The Forrestal Diaries.* New York: Viking, 1951.

Monroe, Elizabeth. "Mr. Bevin's 'Arab Policy.'" In *Middle Eastern Affairs: Number Two.* Edited by Albert Hourani. London: Chatto & Windus, 1961, pp. 9–48.

Nagib, General Mohammed. *My Testimony To History* [in Arabic]. Cairo: Dar Al-Kitab Al-Namuzagi, 1975.

Newcombe, Alan. "Toward the Development of an Inter-Nation Tensiometer." In *Peace Research Society (International), Papers* 13 (1970), 11–28.

Newcombe, Hanna. "The Case for an Arms Embargo." *War/Peace Report* 11 (March 1971), 17–19.

Nimrod, Yoram. "Non-Nuclear Deterrence." *New Outlook* 19 (April–May 1976), 34–42.

Noel-Baker, Philip. *The Arms Race.* London: Atlantic, 1958.

Nutting, Anthony. *Nasser*. New York: Dutton, 1972.

———. *No End of a Lesson*. New York: Potter, 1967.

Patinkin, Don. "The Israel Economy: The First Decade." The Falk Project for Economic Research in Israel, *Fourth Report 1957 and 1958*. Jerusalem, 1959.

Peres, Shimon. *David's Sling*. London: Weidenfeld & Nicolson, 1970.

Pierre, Andrew, ed. *Arms Transfers and American Foreign Policy*. New York: New York University Press, 1979.

Pranger, Robert J., and Dale R. Tahtinen. *Implications of the 1976 Arab-Israeli Military Status*. Washington, D.C.: American Enterprise Institute, 1976.

Quandt, William B. *Decade of Decisions*. Berkeley and Los Angeles: University of California Press, 1978.

Ra'anan, Uri. *The U.S.S.R. Arms the Third World: Case Studies in Soviet Foreign Policy*. Cambridge, Mass.: M.I.T. Press, 1969.

Richardson, Lewis F. *Arms and Insecurity*. Chicago: Quadrangle, 1960.

Rosen, Steven J., and Martin Indyk. "The Temptation to Pre-empt in a Fifth Arab-Israeli War." *Orbis* 20 (Summer 1976), 265–286.

Royal Institute of International Affairs. *British Interests in the Mediterranean and Middle East*. London: Oxford University Press, 1958.

———. *Great Britain and Egypt, 1914–1951*. Information Paper, No. 19, 3d ed. London: Royal Institute of International Affairs, 1952.

Rubner, Alex. *The Economy of Israel*. London: Frank Cass, 1960.

Sablier, Edouard. "La tension en Proche-Orient et la politique des grandes puissances." *Politique Etrangère* 20 (January–February 1955), 21–26.

Safran, Nadav. *From War to War: The Arab-Israeli Confrontation, 1948–1967*. New York: Pegasus, 1969.

Schelling, Thomas C. *Arms and Influence*. New Haven and London: Yale University Press, 1966.

Schelling, Thomas C., and Morton H. Halperin. *Strategy and Arms Control*. New York: Twentieth Century Fund, 1961.

Schiff, Zeev. *A History of the Israeli Army*. San Francisco: Straight Arrow, 1974.

Seale, Patrick. *The Struggle for Syria*. London: Oxford University Press, 1965.

Shamir, Moshe. "Arab Military Lessons from the October War." In *Military Aspects of the Israeli-Arab Conflict*. Edited by Louis Williams. Tel Aviv: University Publishing Projects, 1975, pp. 172–178.

Sheehan, Edward R. F. *The Arabs, Israelis, and Kissinger*. New York: Reader's Digest Press, 1976.

Sheffer, Gabriel, ed. *Dynamics of a Conflict*. New York: Humanities Press, 1975.

Shlaim, Avi. "Failures in National Intelligence Estimates: The Case of the Yom Kippur War." *World Politics* 28 (April 1976), 348–380.

———. "The Gaza Raid, 1955." *Middle East International*, No. 82 (April 1978), pp. 25–28.

Singer, J. David. "Threat-Perception and the Armament-Tension Dilemma." *Journal of Conflict Resolution* 2 (March 1958), 90–105.

Slater, Leonard. *The Pledge*. New York: Simon and Schuster, 1970.

Smith, Gaddis. *Dean Acheson.* New York: Cooper Square, 1972.

Smith, Hedrick. "The U.S. Assumes the Israelis Have A-Bomb or its Parts." *New York Times,* July 18, 1970.

Smolansky, Oles M. *The Soviet Union and the Arab East under Khrushchev.* Lewisburg, Penn.: Bucknell University Press, 1974.

Spain, James W. "Middle East Defense: A New Approach." *Middle East Journal* 8 (Summer 1954), 251–266.

Stanley, John, and Maurice Pearton. *The International Trade in Arms.* London: Chatto & Windus (for the International Institute for Strategic Studies), 1972.

"State Department Pursues Stubborn Policy in Rearming of Arabs." *New Palestine,* March 1950, p. 17.

Stephens, Robert. *Nasser: A Political Biography.* New York: Simon and Schuster, 1971.

Stockholm International Peace Research Institute. *The Arms Trade with the Third World.* New York: Humanities Press, 1971.

Sutton, John, and Geoffrey Kemp. *Arms to Developing Countries: 1945–1965.* Adelphi Paper, No. 28. London: International Institute for Strategic Studies, October 1966.

Tahtinen, Dale. *Arab-Israeli Military Status in 1976.* Washington, D.C.: American Enterprise Institute, 1976.

Thayer, George. *The War Business: The International Trade in Armaments.* New York: Simon and Schuster, 1969.

Trevelyan, Humphrey. *The Middle East in Revolution.* London: Macmillan, 1970.

Tsur, Jacob. *Prélude à Suez: Journal d'une ambassade, 1953–1956,* Paris: Presses de la Cité, 1968.

Tueni, Ghassan. "After October: Military Conflict and Political Change in the Middle East." *Journal of Palestine Studies* 3 (Summer 1974), 114–130.

United Arab Republic. Ministry of National Guidance. *Collected Speeches, Declarations and Statements of President Gamal Abdel Nasser.* Part I: 23 July 1952–January 1958 [in Arabic]. Cairo: Ministry of National Guidance, n.d.

United States. Arms Control and Disarmament Agency. *The International Transfer of Conventional Arms.* A Report to the Congress pursuant to Section 302 of the Foreign Relations Authorization Act of 1972 (Public Law 92–352), April 12, 1974.

———. *World Military Expenditures and Arms Transfers 1967–1976.* Washington, D.C.: Government Printing Office, July 1978.

United States. Congress. House of Representatives. Committee on Foreign Affairs. *Economic and Military Cooperation with Nations in the General Area of the Middle East. Hearings.* 85th Congress, 1st session, 1957.

———. *The Mutual Security Program. Hearings.* 82d Congress, 1st session, 1951.

United States. Congress. House of Representatives. Committee on International Relations. *Conventional Arms Transfer Policy: Background Information.* Committee Print. 95th Congress, 1st session, 1978.

United States. Congress. Senate. *Senate Delegation Report on American Foreign*

Policy and Nonproliferation Interests in the Middle East. 95th Congress, 2d session, 1977.

United States. Congress. Senate. Committee on Foreign Relations. *Mutual Security Act of 1953. Hearings.* 83d Congress, 2d session, 1953.

————. *The Situation in the Middle East. Hearing.* 84th Congress, 2d session, 1956.

———— and Committee on Armed Services. *The President's Proposal on the Middle East. Hearings.* 85th Congress, 1st session, 1957.

United States. Department of State. *Foreign Relations of the United States.* Issues for 1947 through 1950 of Vol. 5: *The Near East and Africa.* Washington, D.C.: Government Printing Office.

Van Cleave, William. "Nuclear Technology and Weapons." In *Nuclear Proliferation: Phase II.* Edited by Robert M. Lawrence and Joel Larus. Lawrence, Kansas: University Press of Kansas, 1974, pp. 30–68.

Verguèse, Dominique. "Science and Technology: Israel's Key to Survival." *Le Monde Weekly,* July 29–August 4, 1971.

Vital, David. "Double-Talk or Double-Think? A Comment on the Draft Non-Proliferation Treaty." *International Affairs* 44 (July 1968), 419–433.

Wallace, Michael D. "Status, Formal Organization, and Arms Levels as Factors Leading to the Onset of War, 1820–1964." In *Peace, War, and Numbers.* Edited by Bruce M. Russett. Beverly Hills, Calif.: Sage Publications, 1972, pp. 49–69.

Waterbury, John. *Egypt: Burdens of the Past, Options for the Future.* Hanover, N.H.: American Universities Field Staff, n.d.

Weller, Jac. "Israeli Arms Production." *Ordnance* 55 (May–June 1971).

Wheelock, Keith. *Nasser's New Egypt.* New York: Praeger, 1960.

Wiltz, John E. *In Search of Peace.* Baton Rouge: Louisiana State University Press, 1963.

Zayid, Mahmud Y. *Egypt's Struggle for Independence.* Beirut: Khayats', 1965.

NEWSPAPERS AND OTHER SERIAL PUBLICATIONS

(*Only newspapers and other serial publications that were exhaustively scanned for data and information are cited here: those selectively consulted for specific material are cited in the footnotes only.*)

Akhbar El-Yom (Cairo), 1950–1951.

Al-Ahram (Cairo), 1950–1955.

Brassey's Annual: The Armed Forces Yearbook. New York: Macmillan, 1951–1953.

Cahiers de l'Orient contemporain (Paris), 1950–1955.

Jane's Fighting Ships. London: Sampson Low, Marston, 1951–1956.

Jerusalem Post (Jerusalem), 1950–1955.

Military Balance. London: International Institute for Strategic Studies, 1972–1978.

New York Times (New York), 1949–1955.

Stebbins, Richard P., ed. *The United States in World Affairs.* New York: Harper (for the Council on Foreign Relations), 1950–1955.

Stockholm International Peace Research Institute. *Yearbook of World Armaments and Disarmament,* 1969–1977.

Times (London), 1949–1955.

United States. Arms Control and Disarmament Agency. *Documents on Disarmament.* Washington, D.C.: Government Printing Office, 1945–1959, 1967–1968, 1970–1971.

INTERVIEWS

Atherton, Alfred L.	U.S. diplomat; former Assistant Secretary of State for the Near East and South Asia; currently Ambassador to Cairo; interviewed in Washington, D.C., January 29, 1973.
Awad Al-Quni, Mohamed	Retired Egyptian diplomat; was Counsellor of Embassy in Washington, 1949–1952; Director of the Political Department at the Ministry of Foreign Affairs, 1952–1955; was Ambassador to Moscow when the "Czech" arms deal was concluded; interviewed in Cairo, August 12, 1973.
Badeau, John S.	Former U.S. diplomat and educator; was President, American University at Cairo, 1945–1953, and later Ambassador to Cairo, 1961–1964; interviewed in Washington, D.C., January 30, 1973.
Badri, Gen. Hassan Al-	Egyptian army officer; was Chief-of-Staff of Egyptian forces in Sinai in the 1950s; later became senior military advisor to Presidents Nasser and Sadat; interviewed in Cairo, August 7, 1973.
Bahaeddine, Ahmed	Leading Egyptian journalist; former editor-in-chief of *Al-Ahram*; interviewed in Cairo, July 19, 1973.
Bashir, Tahsin	Egyptian diplomat; former official government spokesman; interviewed in Cairo, July 17, 1973.
Beeley, Sir Harold	Retired British diplomat; was Counsellor of Embassy in Washington, 1953–1955, and later served as Ambassador to Cairo; interviewed in London, June 15, 1973.

Bowie, Robert — Director of Policy Planning at the U.S. Department of State, 1953–1955; interviewed in Washington, D.C., February 6, 1973.

Chase, Peter — Political officer under Ambassador Byroade at the U.S. embassy in Cairo, 1954–1957; interviewed in New York City, February 5, 1973.

Copeland, Miles — Former U.S. Central Intelligence Agency operative; was posted in Cairo, 1953–1955; interviewed in London, June 14, 1973.

Cremeans, Charles — Former U.S. Central Intelligence Agency analyst; was on special assignment in Cairo, 1955; interviewed in Washington, D.C., January 26, 1973.

Dessouki, Salah — Assistant to Egypt's Minister of the Interior, under both Nasser and Zakaria Mohieddin, during 1952–1955; interviewed in Beirut, June 29, 1973.

Gallman, Waldemar J. — Retired U.S. diplomat; was Ambassador to Baghdad, 1954–1959; interviewed in Washington, D.C., January 29, 1973.

Ghaleb, Gen. Abdel-Hamid — Former Egyptian military officer and diplomat; was Military Attaché to Washington and led arms purchase mission to the U.S. in 1955; interviewed in Beirut, August 30, 1973.

Ghali, Butrus B. — Former Editor-in-Chief of the Cairo journal *International Politics*; currently Egypt's Minister of State for Foreign Affairs; interviewed in Cairo, July 8, 1973.

Hare, Raymond — Retired U.S. diplomat; was Ambassador to Jeddah, 1950–1953; to Beirut, 1953–1954; and to Cairo, 1956–1960; later became Assistant Secretary of State for the Near East and South Asia; interviewed in Washington, D.C., January 25, 1973.

Hart, Parker — Former U.S. diplomat; was Director of the State Department's Office of Near

Eastern Affairs, 1952–1955, and Deputy Chief of Mission in Cairo, 1955–1960; later became Assistant Secretary of State for the Near East and South Asia; interviewed in Washington, D.C., January 25 and February 6, 1973.

Henderson, Loy

Former senior U.S. diplomat; was Director for the Near East and Africa at the State Department in 1945–1948, and Ambassador to Teheran, 1951–1955; interviewed in Washington, D.C., January 27, 1973.

Howard, Harry

Advisor to the Near East Office at the Department of State, 1949–1956, and its unofficial historian; interviewed in Washington, D.C., January 30, 1973.

Idriss, Gen. Muhsin

Member of the office of the Commander-in-Chief, Egyptian Armed Forces, in charge of weapons procurement, 1952–1956; interviewed in Cairo, August 12, 1973.

McGhee, George C.

Former senior U.S. diplomat and businessman; was Assistant Secretary of State for the Near East, South Asia, and Africa, 1949–1951; interviewed in Washington, D.C., February 1, 1973.

Malik, Charles

Leading former Lebanese diplomat and educator; was Minister, later Ambassador to Washington, 1945–1955; became Minister of Foreign Affairs, 1956–1958; interviewed in Rabieh, Lebanon, August 31, 1973.

Muhieddin, Khalid

Member of the Revolutionary Command Council that ruled Egypt following the 1952 revolution; interviewed in Alexandria, August 10, 1973.

Nutting, Sir Anthony

Britain's Minister of State for Foreign Affairs, 1954–1956; interviewed in London, June 14, 1973.

Oudah, Abd Al-Malik

Egyptian educator and research member of *Al-Ahram*'s Center for Political and Strategic Studies; interviewed in Cairo, August 11, 1973.

Paul, Norman S.

Director for the Near East of the U.S. Foreign Operations Administration, 1952–1955; later became Under-Secretary of the Air Force; interviewed in Washington, D.C., February 1, 1973.

Rif'at, Kamaleddin

Prominent member of the Free Officer group that carried out the 1952 Egyptian revolution; cabinet minister and later Ambassador to London; interviewed in London, June 15, 1973.

Roosevelt, Kermit

Former U.S. Central Intelligence Agency official with broad Middle East field experience; was advisor to the Secretary of State on Middle Eastern affairs, 1947–1957; interviewed in Washington, D.C., January 30, 1973.

Souki, Samyr

Press Counsellor at the Egyptian Embassy in Washington, 1953–1954; interviewed in Beirut, June 27, 1973.

Stoddard, Philip

Director of Near East Research, Intelligence and Research Bureau of the U.S. Department of State; interviewed in Washington, D.C., January 31, 1973.

INDEX

Designer:	Al Burkhardt
Compositor:	William Clowes
Printer:	Braun-Brumfield, Inc.
Binder:	Braun-Brumfield, Inc.
Text:	Monotype Plantin
Display:	Typositor Columna
Cloth:	Holliston Roxite B 53575
Paper:	50 lb P&S offset, B-32